GERMAN
for Business

Astrid Küllmann-Lee

Hugo's Language Books Limited

'German for Business' is also available in a pack
with four cassettes: ISBN 0 85285 173 1

Written by

Astrid Küllmann-Lee MSc (Econ)

Cover photo (Spectrum): Deutsche Bank, Frankfurt

Set in Helvetica 55 & 65 by
Typesetters Ltd, Hertford
Printed and bound in Great Britain by
Courier International Ltd
East Kilbride

PREFACE

'German for Business' is one of Hugo's new language courses specially designed for business and professional people – particularly those wishing to take advantage of the opportunities offered by the Single European Market. The content is not solely applicable to British users, but will greatly aid any English-speaking person needing to learn German for business purposes.

Although this course book is closely modelled on its stable companion 'French for Business', it is by no means a direct translation of that title. Some of the topics are omitted, or replaced by others, and the rate of progression is slower. With French, we assumed that most readers had some prior knowledge of the language; this is not the case with German, so more time must be spent on teaching elementary points of grammar.

Once you have completed the Course you should be linguistically able to deal successfully with most business situations, particularly if you also use the audio tapes which are provided as an optional 'extra' to the book. These recordings of the unit dialogues, selected model sentences, vocabulary and exercises provide an additional dimension to your studies and greatly enhance the learning process.

Despite the need to cover elementary aspects of German, this Course will be suitable for:

a) those who studied German at school some while ago and now need to revise their knowledge thoroughly while continuing their studies in a business context;

b) readers of our 'German in Three Months' course who require the language specifically for business/professional reasons.

c) students for whom German is one of the options on a Business Studies course in colleges of further and higher education.

Whether you're an absolute beginner or not, you'll find 'German for Business' to be a stimulating, fast-moving and methodical course; if you devote the necessary time and effort to each unit (perhaps an hour of concentrated study per day for ten weeks or so), you'll learn the language thoroughly and not be afraid to speak it. Many people claim to 'know' a language, but daren't open their mouths; with Hugo behind you, you'll have all the confidence you need!

METHOD

The method adopted is a very practical one with the emphasis being placed on communication in a realistic context. Each unit's German dialogue is accompanied by an English translation, followed by a study of the individual words used (the Checklist), detailed explanatory notes (Checknotes) and abundant examples of grammar 'in action'. Throughout the Course there are numerous varied, lively and contextualized exercises offering ample scope for practising what you've been taught. Answers to these exercises are at the back of the book. There are also numerous extracts from German magazines – articles, advertisements and so forth – used to illustrate or help explain teaching points, which add a certain authenticity.

THEME OF THE UNITS

The majority of the Course chapters are centred around the activities of a British businessman, Mr Jackson, and his German counterpart, Frau Schneider, and cover a wide variety of business situations (see Contents). It should be noted however that, with the exception of the authentic material, the names of all persons and companies mentioned in the Course are purely fictitious.

THE AUDIO CASSETTES

In addition to the chapter devoted to pronunciation, the first five units' dialogues have been provided with the Hugo system of imitated pronunciation, because we feel it is essential for the student to acquire a correct accent from the outset. Nevertheless, we strongly recommend that you obtain the four audio cassettes which have been produced to accompany this book [Hugo's 'German for Business Cassette Course', ISBN 0 85285 1273 1], as these will make the lessons so much more interesting and entertaining and will, of course, accustom your ear to German as pronounced by native speakers.

We hope that you enjoy 'German for Business' and we wish you every success in your studies.

ACKNOWLEDGEMENTS

In addition to the numerous companies and organizations who have kindly allowed reproduction of their material, special thanks are due to *Der Spiegel* and James P. Miscoll for the article in Unit 12.

We are also very grateful to Ron Overy for his careful editing and for providing so much help and advice at all stages in the preparation of this Course.

CONTENTS

6

INTRODUCTION

The pronunciation of German

You will be pleased to hear that German, unlike English, is pronounced virtually as it is written. It is comparatively easy for an English-speaking person to acquire a good pronunciation. Nevertheless, the opening dialogues in Units 1-5 are transcribed into Hugo's 'imitated pronunciation' to help you get used to the way German is pronounced. Please bear in mind that these descriptions, which are based on standard southern English, are merely approximate to the German sounds. If you wish, you can turn immediately to Unit 1 and begin the first session. You'll find the imitated pronunciation section at the back of the book. However, there are considerable benefits to be gained from studying the following general rules on pronunciation beforehand, even if you simply check them through quickly and refer back to certain points as you proceed through the Course.

THE STRESSED SYLLABLE

It takes a little while to learn where to split German words into syllables, but the imitated pronunciation will show you how it's done. In all languages it is very important to stress the correct syllable, otherwise the word will sound unfamiliar and may be misunderstood. German words are usually stressed on the first syllable, unless they are of foreign origin or begin with an unstressed prefix (be-, ge-, er-, ver-, zer-, emp-, ent-). In the imitated pronunciation of the first five Units, a stress mark ['] precedes the stressed syllable.

THE GLOTTAL STOP

English speakers tend to run their words together, so that the foreigner isn't always sure if s/he's hearing 'an egg' or 'a negg'. This doesn't happen in German. Words and syllables beginning with a vowel have to start with a tightening of the vocal cords as if silently clearing your throat. The London Cockney does this all the time when he omits the 'tt' in 'bottle'.

THE 'IMITATED PRONUNCIATION'

Please make yourself familiar with the following simple comments. You have to say all the syllables, which are separated by hyphens, as if they were part of an English word, but note the following:

[e] as in 'open'
[er] similar to the 'u' in the southern English pronunciation of 'truck' (with a hint of an 'r').
[g] as in 'go'.
[h] one way of pronouncing the German ch, similar to the 'h' in 'Hugo'.
[kh] the other way of pronouncing the German ch, a guttural sound as in the Scottish pronunciation of 'loch'.
[ng] as in 'Hong Kong'.
[ọọ] as in 'goods'.
[y] as in 'by'
[y] as in 'yes'.

[ay] represents the German ä, similar to the initial sound in 'air'.
[ö] the sound of the German ö is not used in English; say [ay] with rounded lips (similar to the final sound in 'her').
[ü] the German ü is another sound not used in English; say [ee] as in 'seen' but with rounded lips. It's like the French 'u' in 'tu'.

PRONOUNCING GERMAN VOWELS

The sound of a German vowel doesn't change and is reminiscent of northern English or Scottish vowel pronunciation. Standard English vowels are not always simple one-sound letters, but may represent different sounds as in fat → fate, win → wine, tot → tote. German vowels, however, can be either long or short – but they are always pronounced 'pure'. For instance, the last syllable of the German word **Konto** (*account*) is pronounced as a single sound [toh], not [toh-ọọ].

The most distinctive difference between the pronunciation of German and English is to be found in the existence of additional vowels in German. Three vowels (**a, o, u**) change their sound when an umlaut (two dots ¨) is placed over them; they then look like this: **ä, ö, ü**.

You may wish to memorize the following notes on vowel sounds:

LONG VOWELS

1. If either **a/e/i/o** or **u** precedes a single consonant and is followed by another vowel it is pronounced long:
   a: [ah] as in 'draft' – Daten (*data*) ['Dah-ten];
   e: [ay] as in 'lane' – Telex (*telex*) ['Tay-lex].

2. If either a/e/i/o or u is followed by h, it is pronounced long:
o: [oh] as in 'note' - Lohn (wages) [Lohn].

3. If i is followed by e (as in the verb ending -ieren), it is long:
ie: [ee] as in 'chief' - exportieren (to export) [eks-por-'tee-ren].

4. These vowels can be pronounced long in other positions too:
u: [oo] as in 'tycoon' - Agentur (agency) [Uh-gen-'tooer].

5. aa/ee/oo are also pronounced long (they don't appear very often):
Seerecht (maritime law) ['Zay-reht].

SHORT VOWELS

Every German vowel is pronounced short, if it is followed by a doubled consonant (or ck), or a combination of consonants (like ng): Zoll (customs) [Tsoll]; Entwicklung (development) [Ent-'vik-loong]; Markt (market) [Marrkt].

a: [u, uh]	as in 'cut'	- Finanz (finance) [Fi-'nunts].
e: [e]	as in 'jet'	- Scheck (cheque) [Shekk].
i: [i]	as in 'sit'	- tippen (to type) ['tip-pen].
o: [o]	as in 'not'	- Konferenz (conference) [Kon-fay-'rents].
u: [oo]	as in 'goods'	- Konkurrenz (competition) [Kon-koo-'rents]

The special German vowels ä, ö and ü are sometimes pronounced short, but they're produced in the same way as the longer version, described below.

SPECIAL VOWELS

ä: [ay] similar to 'pay', but longer:
Diktiergerät (dictating machine)]Dik-'teer-ge-rayt].

ö: [ö] no exact equivalent in English. The sound is similar to 'ur' in 'turnover':
Größe (size, height) ['Grö-se].

ü: [ü] similar to the French 'u' as in 'reçu', but there is no exact equivalent in English:
Broschüre (brochure) [Bro-'shü-re].

y: [ü] seldom appears in German but is normally pronounced [ü]:
Stenotypistin (shorthand typist) [Shtay-noh-tü-'pis-tin].

UNSTRESSED SYLLABLES

When -e and -er occur in unstressed syllables, they have a weaker sound and are pronounced as follows:

e: [e] like the 'e' in 'open':
Bericht (report) (Be-'riht].

er: [*er*] similar to the 'u' in 'truck':
Fernsprecher (official name for the *telephone*) ['Fairn-shpre-*her*].

VOWEL COMBINATIONS

ai/ei: [y] like 'y' in 'by':
Thailand (*Thailand*) ['Ty-lunt]; Streik (*strike*) [Shtryk].

au: [ow] like 'ow' in 'Dow Jones':
kaufen (*to buy*) ['kow-fen]; Aufgabe (*task*) ['Owf-gah-be].

äu/eu: [oy] like 'oy' in 'employ':
Verkäuferin (*saleswoman*) [Fair-'koy-fe-rin]; deutsch (*German*) [doytsh].

ie: [ee] as in 'chief':
importieren (*to import*) [im-por-'tee-ren].

PRONOUNCING GERMAN CONSONANTS

Pronounce the German consonants as in English, but bear the following differences in mind:

b: as in English, but at the end of a word or syllable like 'p':
Schreibkräfte (*clerical staff*) ['Shryp-krefte].

c: is only used in front of 'k'.

ch: • after clear vowels (e/ei/i/ie/ä/eu/äu/ü) similar to the 'h' in Hugo:
ich (*I*) [i*h*].
• after dark vowels (a/au/o/u) as in the guttural Scottish pronunciation of 'loch':
Buch (*book*) [Bookh]

d: as in English, but at the end of a word or syllable like 't':
dringend (*urgent*) ['dri*ng*-ent].

g: as in 'go', but at the end of a word or syllable like 'k' or 'kh':
geben (*to give*) ['gay-ben]; Betrag (*amount*) [Be-'trakh]; Zug (*train*) [Tsookh or Tsook].
like 'h' in Hugo in the ending -ig:
wichtig (*important*) ['vi*h*-ti*h*].

h: as in English, but when placed after a vowel it is silent:
Hafen (*port*) ['Hah-fen]; Bahn (*path; tram/railway*) [Bahn].

j: like 'y' in 'yes':
Jahresbericht (*annual report*) ['Yah-res-be-ri*h*t].

ng: as in 'singer', <u>not</u> 'finger':
Zeitungen (*newspapers*) ['Tsy-toong-en].

qu: like 'kv':
Quittung (receipt) ['Kvi-tꞎong].

r: is pronounced more distinctly in German and at the back of the throat:
Rabatt (discount) [Ruh-'but].

s: • at the beginning of words and syllables like English 'z':
Sie (you) [Zee];
• at the end of a word or syllable like 's' in 'see':
Büros (offices) [Bü-'rohs];
• before p or t in the <u>same</u> syllable like 'sh', but as 's-t' when in <u>different</u> syllables:
Spediteur (forwarding agent) [Shpay-di-'töer]; Steno (shorthand) ['Shtay-noh]; Leistung (performance, output) ['Lys-tꞎong].

sch: like 'sh' in English:
Schaufenster (shop window) ['Show-fens-ter].

ss/ß: like 's' in 'sell':
Großbritannien (Great Britain) [Grohs-bri-'tun-i-en).

th: <u>never</u> as in 'the' or 'thin', it is always pronounced as 't':
Theorie (theory) [Tay-oh-'ree].

v: normally like 'f':
Vertreter (representative) [Fair-'tray-ter].

z: like 'ts' in 'exports':
Zoll (customs/duty) [Tsoll].

THE GERMAN ALPHABET

It's very important to be able to pronounce the letters of the alphabet the German way, as you may have to spell your name. (See the end of Unit 5.) This is what the German alphabet sounds like:

A ah	H hah	O oh	V fow
B bay	I ee	P pay	W vay
C tsay	J yot	Q koo	X iks
D day	K kah	R air	Y 'üp-si-lon
E ay	L ell	S ess	Z tsett
F eff	M emm	T tay	
G gay	N enn	U oo	

UNIT 1

At the reception desk

If you have the audio cassettes, please listen to the dialogue in Unit 1 several times before looking at the text. Then, study this German conversation for a few moments before comparing it with the English translation which follows. At this stage you only need to have a general idea of the meaning.

Mr Jackson, a British businessman, has arranged to see Frau Schneider of Futura Büromaschinen in Frankfurt. He goes up to the reception desk.

Mr Jackson:	Guten Tag. Mein Name ist Jackson. Ich habe einen Termin bei Frau Schneider.
Empfangsdame:	Guten Tag, Herr Jackson. Einen Augenblick, bitte. Ich sage Frau Schneiders Sekretärin Bescheid. Nehmen Sie doch bitte Platz!

(The receptionist phones through to Frau Schneider's office.)

Empfangsdame:	Herr Jackson, Frau Schneiders Sekretärin kommt sofort. Ihr Büro ist im ersten Geschoß.
Mr Jackson:	Vielen Dank.

TRANSLATION

Mr Jackson:	Good morning (*literally* 'good day'). My name is Jackson. I have an appointment with Mrs Schneider.
Receptionist:	Good morning, Mr Jackson. Just a moment, please. I('ll) inform Mrs Schneider's secretary (*lit.* 'I tell Mrs Schneider's secretary information'). Please take a seat.
Receptionist:	Mr Jackson, Mrs Schneider's secretary is on her way (*lit.* 'is coming immediately'). Her office is on the first floor.
Mr Jackson:	Thank you very much (*lit.* 'Many thanks').

Imitated Pronunciation: If you don't have the cassettes which accompany "German for Business" and you'd like help with the pronunciation of the dialogues in Units 1-5, turn to the Imitated Pronunciation section at the back of the book.

Checklist 1

Masculine nouns:

der	*the* (used with masc. nouns)
der Tag	*the day*
der Name	*the name*
der Termin	*appointment*
der Herr	*the gentleman*
(Herr -)	*(Mr -)*
der Bescheid	*the notification*
der Augenblick	*the moment*

Feminine nouns:

die	*the* (used with fem. nouns)
die Karte	*the card* (here: *business card*)
die Frau	*the woman, wife*
(Frau -)	*(Mrs -, Ms -)*
die Empfangsdame	*the receptionist*

Neuter nouns:

das	*the* (used with neut. nouns)
das Büro	*the office*
das Geschoß	*the floor, storey*

Adjectives:

gut, guten	*good*
ihr	*her*

Verbs/verbal expressions:

ich habe	*I have*
nehmen	*to take*
Nehmen Sie Platz!	*Take a seat!*
sagen	*to say, tell*
Bescheid sagen	*to inform* (orally)

Other words/expressions:

bitte	*please*
doch	(often used orally to make requests sound more polite; used additionally to 'bitte')
sofort	*at once, immediately*

CHECKNOTES

1 Capital letters

You will have noticed that all nouns start with a capital letter in German. At the beginning of your German studies, it is a good idea to highlight or circle all the capital letters in a text until it has become a habit to use these when you write in German.

Note: The word **Sie** is spelt with a capital letter when used as the polite form of address (meaning: 'you'); when it is spelt **sie** the meaning can be either 'she/her' or 'they/them'.

Unlike the English 'I', the German **ich** does not have a capital when appearing in the middle of a sentence, nor do adjectives denoting the country of origin, e.g.: **deutsche Ware** ('German goods').

2 Gender of German nouns
Definite article ('the')

Every German noun has a grammatical gender and the definite article used reflects this fact. 'The' is expressed as follows:

der (masculine singular) → **der Vertrag**   *the contract*
die (feminine singular)   → **die Bank**   *the bank*
das (neuter singular)   → **das Geschäft** *the business, the shop*

Unfortunately, there are few rules that can help you to determine the gender of German nouns. The best rule of all is to learn the definite article together with the noun. (In order to make it easier to remember them, you could highlight them consistently in three different colours. You should also learn the plural form of the noun.)

Generally speaking, however, nouns ending in **-ung, -heit, -keit, -schaft** and **-ion** are feminine, as well as those referring to female persons (these often end in **-in**).

Nouns denoting male persons or professions (and often ending in **-er**), the days of the week and months, and most rivers and mountains, are masculine.

Nouns derived from verbs are neuter (e.g.: **schreiben**, 'to write' → **das Schreiben** 'the letter/memo'), and so are all diminutive forms ending in **-chen** and (less frequently) **-lein**.

3 Plural 'the'

You'll be pleased to hear that there's only one word for 'the' in the plural: **die**. However, the nouns themselves change in a variety of ways; these changes are always indicated in our Checklists and in dictionaries. We'll be discussing this again later in the Course.

die (masculine plural) → **die Verträge** *the contracts*
die (feminine plural) → **die Banken** *the banks*
die (neuter plural) → **die Bücher** *the books*

4 Indefinite article ('a', 'an')
Possessive adjectives ('my', 'his')

There are two German words for expressing 'a/an': **ein** (masculine and neuter), **eine** (feminine). Here are some examples:

der Name → **ein Name** *the name* → *a name*
das Büro → **ein Büro** *the office* → *an office*
die Frau → **eine Frau** *the woman* → *a woman*

The same pattern is used for the possessive adjectives **mein** ('my') and **sein** ('his'):

	a/an	*my*	*his*
(masc.)	**ein Name**	**mein Name**	**sein Name**
(neut.)	**ein Büro**	**mein Büro**	**sein Büro**
(fem.)	**eine Frau**	**meine Frau**	**seine Frau**

5 Subject (nominative case); direct object (accusative case)

Please study these sentences:

Mein Name ist Jackson.	m.nom.sing.	**Sein Name ist Miller.**
Mein Büro ist in London.	n.nom.sing.	**Sein Büro ist in Köln.**
Meine Frau ist in Paris.	f.nom.sing.	**Seine Frau ist in Rom.**

This pattern alters slightly when we change the grammatical subject to **ich** ('I') and the verb to **kennen** ('to know'), which requires a direct object: our nominative cases change to accusative:

Ich kenne den Namen*.	m.acc.sing.	**Ich kenne seinen Namen*.**
Ich kenne das Büro.	n.acc.sing.	**Ich kenne sein Büro.**
Ich kenne die Frau.	f.acc.sing.	**Ich kenne seine Frau.**

Now the difference between masculine and neuter is obvious.

* A small group of masculine nouns (which includes **Name**) add an **-n** in all cases except the nominative singular.

6 Greetings

Guten Tag (literally 'good day') can be used any time of the day. Certainly this holds good for business purposes, which saves you worrying about which one to use!

Guten Morgen ('good morning') is used until midday.

Guten Abend ('good evening'): normally only used after working hours.

Gute Nacht ('good night'): used only before going to bed.

The German word for 'good' is **gut**, but it becomes **guten** in **Guten Tag** and **Guten Morgen** because these expressions are in the accusative case. Just think of them as shortened versions of:

(Ich wünsche Ihnen einen) guten   *(I wish you a) good morning/day.*
Morgen/Tag!

7 Adjectival endings

In a sentence like 'The desk is new' the English and German constructions are very similar: **Der Schreibtisch ist neu**. However, if you wanted to say 'a new desk' (i.e. if you wanted to put **neu** in front of **Schreibtisch**) you'd need to add a masculine adjectival ending to **neu**; this is because German adjectives take the gender, case and number (singular or plural) of the noun they precede. This will be introduced gradually but in the meantime here are some examples of what we mean, using the adjectives **gut** ('good'), **neu** ('new'), **erst-** ('first') and **deutsch** ('German'):

Ich habe ein gutes Geschäft.	(n., acc., sing.)	*I have a good business.*
Ich habe eine neue Sekretärin.	(f., acc., sing.)	*I have a new secretary.*
Ich habe einen deutschen Namen.	(m., acc., sing.)	*I have a German name.*
Ich kenne sein erstes Geschäft.	(n., acc. sing.)	*I know his first shop.*

Do note that the ending of the adjective in German is not always the same after **der/die/das** as after **ein/mein/sein**. Just look at these examples:

Nominative case
der deutsche Name / die   neue Sekretärin / das gute Geschäft
ein deutscher Name / eine neue Sekretärin / ein gutes Geschäft

Accusative case

den deutschen Namen / die   neue Sekretärin / das erste Geschäft
einen deutschen Namen / meine neue Sekretärin / sein erstes Geschäft

Did you notice that the adjectival endings which follow **ein/mein/ sein** mirror the corresponding definite article?

8 Verbs – the present tense

The verb **kommen** ('to come') shows the typical endings for each person:

Singular (one person)
ich komme	*I come*
du kommst	*you come* (informal)
Sie kommen	*you come* (formal)
er kommt	*he comes*
sie kommt	*she comes*
es kommt	*it comes*

Plural (more than one person)
wir kommen	*we come*
ihr kommt	*you come* (informal)
Sie kommen	*you come* (formal)
sie kommen	*they come*

9 Forms of address

As a business person you will normally find yourself in formal situations where you have to address your business acquaintances and even your colleague(s) as **Sie.**

Generally speaking, the informal address (**du** and **ihr**) is used when speaking to relatives, children and animals. (The equivalent of the German **du** is 'thou' in older forms of English.) We are going to omit the **du** and **ihr** forms, until the formal **Sie** is firmly established in your German responses.

10 Imperative (giving orders, making requests)

Study the following:

Nehmen Sie (bitte Platz)!	*Take (a seat, please)*
Kommen Sie!	*Come*
Gehen Sie!	*Go*
Warten Sie!	*Wait*

You may find it easier to remember this by linking the German two-word imperative to older English forms like 'Hark ye'.

11 Sounds requiring special attention

Remember that the German **ch** sounds sometimes like 'h' in the English word 'huge' and sometimes like 'ch' in the Scottish 'loch' (see chapter on Pronunciation). In the numbers **acht** ('eight') and **achtzehn** ('eighteen') you must use the Scottish sound. The ending **-ig** is normally pronounced like the word **ich**. Only when **ch** is followed by **s** does it sound like 'ks' in English, e.g. **sechs** ('six'). The German **sch** is like an English 'sh', and **z** sounds like 'ts'. Note that this sound comes up in most numbers.

12 Numbers

In your business transactions you will need to be familiar with German numbers. You really should drill yourself to say them aloud while learning, until you have mastered the correct pronunciation. If you don't, confusion could arise later on.

Please make a special effort to pronounce **-zehn** quite long, so that it sounds distinctly different from **-zig**! Note also that the German numbers 4 and 5 start with the same 'f'-sound, although they are spelt differently (one with a v, the other with an f).

1	**eins**	11	**elf**		
2	**zwei**	12	**zwölf**	20	**zwanzig**
3	**drei**	13	**dreizehn**	30	**dreißig**
4	**vier**	14	**vierzehn**	40	**vierzig**
5	**fünf**	15	**fünfzehn**	50	**fünfzig**
6	**sechs**	16	**sechzehn**	60	**sechzig**
7	**sieben**	17	**siebzehn**	70	**siebzig**
8	**acht**	18	**achtzehn**	80	**achtzig**
9	**neun**	19	**neunzehn**	90	**neunzig**
10	**zehn**				

Did you notice some irregularities in the second and third columns? Some of the numbers there don't follow the pattern of [basic number] + **-zehn/-zig**.

100 **(ein-) hundert**
1100 **elfhundert**
1900 **neunzehnhundert**

13 Stressed and unstressed syllables

Remember that German words are usually stressed on the first syllable: **'gu-ten**, **'Na-me**, **'Au-gen-blick**, but there are exceptions: **so-'fort**, **Ter-'min**. The **-e**, **-en** and **-er** endings (unstressed syllables) are pronounced weak (see chapter on Pronunciation).

14 Colours

Colour is important in many aspects of business; study the following:

rot	*red*	**grau**	*grey*
blau	*blue*	**gelb**	*yellow*
braun	*brown*	**grün**	*green*
violett	*mauve*	**weiß**	*white*
schwarz	*black*		

These words take adjectival endings, when put in front of nouns:

Ich sehe ein weißes Taxi, ein schwarzes Fahrrad, eine blaue Straßenbahn, einen grünen Lieferwagen, ein graues Auto, ein gelbes Postauto, einen braunen Lkw (=Lastkraftwagen) und ein rotes Feuerwehrauto.

I see a white taxi, a black bicycle, a blue tram, a green delivery van, a grey car, a yellow post van, a brown lorry and a red fire engine.

This is a very good game to play ... rather than just making out lists of nouns, imagine different situations and surroundings, and say aloud the things you can see.

Comprehension Practice 1

*Re-read or listen again to the conversation between Mr Jackson and the receptionist at the beginning of this Unit, and then say whether the following statements are correct (**richtig**) or wrong (**falsch**):*

New words:
der Mann *man*
am Empfang *at reception*

1 Der Mann ist Herr Jakobs.	richtig/falsch
2 Die Sekretärin kommt sofort.	richtig/falsch
3 Herr Jackson hat einen Termin.	richtig/falsch
4 Ein deutscher Herr ist am Empfang.	richtig/falsch
5 Das Büro ist im ersten Geschoß.	richtig/falsch
6 Frau Schneider ist im Büro.	richtig/falsch

FLUENCY PRACTICE 1
Numbers

Please write out and say aloud the following numbers, then check them against the list in Checknote 12:

11; 8; 80; 7; 17; 6; 5; 12; 70; 50;
30; 1; 3; 10; 9; 90; 20; 40; 60.

FLUENCY PRACTICE 2
Introducing yourself

Re-read or listen again to the conversation at the beginning of this Unit and then take part in this short conversation:

You:	*(Say 'Hello' to the receptionist, tell her your name and that you've an appointment to see Frau Schneider.)*
Empfangsdame:	Guten Tag. Nehmen Sie bitte einen Augenblick hier Platz.
You:	*(Thank her!)*

FLUENCY PRACTICE 3
Describing your room/office

New words:
der Teppich *carpet*
die Gardine *curtains*

die Pflanze   *plant*
die Tapete   *wallpaper*
das Sofa   *sofa*

When describing the furnishings to someone who doesn't know what your room or office is like, you'd say: **Der Teppich ist braun** – or whatever colour it might be. Please describe the following items, giving them one of the colours you've learnt in this Unit.

1 Der Teppich ist ....
2 Die Gardine ist ....
3 Die Pflanze ist ....
4 Der Schreibtisch ist ....
5 Das Sofa ist ....
6 Die Tapete ist ....

FLUENCY PRACTICE 4
Find the hidden words

```
S C H D O C H E W A G E N D
G A U G E N B L I C K T E N
B I T T E Z B E S C H E I D
S P R E T E R M I N M B E I
S O F O R T S A G E N M I L
D M O D I E K A R T E S C H
K E M P F A N G S D A M E N
P L A T Z N F H M E N E I N
```

Did you find 15 words from Unit 1?

FLUENCY PRACTICE 5
Unscramble the 'coded' dialogue

There seems to be something wrong with the word processor! Please turn the following scrambled conversation between the receptionist and Mr Müller into readable information by inserting the necessary gaps and punctuation:

gutentagmeinnameistmüllerichhabeeinenterminbeifrauwalter
gutentagherrmüllereinenaugenblickbitteichsagefrauwalter
bescheidvielendank

It's a good idea to write down your answers to the Fluency Practices, as this will help your memory to store all the new information it has to cope with. Be careful, though, with the capital letters!

UNIT 2

Introducing yourself

Again, if you have the audio cassettes, please listen to the dialogue in this Unit several times, before looking at the German text.

Frau Schneider's secretary has now arrived at the reception desk.

Sekretärin:	Guten Tag. Kann ich Ihnen helfen?
Mr Jackson:	Guten Tag. Mein Name ist Jackson.
Sekretärin:	Entschuldigung, wie heißen Sie?
Mr Jackson:	Jackson. Ich komme aus England. Ich bin Verkaufsleiter bei Excel-Equip. Hier ist meine Karte. Ich bin für elf Uhr bestellt.
Sekretärin:	Ach ja, Herr Jackson. Frau Schneider erwartet Sie. Kommen Sie bitte mit!

TRANSLATION

Secretary:	Good morning. Can I help you?
Mr Jackson:	Good morning. My name is Jackson.
Secretary:	Sorry, what is your name?
Mr Jackson:	Jackson. I come from England. I'm (the) sales manager for Excel-Equip. Here is my (business) card. I have an appointment at eleven o'clock (*lit.* 'I am for eleven o'clock booked in.')
Secretary:	Oh, yes. Mr Jackson. Frau Schneider is expecting (*lit.* 'expects') you. Please follow me (*lit.* 'Come please with!').

Checklist 2

Masculine nouns:

der Verkauf	*(Engl.pl.) sales*
der Leiter	*the manager*
der Verkaufsleiter	*the sales manager*

Feminine nouns:

die Uhr	*the clock*
elf Uhr	*eleven o'clock*
die Entschuldigung	*the apology*
(Entschuldigung!	*Sorry!)*
die Sekretärin	*the secretary*

Verbs/verbal expressions:

ich kann	*I can*
helfen	*to help*
ist	*is*
ich komme	*I come*
ich heiße	*I am called*
Sie heißen	*you (polite form of address) are called*
Sie kommen	*you come / you are coming*
ich bin	*I am*
ich bin bestellt	*I have an appointment (lit. 'I am booked in')*
ich erwarte Sie	*I expect / am expecting you*
Frau S. erwartet Sie	*Mrs S. is expecting you (lit. 'expects you')*
sie ist	*she is*
mit|kommen	*to come along* (with someone)
[see Checknote 21 for an explanation of the vertical stroke]	
Kommen Sie mit!	*Come with me!*

Other words/expressions:

wie?	*how? / what?*
aus	*from* (a town or country)
bei	*with, at* (used with the name of a company)
hier	*here*
für	*for*
ach (ja)!	used to express surprise or when remembering something.
ja	*yes*

CHECKNOTES

15 Questions

Most questions start with a question word like **wer?** ('who?'), **wo?** ('where?'), **wann?** ('when?'), **warum?** ('why?') and **wie?** ('how?'), and are followed by an inversion. For example:

Wer ist am Empfang?	*Who is at reception?*
Wann kommt Herr Jackson?	*When is Mr Jackson coming?*
Warum kommt er nach Frankfurt?	*Why is he coming to Frankfurt?*
Wie geht es Ihnen?	*How are you?*
Wo ist das Büro?	*Where is the office?*

Questions which do not contain a question word at the beginning also show inversion (this way of asking questions can be used for all verbs in German):

Kann ich .... ?	*Can I .../May I .... ?*
Kommt er?	*Is he coming?*
Wartet sie?	*Is she waiting?*

Note: In German one does not use 'do' and 'don't' in questions and negations!

16 Indirect object (dative case)

You may have wondered about this strange word **Ihnen** which came up in the first line of the dialogue. It is the dative case of **Sie**, denoting the indirect object of a sentence. In English you need to use a preposition to denote the indirect object, e.g. '<u>to</u> you', '<u>for</u> you'.

17 Understanding how German verbs function

A good way of unravelling difficult German sentences is to look at the verb. A verb can have:

a) no object
b) a direct object (accusative case)
c) a direct object + indirect object (dative case)

Study the following:

a) Verbs which do not need an object (**essen, steigen, sinken**):

Ich esse.	*I eat/am eating.*	(accusative)
Es steigt.	*It goes up/rises.*	(intransitive*)
Sie sinken.	*They go down/decrease.*	(intransitive*)

[*Verbs which never have a direct object (accusative) to follow are called 'intransitive'.]

b) Verbs which take one (direct) object (**kennen, kaufen, haben, essen**):

Ich kenne den Verkaufsleiter.	*I know the sales manager.*
Ich kaufe einen Computer.	*I('m) buy(ing) a computer.*
Sie hat einen neuen Chef.	*She has a new boss.*
Ich esse ein Steak.	*I eat a steak.*

[Verbs which normally take a direct object are 'transitive'.]

c) Verbs which can take more than one object (**geben, kaufen**):

Ich gebe ihm einen Brief.	*I give a letter to him.*
Er kauft ihr einen Computer.	*He buys a computer for her.*

As you can see, **kaufen** may be used in different ways and in this course book it would be listed in the following style: **kaufen** acc.(dat.). The (dat.) in brackets indicates that the indirect object is optional. Applying the same use of brackets, we find **essen** (acc.), **kennen** acc., **haben** acc. and **geben** acc. (dat.)

18 Pronouns

Nouns can be replaced by pronouns – just as they can be in English – in the following way:

der Verkaufsleiter	**- er**	*(he)*
die Sekretärin	**- sie**	*(she)*
das Geschäft	**- es**	*(it)*

However, the pronoun 'it' has three German equivalents, depending on the grammatical gender of the noun it refers to:

der Name - er	*the name - it*	
die Karte - sie	*the card - it*	
das Büro - es	*the office - it*	

19 Compound nouns

If two nouns are combined into a single word, this is called a compound noun and there are lots of them in German. You've seen one in this Unit: **der Verkauf + der Leiter = der Verkaufsleiter**. Many compound nouns have a linking **-s-** in the middle (some an **-n-** or **-en-**) holding the two parts together. Others have no such linkage. As you'll see from the following examples, the final noun determines the gender of the compound noun:

die Augen (pl.) + der Blick → der Augenblick *(moment)*
der Verkauf + die Leiterin → die Verkaufsleiterin *(sales manager, f.)*

der Verkauf + das Büro → das Verkaufsbüro *(sales office)*
der Kredit + die Karte → die Kreditkarte *(credit card)*

20 bitte, 'please'

You may be a little surprised to learn that **bitte** is not always placed at the beginning or at the end of a statement. It is much more common to put this and other particles in the middle of a sentence, especially if you want to sound friendly! For example:

Kommen Sie bitte mit!	*Please follow me!*
Kommen Sie bitte herein!	*Come in, please!*
Sprechen Sie bitte langsam!	*Please speak slowly!*

21 Separable verbs

Mitkommen is a separable verb, which means **mit** goes to the end of the sentence, when it is the only verb in that sentence:

(Statement)	**Ich komme mit.**	*I come with (you).*
(Imperative)	**Kommen Sie mit!**	*Come with me!*

Note (i): separable verbs are always stressed on the first syllable.
   (ii): **mit** can also be used as a preposition.

In the Checklists, to help you, we have used a vertical stroke to indicate which are the separable verbs. Here are some more examples:

an|bieten *(to offer)*	→	ich biete an	*I offer*
vor|stellen *(to introduce)*	→	er stellt vor	*he introduces*
aus|nutzen *(to make use of)*	→	sie nutzt aus	*she makes use of*
herein|kommen *(to enter, come in)*	→	sie kommen herein	*they enter*

22 Professions

Unlike English (where you'd say 'He is a̲ teacher'), in German no indefinite article is used in front of job titles. Examples:

Er ist Verkaufsfahrer.	*He is [a] delivery van driver*
Sie ist Kontoristin.	*She is [an] accounts clerk*
Er ist Ingenieur.	*He is [an] engineer*
Er ist Steuerfachmann.	*He is [a] tax expert*
Sie ist Einkaufsleiterin.	*She is [a] purchasing manager*
Sie ist Buchhalterin.	*She is [a] bookkeeper*

23 Nationality

Similarly in German, when stating your nationality, you say:

male, sing.	female, sing.	adjective
Ich bin Engländer.	Ich bin Engländerin.	englisch
Ich bin Brite.	Ich bin Britin.	britisch
Ich bin Amerikaner.	Ich bin Amerikanerin.	amerikanisch

Note that you cannot use an adjective in German and say 'I am English/American'; you must use the noun: **Ich bin Engländer(in)/ Amerikaner(in)**. The words **Englisch, Deutsch** (with capital letters) refer to the language.

Please study the names of some European countries and the names for their male and female inhabitants (plus the related adjectives):

Country	inhabitant, m.	inhabitant, f.	adjective
England	der Engländer	die Engländerin	englisch
Wales	der Waliser	die Waliserin	walisisch
Belgien	der Belgier	die Belgierin	belgisch
Luxemburg	der Luxemburger	die Luxemburgerin	luxemburgisch
Italien	der Italiener	die Italienerin	italienisch
Spanien	der Spanier	die Spanierin	spanisch
Schottland	der Schotte	die Schottin	schottisch
Frankreich	der Franzose	die Französin	französisch
Dänemark	der Däne	die Dänin	dänisch
Irland	der Ire	die Irin	irisch
Portugal	der Portugiese	die Portugiesin	portugiesisch
Griechenland	der Grieche	die Griechin	griechisch
Deutschland	der Deutsche	die Deutsche	deutsch

The above countries are neuter, but some countries are masculine and others are feminine. Learn the following:

der Libanon (m.sing.): der Libanese, die Libanesin; libanesisch
die Schweiz (f.sing.): der/die Schweizer/in; schweizerisch
die Niederlande (pl.): der/die Niederländer/in; niederländisch
die Vereinigten Staaten von Amerika (pl.) = die U S A (pl.): der/die Amerikaner/in; amerikanisch

24 Everyday expressions of time

Please study these indications of time:

(Es ist) ein Uhr / zwei Uhr / drei Uhr / vier Uhr ...
(It's) one o'clock/two o'clock/three o'clock/four o'clock ...

Note that **nach** means 'past' and **vor** means 'to':

8.05	fünf nach acht	8.55	fünf vor neun
8.10	zehn nach acht	8.50	zehn vor neun
8.20	zwanzig nach acht	8.40	zwanzig vor neun

However, at the half hour stage, the Germans think forward to the following hour ('half on the way to ...'), like this:

6.30	halb sieben	('half to seven' = half past six)
12.30	halb eins	('half to one' = half past twelve)
1.30	halb zwei	('half to two' = half past one)

It's a useful exercise to draw twelve clocks showing 'half past ...' and to write the German expression of time next to it, so that you can visualize it better. When you have made yourself familiar with this way of looking at the half hour, you can take the next step and study some other colloquial expressions of time:

11.25	fünf vor halb zwölf	11.35	fünf nach halb zwölf
2.25	fünf vor halb drei	2.35	fünf nach halb drei

This may appear a little complicated, but it is the normal, conversational way of indicating time. You will find simpler and more formal ways in Checknote 57.

25 Prepositions used in expressions of time

When giving a very rough indication of time you say:

*am Morgen/am Mittag/am Nachmittag/am Abend
in the morning/at midday/in the afternoon/in the evening*

*am is a contraction of **an + dem** (dative masc.sing.).

We usually translate 'at' as **um** (please make sure that you pronounce **um** correctly as 'oom'):

um neun Uhr/um zehn Uhr abends/um Mitternacht
at nine o'clock/at ten p.m.(every evening)/at midnight

Study also the following expressions (**im** is the contracted form of **in + dem**):

im Januar/im Sommer/im Jahre 1990   (dative masc.sing.)
in January/in summer/in the year 1990

in der Nacht/in der Zwischenzeit   (dative fem.sing.)
at night/in the meantime

Note: In German there is no 'in' before year numbers! You can simply say **neunzehnhundertneunzig** ('1990') or **im Jahr(e) 1990** ('in the year 1990').

26 General expressions of time

The following words and expressions are used a thousand times every day in German-speaking countries. Learn them as soon as you can:

heute	*today*
heute morgen	*this morning*
heute mittag	*this lunchtime*
heute abend	*this evening/tonight*
morgen	*tomorrow*
morgen früh	*tomorrow morning*
morgen mittag	*tomorrow lunchtime*
morgen abend	*tomorrow/tomorrow night*
übermorgen	*the day after tomorrow*
nächste Woche	*next week*
nächsten Monat	*next month*
nächstes Jahr	*next year*
gestern	*yesterday*
vorgestern	*the day before yesterday*
vorige Woche/letzte Woche	*last week*
vorigen Monat/letzten Monat	*last month*
voriges Jahr/letztes Jahr	*last year*

In letters you may find the abbreviation **d.M.**; this refers to the current month (equivalent to the English 'inst.').

27 Present tense endings

In German dictionaries all verbs are given in the infinitive form, i.e. the stem plus the infinitive ending **-en**. You are already familiar with **komm-en**, 'to come'; **erwart-en**, 'to expect'; **kenn-en**, 'to know (a person)'. Get into the habit of thinking in terms of this stem, as you have to put different endings on it when conjugating a German verb.

In an English present tense, only the third person singular has an ending to be remembered (s): 'I sell, you sell, we sell, they sell, he/she/it sells'. In German, as you saw in Checknote 8, you are faced with a variety of different endings. We would like to introduce you now to three important verbs in the present tense: **sag-en**, 'to say'; **bestell-en**, 'to order'; **telefonier-en**, 'to phone'. Notice how we've separated the endings from the stems. Note also that **ich telefoniere**, for example, means both 'I phone' and 'I am phoning'. Before we start, here is a reminder: **ich** = 'I'; **er** = 'he'; **sie** = 'she'; **wir** = 'we'; **sie** = 'they'; **Sie** = 'you', formal form of address (both singular and plural).

a) ich sag-e; ich bestell-e; ich telefonier-e

In spoken German, the **-e** ending is often swallowed and people will say **ich sag', ich bestell', ich zeig'**. Take care not to use the infinitive (i.e. the dictionary form) when talking about yourself.

b) er/sie sag-t; er/sie bestell-t; er/sie telefonier-t

Sometimes an **-e-** is inserted in the **er/sie** form before the **-t**, especially when the stem of the verb ends in **-t** or **-d**, e.g.: **antworten** ('to answer') → **er antwort-et**.

c) wir/sie/Sie sag-en; wir/sie/Sie bestell-en; wir/sie/Sie telefonier-en

As you can see, the plural forms look just like the infinitives.

28 Weak verbs: simple past

Verbs are classified as 'weak' or 'strong' according to the way they form the past tense. In English, weak verbs add -ed, -d or -t to form the simple past ('dance/danced', 'walk/walked', 'dream/dreamt') or they stay the same ('cut/cut'); German weak verbs add **-te** in the singular and **-ten** in the plural. For example:

bestellen (*to order*)	→ ich bestellte	*I ordered*
verkaufen (*to sell*)	→ er verkaufte	*he sold**
zeigen (*to show*)	→ sie zeigte	*she showed*
bestätigen (*to confirm*)	→ wir bestätigten	*we confirmed*
erwarten (*to expect*)	→ sie erwarteten	*they expected*

[*In English, *to sell* is a 'strong' verb – see the next Checknote.]

29 Strong/irregular verbs: simple past

Strong verbs in English are those which form their past tense by changing the stem vowel ('write/wrote', 'buy/bought', 'stand/stood'); the same principle applies to strong verbs in German. These don't have a special ending in the singular, but the plural ending is **-en**:

sprechen (*to speak*)	→ ich sprach	*I spoke*
treffen (*to meet*)	→ er traf	*he met*
schreiben (*to write*)	→ sie schrieb	*she wrote*
besprechen (*to discuss*)	→ wir besprachen	*we discussed*
bitten (*to request*)	→ sie baten	*they requested*

Comprehension Practice 2

*Re-read or listen again to the conversation between the secretary and Mr Jackson at the beginning of this Unit and then say whether these statements are true or false (**richtig oder falsch**).*

1 Herr Schneider erwartet Frau Jackson.	richtig/falsch?
2 Herr Jackson kann Deutsch.	richtig/falsch?
3 Excel-Equip ist in Deutschland.	richtig/falsch?
4 Die Sekretärin kann Englisch.	richtig/falsch?
5 Herr Jackson ist für zwölf Uhr bestellt.	richtig/falsch?
6 Herr Jackson kommt aus England.	richtig/falsch?

FLUENCY PRACTICE 6
Job titles

Mr Jackson has been handed an organizational chart of Bürotex.
The names of the persons he is likely to meet are entered on it:

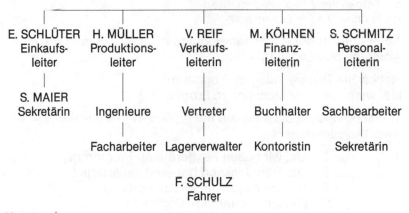

E. WAGENKNECHT
Geschäftsführer

E. SCHLÜTER	H. MÜLLER	V. REIF	M. KÖHNEN	S. SCHMITZ
Einkaufs-leiter	Produktions-leiter	Verkaufs-leiterin	Finanz-leiterin	Personal-lciterin

S. MAIER
Sekretärin   Ingenieure   Vertreter   Buchhalter   Sachbearbeiter

Facharbeiter   Lagerverwalter   Kontoristin   Sekretärin

F. SCHULZ
Fahrer

New words:

der Geschäftsführer	*managing director*
der Produktionsleiter	*production manager*
die Finanzleiterin	*financial controller, f.*
die Personalleiterin	*personnel manager, f.*
der/die Vertreter	*(sales) representative/s*
der/die Sachbearbeiter	*clerk/s*
der/die Facharbeiter	*skilled worker/s*
der/die Lagerverwalter	*warehouse manager/s*

Please answer the following questions with short one-word answers, as oral communication doesn't always use full sentences. Note that **was ist?** aks 'what is (his/her function)?'

1 Was ist Herr Wagenknecht?
2 Was ist Frau Schmitz?
3 Was ist Herr Müller?
4 Was ist Frau Köhnen?
5 Was sind Sie? ('What is your own position?')

Note: In the business world the male job title is sometimes used for female employees, too. Women are always addressed as **Frau** .... regardless of whether they are married or not.

FLUENCY PRACTICE 7
Asking questions

New words:

der Tischrechner	*desk calculator*
das Programm	*range of products*
der Textcomputer	*word processor*
das Faxgerät	*fax machine*
der Fotokopierer	*photocopier*
ich komme aus	*I come from*

An enquiry about a company's range of products (and the reply) would be phrased in this manner:

Haben Sie Tischrechner im Programm?
(Ja, wir haben Tischrechner im Programm.)

The sentences in brackets are the replies to five questions. What were the questions?

1 ....?   (Ja, wir haben Faxgeräte im Programm.)
2 ....?   (Ja, Herr Jackson hat eine Sekretärin.)
3 ....?   (Ja, ich habe einen Fotokopierer.)
4 ....?   (Ja, ich komme aus England.)
5 ....?   (Ja, wir verkaufen Textcomputer.)

FLUENCY PRACTICE 8
What's the time? - Wie spät ist es? (lit. 'How late is it?')

Es ist ....   Es ist ....   Es ist ....   Es ist ....

FLUENCY PRACTICE 9
Naming European nationals

Please give the names for a male and a female inhabitant of the following countries, after revising Checknote 23:

1 Bundesrepublik Deutschland: der ... , die ... .
2 Großbritannien: der ... , die ... . (Or: der ... , die ... .)
3 Frankreich: der ... , die ... .
4 Irland: der ... , die ... .

FLUENCY PRACTICE 10
Role-play

New words:

für	*for*
tun	*to do*
vielleicht	*perhaps*
die Geschäftskarte	*business card*
ja sicher	*yes, of course*

Imagine you are Mr Smith, sales director of Brown Engineering Ltd., visiting a German company. You have arranged to meet Mr Schwarz at three o'clock. Please write down your part in this short conversation with Mr Schwarz' secretary:

Sekretärin: Guten Tag. Was kann ich für Sie tun?

You: *Good afternoon. I'm (called) Richard Smith. I have an appointment with Mr Schwarz, at three o'clock.*

Sekretärin: Ach ja, Herr Smith. Haben Sie vielleicht eine Geschäftskarte?

You: *[while handing over your card] Yes, of course, here is my card.*

Sekretärin: Vielen Dank!

You: *I am the sales director of Brown Engineering Ltd.*

Sekretärin: Kommen Sie bitte mit, Herr Smith.

You: *Thank you.*

UNIT 3

Starting a business meeting

Study the following dialogue in the usual way.

Mr Jackson is shown into Frau Schneider's office, invited to sit down at the conference table and offered a beverage. Finally they touch on his plans to export office equipment to Germany.

Frau Schneider:	Herein!
Sekretärin:	Herr Jackson von Excel-Equip ist hier.
Frau Schneider:	Guten Tag, Herr Jackson. Kommen Sie doch bitte herein! Wir haben erst gestern telefoniert. Es freut mich, Sie kennenzulernen.
Mr Jackson:	Ganz meinerseits, Frau Schneider.
Frau Schneider:	Nehmen Sie bitte hier am Tisch Platz!
Mr Jackson:	Vielen Dank.
Frau Schneider:	Möchten Sie einen Kaffee, oder lieber einen Tee?
Mr Jackson:	Ich trinke gerne einen Kaffee. Bitte schwarz – einen Löffel Zucker.
Sekretärin:	Ein Kaffee. Kommt sofort.

The secretary goes to fetch the coffee.

Frau Schneider:	Herr Jackson, Sie haben mir gestern am Telefon gesagt, daß Sie Bürogeräte nach Deutschland exportieren wollen.
Mr Jackson:	Ja, das stimmt. Wir sind fest auf dem britischen Markt etabliert. Jetzt wollen wir die Vorteile des Europäischen Binnenmarktes ausnutzen.

The secretary brings the coffee.

Sekretärin:	Hier ist Ihr Kaffee. Schwarz, mit Zucker.
Mr Jackson:	Vielen Dank. Das ist sehr nett von Ihnen.
Sekretärin:	Bitte sehr. Gern geschehen!

TRANSLATION

Frau Schneider:	Come in!
Secretary:	Mr Jackson from Excel-Equip is here.
Frau Schneider:	Good morning (good day) Mr Jackson. Please, do come in. We spoke on the telephone only yesterday. How do you do (*lit.* 'it pleases me to meet you')?
Mr Jackson:	How do you do (*lit.* 'completely on my part')?
Frau Schneider:	Take a seat here, at the table (*lit.* 'Take please here at the table a seat').
Mr Jackson:	Many thanks.
Frau Schneider:	Would you like a coffee or would you prefer tea (*lit.* 'Would like you a coffee, or preferably a tea')?
Mr Jackson:	I'd like a coffee (*lit.* 'I drink gladly a coffee'). Black please - one spoon (of) sugar.
Secretary:	One coffee coming up (*lit.* 'One coffee; comes at once')!

The secretary goes to fetch the coffee.

Frau Schneider:	Mr Jackson, you told me on the phone yesterday (*lit.* 'you have to me yesterday on the phone said') that you want to export office equipment to Germany (*lit.* 'that you office equipment to Germany export want').
Mr Jackson:	Yes, that's right. We are firmly established on the British market. Now we want to take advantage of the Single European Market (*lit.* 'We want the advantages of the SEM to make the most of).

The secretary brings the coffee.

Secretary:	Here's your coffee. Black, with sugar.
Mr Jackson:	Thank you very much. That's very kind of you.
Secretary:	You're welcome (*lit.* 'Please very much')! It's a pleasure (*lit.* 'Gladly happened').

Checklist 3

Masculine nouns:

singular	plural	
der Tisch	die Tische	*table*
der Platz	die Plätze	*seat, place*
der Kaffee	-	*coffee*
der Tee	-	*tea*
der Zucker	-	*sugar*
der Löffel	die Löffel	*spoon*
der Vorteil	die Vorteile	*advantage*
der Markt	die Märkte	*market, market place*
der Binnenmarkt	die Binnenmärkte	*internal market*
der Europäische Binnenmarkt		*the Single (European) Market*

Neuter nouns:

das Telefon	die Telefone	*telephone*
das Gerät	die Geräte	*machine, equipment*
das Bürogerät	die Bürogeräte	*office equipment*

Verbs/verbal expressions:

herein|kommen	*to enter, come in*
wir haben	*we have*
telefonieren	*to phone*
wir haben telefoniert	*we spoke on the phone*
sich freuen	*to be pleased*
es freut mich	*I'm pleased*
kennen|lernen	*to make someone's acquaintance*
nehmen	*to take*
Platz nehmen	*to have a seat*
möchten Sie?	*would you like?*
(verb+) lieber	(comparative of 'gern') *to prefer*
(verb+) gern/e	*to like* (doing something)
trinken	*to drink*
ich trinke gerne...	*I like drinking...* (here: *I would like to drink...*)
kommt sofort	(a dish/drink) *coming up*
sagen	*to say*
sie haben gesagt	*you said/have said*
sie haben mir gesagt	*you (have) told me*
wollen	*to want*
exportieren	*to export*
stimmen (impers.:'es')	*to agree, tally*
das stimmt!	*that's right!*
etablieren	*to establish*
wir sind etabliert	*we are established*
aus|nutzen	*to use, utilize, make the most of*
Vorteile ausnutzen	*to take advantage of, make the most of*

Other words/expressions:

Herein!	*Come in!*	fest	*firmly*
erst	*only*	auf (dem Markt)	*in (the market*
gestern	*yesterday*		*place)*
ganz	*completely*	des (genitive case)	*of the*
meinerseits	*on/for my part*	schwarz	*black*
sofort	*at once*	mit	*with*
am Telefon	*on the telephone*	sehr	*very*
daß	*that*	nett	*nice*
nach	*to (a town/country)*	von (+ dat.)	*of; from*

CHECKNOTES

30 Irregular verbs: **haben/sein**

Unfortunately not all German verbs follow the pattern of **kommen**. There are quite a number of irregular verbs, the most important ones being **haben** ('to have') and **sein** ('to be'). Here are their present tenses:

haben		**sein**	
ich habe	*I have*	**ich bin**	*I am*
er hat	*he has*	**er ist**	*he is*
sie hat	*she has*	**sie ist**	*she is*
es hat	*it has*	**es ist**	*it is*
wir haben	*we have*	**wir sind**	*we are*
sie haben	*they have*	**sie sind**	*they are*
Sie haben	*you have*	**Sie sind**	*you are*

In addition to being important independent verbs, **haben** and **sein** are also used as auxiliaries to make up other tenses, just like 'to have' and 'to be' in English (see Checknotes 32/36).

31 Vowel change in the present tense

Unfortunately, some of the most common verbs have irregular forms in the third person singular. For example:

nehmen *(to take)*	Ich nehme	→ er/sie/es nimmt
fahren *(to drive/travel)*	ich fahre	→ er/sie/es fährt
helfen *(to help)*	ich helfe	→ er/sie/es hilft
sehen *(to see)*	ich sehe	→ er/sie/es sieht
empfehlen *(to recommend)*	ich empfehle	→ er/sie/es empfiehlt
sprechen *(to speak)*	ich spreche	→ er/sie/es spricht
geben *(to give)*	ich gebe	→ er/sie/es gibt

Note the special meaning of **es gibt**: literally 'it gives', this also translates 'there is'/'there are'!

As long as the above verbs occur in the **ich** or plural form, you wouldn't be able to tell that they are irregular, but the **er/sie/es** form is a give-away! When learning irregular verbs, it is a good policy to learn this form (the third person singular) after the infinitive.

32 The past tense (simple past vs. present perfect)

You were introduced to the German simple past in Checknotes 28 and 29 but, with the exception of **haben, sein** and the modal verbs (see Checknote 56), this tense is mostly used in written German. In the spoken language a different tense is preferred, i.e. the present perfect. This tense is formed with either **haben** or **sein** + the past participle of the verb and translates the English 'I did' or 'I have done' something. The examples in the following Checknotes will make this clear.

33 The present perfect (weak verbs)

Study the following:

organisieren *(to organize)*	→ ich habe organisiert	*I (have) organized*
installieren *(to install)*	→ er hat installiert	*he (has) installed*
importieren *(to import)*	→ sie hat importiert	*she (has) imported*
exportieren *(to export)*	→ wir haben exportiert	*we (have) exported*
erwarten *(to expect)*	→ ich habe erwartet	*I (have) expected*
verkaufen *(to sell)*	→ er hat verkauft	*he (has) sold*

You'll have noticed that the past participle of verbs ending in **-ieren** is formed by adding **-t** to the stem. Verbs which begin with **er-, ver-, zer-, ge-, be-, emp-, ent-, miß-** (called inseparable prefixes) also fall into this category.

Most weak verbs, however, follow a slightly different pattern:

ge- + stem + ending: **-t**

machen *(to do, make)*	Sie haben gemacht	*you (have) done, made*
fragen *(to ask a question)*	wir haben gefragt	*we (have) asked*
warten *(to wait)*	ich habe gewartet	*I (have) waited*
schicken *(to send)*	sie hat geschickt	*she (has) sent*

Although there are many weak verbs, the most commonly used ones tend to be strong verbs, as given in the next Checknote.

34 The present perfect (strong/irregular verbs)

The strong/irregular verbs are a little more difficult. The pattern is:

ge- + stem (vowel change) + ending: **-en**

schreiben *(to write)*	ich habe geschrieben	*I have written*
geben *(to give)*	er hat gegeben	*he has given*
finden *(to find)*	sie hat gefunden	*she (has) found*
lassen *(to leave behind)*	sie haben gelassen	*they (have) left*
sprechen *(to speak)*	sie hat gesprochen	*she has spoken*

35 The past tense (mixed verbs)

Some German verbs form their past tenses by adding **-te** (simple past) and **-t** (present perfect) just like weak verbs, but they also change the stem vowel like strong verbs. Not surprisingly, they're called 'mixed' verbs. Here's the pattern:

ge- + stem (vowel change) + ending: **-t**

			simple past:
denken	ich habe gedacht	*I (have) thought*	dachte *thought*
bringen	er hat gebracht	*he (has) brought*	brachte *brought*
nennen	sie hat genannt	*she (has) named*	nannte *named*
kennen	er hat gekannt	*he knew/has known*	kannte *knew*
wissen	wir haben gewußt	*we know/have known*	wußte *knew*

36 The present perfect: **haben** or **sein**?

You are probably wondering why all the examples given so far contained the verb **haben**, when we said in Checknote 32 that both **haben** and **sein** are used to form the present perfect. The following Checknotes will make this clear. Verbs taking **haben** are:

1: All verbs which can take a direct object regardless of whether the verb is weak or strong, e.g.:

Er hat die Steuern gesenkt.
He has decreased taxes.

Sie haben hohen Profit gemacht.
They made a high profit.

2: All reflexive verbs (see Checknote 48), such as **sich fragen** ('to ask oneself'). This point is particularly important for those of you who know French, as the rules in that language are different.

Er hat sich gefragt, was er tun soll.
He asked himself what he should do.

3: Verbs which do not take a direct object, provided they do not imply any idea of motion, only of duration, e.g.:

Er hat lange gewartet.
He (has) waited for a long time.

Das Geschäft hat im letzten Jahr stagniert.
Business was bad (lit. 'stagnated') *last year.*

4: Verbs giving a fixed starting or finishing time:

anfangen *(to start)*	wir fingen an	→	wir haben angefangen
aufhören *(to stop)*	wir hörten auf	→	wir haben aufgehört
beginnen *(to begin)*	wir begannen	→	wir haben begonnen

Wir haben mit dem Fotokopieren angefangen.
We started with the photocopying.

Wir haben um fünf Uhr aufgehört.
We stopped at five o'clock.

As you can see, the group of verbs using **haben** to form the present perfect is very large indeed, and includes the verb **haben** itself: **ich habe gehabt** ('I have had/I had').

37 Present perfect: **sein**

A smaller group of verbs uses **sein** to form the present perfect. These are:

1: The verbs **sein** ('to be') → **ich bin gewesen**, and **bleiben** ('to remain'; 'to stay') → **ich bin geblieben**. For example:

Ich bin in Schwierigkeiten gewesen.
I was (have been) in difficulties.

Ich bin zu Hause geblieben.
I stayed home.

2: All verbs which do not take a direct object (i.e. intransitive verbs) and which express either:

a) motion to or from a place:

aufstehen *(to get up)*	ich bin aufgestanden
fahren *(to drive, travel)*	er ist gefahren
fallen *(to fall)*	es ist gefallen
fliegen *(to fly)*	wir sind geflogen
gehen *(to go, walk)*	sie sind gegangen
kommen *(to come)*	ich bin gekommen
reisen *(to travel)*	wir sind gereist
sinken *(to go down, sink)*	es ist gesunken
steigen *(to go up, rise)*	sie sind gestiegen

Er ist viel gereist.	*He travelled extensively/a lot.*
Die Kurse sind gesunken.	*Share prices have fallen/fell.*
Die Zinsen sind gestiegen.	*Interest rates went up.*

or b) a change of state, e.g.:

entstehen *(to develop/arise/start up)*	es ist entstanden
werden *(to become)*	es ist geworden
wachsen *(to grow)*	er ist gewachsen

Der Profit ist gewachsen.	*Profit has grown.*
Hohe Kosten sind entstanden.	*High costs were incurred.*
Er ist Abteilungsleiter geworden.	*He has become head of department.*

Many intransitive verbs are used to explain graphs and charts, to discuss share movements, business performance, etc. and they are therefore quite important.

38 German word order

German word order follows a logic of its own and takes a lot of practice to get right, but rest assured that you will get used to it! In German there are two 'reserved spaces' for the verbs in every main clause or sentence: the second, and the final place:

[1] [2]   [f]
Wir haben erst gestern   telefoniert.
Wir sind fest auf dem britischen Markt etabliert.
Wir wollen die Vorteile ....   ausnutzen.

The verb that shows the personal ending is always the second 'idea' in the sentence; here we have marked its place as [2].

The other 'reserved space' at the end of the sentence, i.e. in the final position, is marked [f]. This is reserved for the past participle or the infinitive (i.e. the one that doesn't show a personal ending).

Note: If there's only one verb in the sentence, the space marked [2] has to be filled with a verb, but the final position is left free.

In English, you can place a comma after the first idea in your sentence and then start again (e.g.: 'Naturally, we want ...'). In German, this isn't possible. Once you've played your first card, your second move is prescribed by the rules of the game! For example:

Jetzt wollen wir die Vorteile ausnutzen.
Now we want to make the best use of (lit. 'utilize') *the advantages.*

Natürlich wollen wir die Vorteile ausnutzen.
Naturally, we want to make the best use of the advantages.

Note the iron rule of German word order: the verb which shows the personal ending has to be the second idea in a main clause!

39 Impersonal sentence opener: es

Es ('it') is used more often in German than in English at the beginning of a sentence; if the subject of a sentence is quite long, i.e. an infinitive phrase, **es** acts as a 'place keeper' for the subject which will follow a little later in the sentence. Here are some examples of its use:

es stimmt	*it's correct*
es gefällt mir	*I like it* (lit. 'it pleases me')
es freut mich zu hören/sehen	*I'm pleased to hear/see*
es ist nützlich, den Vertreter zu kennen	*it's useful to know the rep.*

40 Separable verbs: infinitive phrase with zu

Separable verbs (see Checknote 21), which – in our Checklists – have a vertical stroke after the prefix, insert the **zu** in that place. For example:

infinitive:		infinitive phrase:	
kennen|lernen	→	**kennenzulernen**	*to get to know*
vor|stellen	→	**vorzustellen**	*to introduce*
an|bieten	→	**anzubieten**	*to offer*

As you can see, **zu** becomes part of the separable verb. Study the following:

Es ist nett, Sie kennenzulernen.
It's nice to make your acquaintance.

Es ist wichtig, ihn dem neuen Direktor vorzustellen.
It's important to introduce him to the new director.

Ich bitte ihn hereinzukommen.
I ask him (politely) *to come in.*

41 Introductions

There are several German equivalents of the English 'How do you do?' You can say:

a) **Es freut mich, Sie kennenzulernen.**
b) **Ich bin erfreut, Sie kennenzulernen.** (Very formal)
c) **Ich freue mich, Sie kennenzulernen.** (Informal)
d) **Sehr erfreut.**
e) **Angenehm.** (*lit.* 'Pleasant').

The normal reply to all the above is **Ganz meinerseits** ('The pleasure is all mine'), whether or not the pleasure really is all yours!

42 Translating 'ideas'

It is very useful to be able to detect words you already know hidden in the new words you come across. In this Unit's dialogue you met the compound **meinerseits**. You already know that **mein** means 'my' and you may be able to guess that **seits** has something to do with 'side'. You can thus conclude that **(ganz) meinerseits** means something like '(completely) on my side' and normally means 'on my part'.

This is merely one example (you'll find many others in the Course), illustrating how important it is to translate 'ideas' and not to expect a 'word-for-word' translation.

43 Comparatives and superlatives

Most German adjectives and adverbs form regular comparatives by adding an **-er** suffix in the same way as many English adjectives:

neu	→	**neuer**	*new*	→ *newer*
ruhig	→	**ruhiger**	*quiet*	→ *quieter*

In German, the length of the adjective is not important, i.e. there's no equivalent to the English 'more':

modern	→	**moderner**	*modern*	→ *more modern*
schön	→	**schöner**	*beautiful*	→ *more beautiful*

When used before a noun, the comparative form of the adjective adds the normal adjectival endings, e.g. **eine modernere Fabrik** ('a more modern factory'). Note that German adjectives can be used without any change as adverbs, unlike English where you must add -ly: **sie arbeitet ruhig** ('she works quietly'). However, just as in English, some forms are irregular:

gut	→	**besser** (adj./adv.)	*good*	→ *better*
gern	→	**lieber** (only adv.)	lit. *gladly*	→ *more gladly*
viel(e)	→	**mehr** (adj./adv.)	*much (many)*	→ *more*

Gern and **lieber** are very common German adverbs which cause some confusion for the native English speaker, as these ideas are expressed in English by using either the verb 'like' or 'prefer' (doing something) – see Fluency Practice 14.

In English the superlative form of adjectives ends in -st; 'best', 'dearest', 'fastest': in German it also ends in **-st** but, of course, you must add the various adjectival endings. For example:

der beste Verkäufer *(the best salesman)*
das teuerste Modell *(the dearest model)*
das schnellste Auto *(the fastest car)*

Wir haben die neusten Modelle auf der Messe vorgeführt.
We exhibited the latest models at the trade fair.

Das neue Auto ist nicht nur das beste, sondern auch das teuerste.
The new car is not only the best, but the dearest.

However, you'll have to get used to the little word **am** in front of the superlative form of the adverb (**am besten, am teuersten, am schnellsten**):

Das neue Flugzeug fliegt am schnellsten.
The new plane flies fastest.

Die teuersten Geräte halten am besten.
The dearest machines last longest.

Comprehension Practice 3

Re-read or listen again to the conversation at the beginning of this Unit and then say whether these statements are true or false (richtig/falsch, r/f).

New words:
auch   *also*
sitzen   *to sit* (sie sitzt, sie saß, sie hat gesessen)
schon   *already*
etwas   *something*

Note: **Herr** becomes **Herrn** in all cases of the singular and **Herren** in the plural.

1 Frau Schneider bittet Herrn Jackson hereinzukommen.   r/f
2 Herr Jackson und Frau Schneider haben gestern telefoniert. r/f
3 Die Sekretärin sitzt auch am Konferenztisch.   r/f
4 Excel-Equip ist schon in Deutschland fest etabliert.   r/f
5 Frau Schneider bietet etwas zu trinken an.   r/f
6 Herr Jackson und Frau Schneider wollen die Vorteile des
   Europäischen Binnenmarkts ausnutzen.   r/f

FLUENCY PRACTICE 11
Some of the tasks you may have to carry out in your work

New words:

die Ausstellung	*the exhibition, fair*
die Ausstellungen	*fairs*
der Fotokopierer	*photocopier*
das Faxgerät	*fax machine*
die Ware	*goods*
der Vertrag	*the contract*
der Bestand	*the stock*
der Kunde	*the customer*
die Kunden	*customers*
unterschreiben	*to sign* (er unterschreibt, er unterschrieb, er hat unterschrieben)
warten	*to wait* (sie wartet, sie wartete, sie hat gewartet)

Fill in the correct form of the verb, after revising Checknotes 8, 27:

1 Wir (organize) Ausstellungen.
2 Sie (order) zwei Fotokopierer.
3 Sie (import) deutsche Faxgeräte.
4 Die Firma (sells) gute Ware.
5 Er (telephones) mit Telekom.
6 Ich (sign) den Vertrag.
7 Die Kunden (wait) im Büro.

FLUENCY PRACTICE 12
Talking about what you did/have done (see Checknotes 33, 34)

You will find German word order a little strange for a while, but it is surprising how quickly one gets used to it. Let's practise the past tense normally used in conversation, i.e. the present perfect.

1 Wir (have) Ausstellungen (organized).
2 Sie (have) zwei Fotokopierer (ordered).
3 Sie (have) deutsche Faxgeräte (imported).
4 Die Firma (has) gute Ware (sold).
5 Der Ingenieur (has) mit Telekom (telephoned).
6 Ich (have) den Vertrag (signed).
7 Die Kunden (have) im Büro (waited).

FLUENCY PRACTICE 13
Giving instructions to your secretary/P.A.

Instruct your secretary to carry out the following tasks for you. In a normal office situation you would say **'Machen Sie bitte zehn Fotokopien!'** ('Please make ten photocopies.'):

1 zwei Tassen Kaffee bringen – bring 2 cups of coffee.
2 Herrn XYZ anlrufen – ring Mr XYZ.
3 den Brief von Interop beantworten – reply to Interop's letter.
4 eine Besprechung mit M. vereinbaren – arrange a meeting with M.
5 einen neuen Katalog bestellen – order a new catalogue.

If your secretary is new and you wish to sound a little more polite, you could begin each request with **Könnten Sie ...**: '**Könnten Sie bitte zehn Fotokopien machen**'.

FLUENCY PRACTICE 14
*Comparisons using **gern/lieber***

When offered the choice of tea or coffee. Mr Jackson could have replied: "Ich trinke gern(e) Tee, aber ich trinke lieber Kaffee." *I like drinking tea, but I prefer drinking coffee.* How would the following people comment on their preferences? You'll need to know one new word – **die Messe** ('the trade fair').

1 Sekretärin: Kaffee trinken – Tee trinken.
2 Frau Schneider: bei Bürotec bestellen – bei Excel-Equip bestellen.
3 Mr Jackson: nach Frankreich exportieren – nach Deutschland exportieren.
4 Mr Smith: aus Japan importieren – aus Deutschland importieren.
5 Empfangsdame: am Empfang arbeiten – im Büro arbeiten.
6 Herr Müller: eine Messe organisieren – eine Konferenz organisieren.

ADDITIONAL VOCABULARY

The following important words should form part of every business person's vocabulary; learn them as soon as you can:

der Anrufbeantworter,-	*answerphone*
der Tischrechner,-	*calculator*
der Personalcomputer,-	*micro-computer, PC*
der Textcomputer,-	*word processor*
der Schreibsaal	*typing pool*
die Finanz	*accounts department*
die Werbeabteilung,-en	*advertising department*
das Faxgerät,-e	*fax machine*
das Diktiergerät,-e	*dictating machine*
wieviel?	*how much?*
wieviele?	*how many?*

UNIT 4

Introducing your firm

> *In this Unit you will learn more about the use of the present tense, numbers and German pronunciation, and you will also be introduced to reflexive verbs and relative pronouns. In the dialogue Frau Schneider invites Mr Jackson to talk about his firm.*

Frau Schneider: Herr Jackson, Ihre Firma will also nach Deutschland exportieren. Ich muß gestehen, daß mir der Name Excel-Equip leider nicht vertraut ist. Können Sie mir mehr über Ihre Firma erzählen?

Mr Jackson: Ja sicher! Unsere Firma besteht seit 1970. Wir haben uns auf Büroausstattung spezialisiert; um es genau zu sagen: auf elektronische Bürogeräte. Wir stellen Tischrechner, elektronische Schreibmaschinen, Mikrocomputer, Fernkopierer, Textcomputer, und so weiter her. Mit anderen Worten: wir produzieren alles, was man für ein modernes Büro braucht.

Frau Schneider: Sie haben sich also auf Spitzentechnologie spezialisiert!

Mr Jackson: Ja. Das stimmt. Jetzt suchen wir einen Agenten in Deutschland.

TRANSLATION

Frau Schneider: Mr Jackson, [so] your firm wants to export to Germany. I have to admit that, unfortunately, I am not familiar with the name Excel-Equip (*lit.* 'that to me the name Excel-Equip, unfortunately, not familiar is'). Can you tell me more about your firm?

Mr Jackson: Yes, of course. Our firm has existed (*lit.* 'exists') since 1970. We specialize in office equipment, or more precisely (*lit.* 'in order to say it precisely'), in

47

electronic office machines. We produce calculators, electronic typewriters, microcomputers, fax machines, word processors and so on. In other words (*lit.* 'with other words'), we produce everything that is needed for the modern office.

Frau Schneider: I see that you have specialized in advanced technology (*lit.* '... yourself ... specialized').

Mr Jackson: Yes. That's right. We are now looking for an agent in Germany.

Checklist 4

Masculine nouns:

(singular)	(plural)	
der Computer	die Computer	*computer*
der Mikrocomputer	die Mikrocomputer	*micro-computer*
der Tischrechner	die Tischrechner	*(desk) calculator*
der Textcomputer	die Textcomputer	*word processor*
der Agent	die Agenten	*agent*

Feminine nouns:

die Firma	die Firmen	*firm*
die Ausstattung	die Ausstattungen	*equipment*
die Büroausstattung	die Büroausstattungen	*office equipment*
die Maschine	die Maschinen	*machine*
die Schreibmaschine	die Schreibmaschinen	*typewriter*
die Technik	die Techniken	*technique; technology*
die Technologie		*technology*
die Spitze	die Spitzen	*peak, top, (the best)*
die Spitzentechnologie		*advanced technology*

Neuter nouns:

das Faxgerät	die Faxgeräte	*fax machine*
das Land	die Länder	*country, state*

Adjectives/adverbs:

genau	*precise*
ander-	*different, other*
alles	*everything*
modern	*modern*

Modal verbs:

wollen	*to want to, intend to*
können	*to be able to, can*
müssen	*to have to, must*

Verbs:

erzählen (über) acc.	*to tell, talk (about)*
spezialisieren (refl.) auf acc.	*to specialize in*
her|stellen acc.	*to manufacture, make*
produzieren acc.	*to produce*
suchen acc.	*to look for*
bestehen	*to exist*
(es besteht, es bestand, es hat bestanden)	

Other words/expressions:

seit	*since*
und so weiter	*and so on*
(usw.)	*(etc.)*

CHECKNOTES

44 Verbs + prepositions (+ accusative case)

As in English, a number of verbs are followed by certain prepositions. These verbs take an accusative after the preposition, just like **erzählen über** ('to talk about') which we met in this Unit's dialogue:

berichten über acc.	*to report on*
informieren über acc.	*to inform about*
sehen auf acc.	*to insist on (see to it that...)*
garantieren (für acc.)	*to vouch for*

Examples:

Das TV-Wirtschaftsmagazin berichtet über die Börsenkurse.
The TV programme on economic affairs reports on share prices.

Wir garantieren (für) eine schnelle Ausführung der Bestellung.
We guarantee a prompt oxcoution of the order.

Wir sehen auf gleichbleibend gute Produktqualität.
We see to it that the quality of our products remains constant.
(gleichbleibend = 'constant')

Wir müssen die Kunden über die Preiserhöhungen umgehend informieren.
We have to inform the customers about the price increases immediately.

45 Use of the present tense

After learning about so many features of the German language which seem complicated to an English native speaker, you will be pleased to learn that Germans make life a little easier for themselves by using the present tense, when English speakers would use the present perfect or the future tense. Additional information in the sentence signals the different time scale.

For example, the word **seit** ('since') puts the starting point of an action clearly in the past, but the German verb stays in the present tense:

> Die Firma besteht seit 1970. (lit. 'The firm exists since 1970'.)
> Instead of: *The firm has existed since 1970.*

The same principle applies to the word **morgen** ('tomorrow'). Study the following:

> Ich bestelle morgen eine elektronische Schreibmaschine.
> (lit. 'I order tomorrow an electronic typewriter'.)
> *I'll* (or *I'm going to*) *order an electronic typewriter tomorrow.*

46 Extended infinitives

You'll remember that in the dialogue Mr Jackson said **'um es genau zu sagen'** ('to be precise', lit. 'in order to say it precisely'); here's another example of this construction:

> Herr Jackson ist in Frankfurt, um einen Agenten zu suchen.
> *Mr Jackson is in Frankfurt in order to look for an agent.*

47 Personal pronouns - accusative case

We must look now at the personal pronouns in the accusative case (direct object). The first, **ich** ('I'), becomes **mich** ('me'). Here are the other persons:

er	→	**ihn**	*he*	→ *him*
sie	→	**sie**	*she*	→ *her*
es	→	**es**	*it*	→ *it*
wir	→	**uns**	*we*	→ *us*
sie	→	**sie**	*they*	→ *them*
Sie	→	**Sie**	*you*	→ *you* (polite form)

Let's make some phone calls using the verb **an|rufen** + acc. (direct object):

Herr Müller ...	Ich rufe ihn an.	*I phone him.*
Frau Zander ...	Ich rufe sie an.	*I phone her.*
Direktor Riedel ...	Ich rufe Sie morgen an!	*I'll phone you tomorrow!*

48 Reflexive verbs

If you look up the word 'to specialize' in your German dictionary, you'll find 'sich spezialisieren' or 'spezialisieren, refl.vb', which means that the verb is reflexive. These verbs form their various tenses with the pronouns **mich** ('myself'), **sich** ('yourself', 'himself', etc.), **uns** ('ourselves') and so on. Let's see now how reflexive verbs are conjugated:

Present tense:

ich spezialisiere mich	*I specialize (myself)*
er/sie/es spezialisiert sich	*he/she/it specializes (him/her/itself)*
wir spezialisieren uns	*we specialize (ourselves)*
sie spezialisieren sich	*they specialize (themselves)*
Sie spezialisieren sich	*you specialize (yourself, yourselves)*

Sometimes it's quite obvious why a verb is reflexive (**sich fragen**, 'to ask oneself', or **sich verletzen**, 'to injure oneself'), but very often it's less evident. For example, you'll be surprised to learn that the following verbs are reflexive in German:

sich spezialisieren auf	*to specialize in*
sich interessieren für	*to be interested in*
sich bemühen (um)	*to endeavour, to take trouble (over)*
sich eignen (für)	*to be suitable (for)*
sich ärgern (über)	*to be angry (about)*
sich lohnen	*to be worthwhile*

Here are some examples showing you how these verbs are used:

Die Firma spezialisiert sich auf Spitzentechnologie.
The firm specializes (itself) in advanced technology.

Der Verkaufsleiter bemüht sich um Umsatzsteigerung.
The sales manager is trying hard to increase turnover.

Die Sekretärin ärgert sich über den Chef.
The secretary is annoyed (irritates herself) with the boss.

Wir interessieren uns für die neuen Tischrechner.
We're interested (interest ourselves) in the new desk calculators.

49 Personal pronouns - dative case

You have already met the dative case of the personal pronoun **Sie**: **Ihnen** ('to you'). You'll remember the opening line of Unit 2's dialogue was **Kann ich Ihnen helfen?** ('Can I help you?'). This translation is a simplification of 'Can I be of help to you?'; the word 'to' indicates a need to use the dative case as opposed to the accusative. Study these pronouns:

	dat.				
ich	→	mir	I	→	to me
er	→	ihm	he	→	to him
sie	→	ihr	she	→	to her
es	→	ihm	it	→	to it
wir	→	uns	we	→	to us
sie	→	ihnen	they	→	to them
Sie	→	Ihnen	you	→	to you

As **helfen** is followed by the dative case, we've chosen this verb to show you how they all work in practice:

Er hilft mir.   Er hilft ihr.   Sie hilft ihm.
He helps me. *He helps her.* *She helps him.*

Sie helfen uns.   Wir helfen ihnen.
They help us.   *We help them.*

Take care to distinguish between **ihnen** ('to them') and **Ihnen** ('to you'). Here are some more examples, using other verbs:

Wir schicken Ihnen die Dokumente per Boten.
We('ll) send (to) you the documents by messenger.

Wir geben ihm eine Frist von 30 Tagen.
We set (give to) him a time-limit of 30 days.

Der neue Großrechner spart mir viel Zeit.
The new main-frame computer saves (for) me a lot of time.

You can try and work out the next few examples by yourself, but cover up the English translation on the right first!

Ich schicke ihm ein Fax.	*I('ll) send (to) him a fax.*
Wir schicken ihr eine Fotokopie.	*We('ll) send (to) her a photostat.*
Er gibt uns ein Freiexemplar.	*He gives (to) us a free sample.*
Wir senden Ihnen eine schriftliche Bestätigung.	*We('ll) send (to) you written confirmation.*
Er hilft ihm bei der Übersetzung.	*I (give) help (to) him with the translation.*

50 More numbers

The numbers over twenty (and up to ninety-nine) are a bit tricky, but they may remind you of the old English forms – 'four and twenty ...':

21 **einundzwanzig**
22 **zweiundzwanzig**
23 **dreiundzwanzig**
24 **vierundzwanzig**

36 **sechsunddreißig**
37 **siebenunddreißig**
38 **achtunddreißig**
39 **neununddreißig**

If your business is doing well, you may want to use some higher numbers:

1 000	**(ein) tausend**
1 000 000	**eine Million**
1 000 000 000	**eine Milliarde**

Note: For higher numbers, dots may be used to make them easier to read, but never commas as in English. However, a comma is used to separate the Mark from the Pfennig (smallest currency unit), e.g.:

DM 1.765,35 = eintausendsiebenhundertfünfundsechzig Mark fünfunddreißig
DM   19,99 = neunzehn Mark (und) neunundneunzig (Pfennig)

Normally, **und** and **Pfennig** are omitted.

In English there are three possibilities for 0 ('zero/nought/nil'); in German there's only one word: **null**.

51 **Was** used as relative pronoun

When the German **was** is not used as a question word asking 'what?', it means 'that' or 'which' and is normally preceded by **alles** ('everything') or **etwas** ('something'):

... alles, was man für ein modernes Büro braucht.
... everything (that) one needs for the modern office.

This sentence demonstrates a tendency in German to send the verb to the end of a sentence. We'll study this construction closer when we tackle subclauses.

Was is also used, if the subclause refers back to the preceding idea:

Er sagte telefonisch ab, was ich nicht erwartet hatte.
He cancelled [his appointment] by phone, which I hadn't expected.

52 Relative pronouns
   ('who', 'whom', 'which', 'that')

In addition to meaning 'the', the various forms of **der/die/das** can also be used as relative pronouns. Consider the following (and, at the same time, make a special note of the German word order):

Der Mann, der da steht, ...
The man who is standing there, ...   masc. nom. sing.

Der Lieferung, die gekommen ist, ...
The delivery which came ...   fem. nom. sing.

Das Scheckbuch, das ... enthält, ...
The chequebook which contains ...   neut. nom. sing.

Herr Jackson, den ich gestern gesehen habe, ...
Mr Jackson whom I saw yesterday ...   masc. acc. sing.

Of course, if the **der/die/das** is preceded by a preposition which requires a specific 'case', then the correct ending must be used. For example:

Das Kaufhaus, in dem er arbeitet, ...
The department store in which he works ...   neut. dat. sing.

Die Sekretärin, mit der ich gestern sprach, ...
The secretary with whom I spoke yesterday ...   fem. dat. sing.

Sometimes it's the verb that requires a particular case:

Der Lieferant, dem wir geholfen haben, ...
The supplier we helped ...   masc. dat.sing.

You will have noticed that **der** (masc.) and **das** (neut.) become **dem** and **die** (fem.) changes to **der** in the dative case.

As usual, the plural forms are easier to handle, as there is only **die** (nom. and acc.) and **denen** (dat.) for all three genders:

Die Büros, die ich gesehen habe, ...
The offices which I have seen, ...   neut. acc. pl.

Die Arbeiter, die ich entlassen habe, ...
The workers whom I (have) laid off, ...   masc. acc. pl.

Die Rechnungen, die ich geschickt habe, ...
The bills which I (have) sent out, ...   fem. acc. pl.

Die Kunden, denen wir einen Rabatt versprochen haben, ...
The customers to whom we promised a discount ...   masc. dat. pl.

53 Remembering the gender of nouns

One of the niggly points of German is the fact that you have to remember the gender of every noun. This is not a particularly difficult task, but it is one that requires constant practice and revision. Please remember, however, that if you do make a mistake, it's not a catastophe!

When speaking German, you can get away with shortening the definite article in most cases to **de'**, as native speakers of German will automatically substitute the appropriate ending without being conscious of doing it. This is, in fact, a feature of German dialects.

54 Pronunciation: ä, ö, ü

To give you a rest from German grammar, we take another look at specific pronunciation problems. As you know, the sounds of the letters **a, o** and **u** are modified when they have an **Umlaut** (two dots ¨) above them; in fact, the word Umlaut means 'change of sound'. The points to remember are:

ä: sounds similar to 'ey' in 'they', but longer. Some American pronunciations of 'happy' use the same sound. Or, Imagine an upper-class English character in one of Noël Coward's plays saying I'm so very hEppy to know you; that's close to the German **ä**. Compare:

anders (*different*) ... **ändern** (*to modify*).

ö: no equivalent in English; it sounds like 'ur' in 'turnover'. Compare:

oben (*above*) ... **hören** (*to hear*).

ü: no equivalent in English; the sound is very similar to French 'u' in 'reçu'. Compare:

Hut (*hat*) – remember to say 'hoot', not 'hut' ... **Hüte** (*hats*).

55 Long and short vowels

It is also essential to distinguish between German long and short vowels, otherwise there will be confusion – e.g.:

(long)		(short)	
wen	*whom*	wenn	*if*
schief	*crooked*	Schiff	*ship*
fühlen	*to feel*	füllen	*to fill*

Just imagine the misunderstandings there would be in English If a foreigner constantly said 'I leave' when he meant 'I live', and 'feel it' when he should have said 'fill it'!

56 Modal verbs

Examples of modal verbs in English are: 'I can', 'you must', 'she may', etc. Study these German modals:

wollen	*(to want to)*	ich/er/sie/es will	wir/sie/Sie wollen
können	*(to be able to, can)*	ich/er/sie/es kann	wir/sie/Sie können
müssen	*(to have to, must)*	ich/er/sie/es muß	wir/sie/Sie müssen
dürfen	*(to be allowed to, may)*	ich/er/sie/es darf	wir/sie/Sie dürfen

Normally, these verbs are followed by another verb, but there are some exceptions (cf. Comprehension Practice 2: Herr Jackson kann Deutsch).

Please study the following examples carefully and then, for additional practice, try covering up the German sentences and translating back into English:

Er will einen Container bestellen.	*He wants to order a (freight) container.*
Sie kann den Liefertermin bestätigen.	*She is able to confirm the delivery date.*
Ich muß die Verzögerung aufholen.	*I have to make up for the delay.*
Er darf keinen Fehler machen.	*He is not allowed to make any mistake.*

Note: Unlike the English ('want to', 'be able to', 'have to'), the German modal auxiliary is never followed by **zu**.

57 Formal expressions of time

In Checknote 24 you learned how to express the time. Another, more formal way is as follows:

11.25 = elf Uhr fünfundzwanzig   11.35 = elf Uhr fünfunddreißig
2.25 = zwei Uhr fünfundzwanzig   2.35 = zwei Uhr fünfunddreißig

There is no equivalent for the English abbreviation a.m./p.m. In German one has to add **morgens** ('in the morning'), **mittags** ('at midday'), **nachmittags** ('in the afternoon'), **abends** ('in the evening') or **nachts** ('at night') - e.g. **fünf Uhr morgens** ('5 a.m.').

The 24-hour clock is widely used for official timetables. Please study the following examples:

20.35 = zwanzig Uhr fünfunddreißig   17.05 = siebzehn Uhr fünf
07.56 = sieben Uhr sechsundfünfzig   00.10 = null Uhr zehn

58 German addresses

Again, as a temporary respite from grammar, we would like to give you some useful words in connection with the German postal service. Note the following:

die Adresse	*address* (note the German word has only one 'd')
die Hausnummer	*house number*
die Straße	*street*
der Straßenname	*street name*
die Stadt, Städte	*town*
der Städtename	*name of the town*

die Postleitzahl	*postcode*
die Postfach	*P.O. Box*
die Telefonnummer	*telephone number*

German addresses are now written in the standard order (name/ street/town) but the house number is still placed after the street name, e.g.: **Schloßstraße 147.**

Postcodes are put in front of the town's name, its size being reflected by the number of zeros shown; big cities rate three (7000 Stuttgart), smaller places have two or less (7800 Freiburg, 7840 Müllheim). If you were given an address in 4330 Mülheim, you'd know it was near 4000 Düsseldorf, not the Mülheim near 5000 Köln.

Reading out the names of German towns along with their postcodes not only helps you practise saying long numbers but you also become acquainted with placenames, thus killing two birds with one stone ("Zwei Fliegen mit einer Klappe schlagen" ... the Germans "catch two flies with one flap"!). See Fluency Practice 17 for a selection.

Letters are not used in postcodes, but another number may appear after the name of the town, indicating the district; for example, the number 1 normally means **Altstadt**, or '(old) town centre'. Here is a typical address:

Dr. Werner Müller
Lindenstraße 569
5000 Köln 1

59 Telephone numbers

German telephone numbers are split up into double digits, starting from the end, and are often printed in this way to make them easier to read. Area codes start with 0 when inside the country. The area code for a city is fairly short (München 089), but the area code for a small town may well be longer, e.g.: 0 22 03 (**null zwelundzwanzig null drei**).

On the telephone you may hear people using **zwo**, which is a variation of **zwei**, in order to distinguish the number 2 from 3 (**drei**). The number 02237 843657 is, therefore, read as: 0 22 37-84 36 57.

Comprehension Practice 4

Richtig oder falsch?

New words:
der Handelsvertreter   *sales rep.*
der Spezialist   *specialist*
die Büroeinrichtung   *office furniture*

1 Herr Jackson will nach Amerika exportieren.   r/f
2 Die Firma besteht seit 1990.   r/f
3 Sie stellen alles her, was man für ein modernes Büro braucht.   r/f
4 Herr Jackson ist Spezialist für Büroeinrichtung.   r/f
5 Die Firma hat sich auf Spitzentechnologie spezialisiert.   r/f
6 Excel-Equip sucht einen Handelsvertreter.   r/f

FLUENCY PRACTICE 15
Requests using personal pronouns

Please complete the following requests after revising Checknote 49.
You'll also need to study the following vocabulary.

New words:
die Bestellung   *order*
die Rechnung   *bill, invoice*
die Preisliste   *price list*
das Telefonbuch   *telephone directory*

1 Geben Sie (me) bitte die Bestellung!
2 Geben Sie (her) bitte das Telefonbuch!
3 Geben Sie (him) bitte die Rechnung!
4 Geben Sie (them) bitte die neuen Preislisten!

FLUENCY PRACTICE 16
Practising telephone numbers

Please read out the following numbers from your personal organizer:

Müller	57 83 38	Schuster	6 23 26 34
Maier	80 20 60	Kaufmann	2 19 81
Bürger	5 18 97 39	Freund	33 44 99

FLUENCY PRACTICE 17
German postcodes

Read out aloud the following postcodes and town names:

1000 Berlin. 2000 Hamburg. 3000 Hannover. 4000 Düsseldorf. 5000 Köln. 6000 Frankfurt. 7000 Stuttgart. 8000 München. 5300 Bonn. 2800 Bremen. 6500 Mainz. 5400 Koblenz. 7400 Tübingen. 2300 Kiel. 6540 Simmern. 7750 Konstanz. 4050 Mönchen-Gladbach. 2242 Büsum. 6635 Schwalmbach.

FLUENCY PRACTICE 18
Using relative pronouns

Please insert the correct relative pronoun, paying particular attention to the gender, number and case of the noun it refers to. (There are two new words to note: **der Bericht**, 'report'; **ein|laden**, 'to invite'.)

1 Die Rechnung, ____ ich gefunden habe, ist bezahlt.
2 Das Auto, ____ ich kaufen möchte, ist sehr teuer.
3 Der Bericht, ____ heute ankam, ist sehr interessant.
4 Der Mechaniker, ____ ich bestellt habe, ist hier. (= 'has arrived')
5 Die Kunden, ____ ich eingeladen habe, sind in der Empfangshalle.
6 Ich habe ihm alles gegeben, ____ ich hatte.

DICTIONARY PRACTICE 1
Going to the cinema

This magazine extract [from Cosmopolitan 2/91] invites you to take some time off and to go along to the cinema where you can see some excellent films. Read the article, answer the questions in English, and then check with the Key. We're not helping you with the words this time, as you must get used to consulting your dictionary quickly and correctly.

TREFFPUNKT KINO

Sagen Sie alle Verabredungen ab! Kaufen Sie Gummibärchen und eine Zeitung mit Kinoprogrammen, und überreden Sie gute Freunde zu einem Abend vor der großen Leinwand. Im Februar starten elf wunderbare Filme, jeder auf andere Art und Weise sehenswert!

---

1 What should you cancel?
2 What must you buy?
3 What should you persuade your friends to do?
4 How many films are being shown?
5 When do they begin?

UNIT 5

Setting up business on the Continent

This Unit takes a closer look at the dative case and comparisons, and you'll learn more about asking questions. We also introduce the formal future tense.

The conversation between Mr Jackson and Frau Schneider turns to problems of logistics and high rents.

Frau Schneider:	Herr Jackson, darf ich Sie noch mal fragen, warum Sie nach Deutschland exportieren wollen?
Mr Jackson:	Wir wollen expandieren. Wir haben schon eine Niederlassung in Frankreich und ich kann Ihnen versichern, daß wir dort einen sehr guten Ruf haben.
Frau Schneider:	Wo befindet sich denn Ihre französische Niederlassung?
Mr Jackson:	An der Peripherie von Paris. Das ist verkehrstechnisch günstiger als im Zentrum.
Frau Schneider:	Unsere Büros liegen im teuren Westend von Frankfurt. Wenn die Mieten weiter so stark steigen wie in den letzten Jahren, dann werden auch wir eines Tages in die Außenbezirke ziehen müssen.
Mr Jackson:	Sie wissen sicher, wie extrem hoch die Mieten in Paris sind.
Frau Schneider:	Allerdings! Aber was soll man da tun? Es bleibt einem nichts anderes übrig als zu zahlen!

TRANSLATION

Frau Schneider:	Mr Jackson, may I ask you again why you want to export to Germany?
Mr Jackson:	We want to expand. We already have a branch in France and I can assure (to) you that we have a very good reputation there.

Frau Schneider:	Where is your French branch situated, then?
Mr Jackson:	On the outskirts (*lit.* 'periphery') of Paris. From a logistical point of view it's more advantageous than in the centre.
Frau Schneider:	Our offices are situated in the expensive 'Westend' of Frankfurt. If (the) rents continue to go up as much (*lit.* 'steeply') as in the last [few] years, we'll also have to move into the suburbs one day.
Mr Jackson:	I'm sure you know how extremely high the rents are in Paris.
Frau Schneider:	Absolutely! But what should one do? One can't do anything but pay (*lit.* 'It remains to one nothing else but..')!

Checklist 5

(Note: German plural endings are given after the comma.)

Masculine nouns:

der Ruf	*reputation*
der Bezirk, -e	*area, administrative district*
der Außenbezirk, -e	*outlying district*
der Tag, -e	*day*
der Verkehr	*traffic*

Feminine nouns:

die Niederlassung,-en	*branch, agency*
die Peripherie, -n	*outskirts*
die Miete, -n	*rent*

Neuter nouns:

das Zentrum, -tren	*centre*
das Ende	*end*
das Wootend	*business centre of Frankfurt*
das Jahr, -e	*year*

Verbs:

expandieren	*to expand*
befinden (refl.) in (dat.)	*to be situated in*
werden (aux.)	*will/shall*
wissen (acc.)	*to know* (a fact)
sollen (modal)	*to be expected to*
übrig|bleiben (intr.)	*to remain*
zahlen (acc.)	*to pay* (a bill)
ziehen in/nach acc.	to move to

Verb forms for memorizing:
es befindet, befand, hat sich befunden
es zieht an, zog an, hat angezogen
er weiß, wußte, hat gewußt
es bleibt, blieb, ist geblieben
sie zahlt, zahlte, hat gezahlt
sie zieht, sie zog, sie ist gezogen

Adjectives/adverbs:

-technisch (suffix)	*of a technical nature*
verkehrstechnisch	*traffic-wise*
günstig	*convenient, favourable*
günstiger	*more convenient*
teuer	*expensive*
stark	*strong*
letzt-	*last*
sicher	*sure; safe*
extrem	*extremely*
hoch	*high*

Other words/expressions:

mal = einmal	*once*
noch (ein)mal	*once more*
schon	*already*
in + dat.	*in (a place)*
daß	*that*
dort	*there*
sehr	*very*
denn	*then* (= emphasis; often untranslated)
dann	*then* (= 'in that case')
an + dat.	*on*
das ist	*that is*
als	*than*
im = in dem	*in the*
unser (m. & n.),	*our*
unsere (f.)	*our*
wenn ..., (dann)	*if..., (then)*
weiter (+ verb)	*to continue to*
so + adj. ... wie	*as + adj. ... as*
auch	*too, also*
eines Tages (gen.)	*one day*
allerdings!	*quite! certainly!*
man (dat.: einem; acc.: einen)	*one, people*
nichts	*nothing*
nichts anderes als	*nothing but*
da	*in such a case*

CHECKNOTES

60 Dative case of der/die/das

We must now look a little more closely at the dative case. You'll find it useful to memorize this pattern:

	masc. sing.:	fem. sing.:	neut. sing.:	m./f./n. pl.
nom.	**der**	**die**	**das**	**die**
dat.	**dem**	**der**	**dem**	**den**

In the dative case plural, not only do **der/die/das** change to **den**, but the noun itself also takes an ending, i.e. **-n.**

Let's see how it works in practice using the verb **geben,** which takes an indirect object (in the dative case) and a direct object (in the accusative case). Here are some examples:

Geben Sie der Sekretärin einen Textcomputer.
Give the secretary a word processor.

Geben Sie dem Direktor einen Kaffee.
Give the director a coffee.

Geben Sie dem Büro einen neuen Anstrich.
Give the office a new coat of paint.

Geben Sie den Kunden die Werbegeschenke.
Give the customers the advertising gifts.

Note that, in German, we give 'to the secretary', 'to the customers', etc. and note also the German word order ('to the customers the gifts'), i.e.: when two nouns are used, the dative case precedes the accusative case.

61 Dative case of ein, eine

The dative case of **ein** mirrors that of **der, die, das:**

	masc.	fem.	neut.
the (sing.)	**dem**	**der**	**dem**
a, an	**einem**	**einer**	**einem**

Please study these sentences:

Ich empfehle einem Reisenden (m.) ein gutes Hotel.
I recommend a good hotel to a traveller.

Wir liefern einer Firma (f.) neue Ware.
We deliver new stock to a firm.

Sie raubten einem Mädchen (n.) das Bargeld.
They stole the cash from a girl.

No, your eyes are not deceiving you; **Mädchen** ('girl') is neuter!

62 Dative case: adjectives

Learn three new words: **pensionert** ('retired'), **klein** ('small'), and **jung** ('young'), and then study these sentences:

a) **geben** (dat.) acc. *to give*

Geben Sie der   neuen Sekretärin einen Textkomputer!
Geben Sie dem pensionierten Direktor einen Kaffee!
Geben Sie dem   kleinen Büro einen neuen Anstrich!

b) **gehören** dat. *to belong to*

Der Kalender gehört einer neuen Sekretärin.
The calender belongs to a new secretary.

Der Schreibtisch gehört einem pensionierten Direktor.
The desk belongs to a retired director.

Der Sportwagen gehört einem jungen Mädchen.
The sports car belongs to a young girl.

Yes, unfortunately, adjectives have endings too in the dative case! You'll have seen that any adjective, following the dative forms **dem/der** and **einem/einer**, takes the ending **-en**.

63 Verbs taking a direct and an indirect object

Geben, of course, is not the only verb that can take two objects; there are others:

Ich kann Ihnen das bestätigen.	*I can confirm that to you.*
Ich kann Ihnen das versichern.	*I can assure you of that.*
Ich will Ihnen das erklären.	*I want to explain that to you.*
Ich vertraue ihm den Schlüssel an.	*I trust him with the key.*
Ich empfehle ihm die beste Ware.	*I recommend the best goods to him.*

64 Prepositions taking the dative case

Who was it who said it's the little things in life that really matter? Well, the same could be said of those little German words - the prepositions. You couldn't hold a conversation for long without using them. Here are some that take the dative case:

ab   *from* (a starting point)
aus   *out of*

außer	*except*
bei	*near, at; while*
dank	*thanks to; owing to*
mit	*with; at the age of*
nach	*to* (a town or country); *after* (indication of time or date)
seit	*since*
von	*from*
zu	*at* (+ general indication of time); *to* (a target)

Here are some examples:

ab Spediteur	*ex shipping agent*
aus dem Safe	*out of the safe*
bei dem (beim) Empfang	*at reception* (hotel)
mit dem Auto	*by car*
nach dem Essen	*after dinner*
seit dem Einbruch	*since the burglary*
von dem (vom) Makler	*by the agent, broker*
zu Ostern	*at Easter*
zu der (zur) Messe	*to the fair/exhibition*

Some prepositions can go before or after the noun, as the following examples show:

entsprechend	*according to*
zufolge	*according to*
gegenüber	*opposite*

den neuen Anweisungen entsprechend	*according to the new instructions*
gegenüber dem roten Rathaus	*opposite the red town hall*
der internationalen Presse zufolge	*according to reports by the international press*

Sometimes the preposition is contracted with the definite article:

bei + dem → beim
von + dem → vom
zu + dem → zum
zu + der → zur

65 Prepositions taking either dative or accusative

There's one other group of German prepositions we must mention and they're rather special, because they sometimes take the dative and sometimes the accusative case. If you can ask the question **wo?** ('where?'), then you use the dative. If movement or change is implied, the accusative is used. For the time being we're only concerned with the dative. Here are those special prepositions; keep referring back to them until you've learned them:

an	*at*	**über**	*over, above*
auf	*on*	**unter**	*under*
hinter	*behind*	**vor**	*in front of*
in	*in*	**zwischen**	*between*
neben	*next to*		

Now, let's imagine you've mislaid an important letter. Where could it be? **Der Brief liegt ...**

an der Rezeption	*at reception*
auf dem Schreibtisch	*on the desk*
hinter der Tür	*behind the door*
in dem (im) Restaurant	*in the restaurant*
neben dem Schrank	*next to the cupboard*
über dem Fenster	*above the window*
unter dem Teppich	*under the carpet*
vor der Tür(e)	*in front of the door*
zwischen den Akten	*between the files*

When a German tells you something in confidence, he or she might say **"unter uns gesagt"** ('just between us').

66 Bei: special uses

It's interesting that **bei** sounds like the English word 'by', because it's rarely used in that sense! The preposition **bei** can have many different meanings; let's study some of them:

bei Frankfurt	*near Frankfurt*
bei mir	*at my place* (or 'on/with me')
sie wohnt bei ihrer Schwester	*she lives with her sister*
wir arbeiten bei einer großen Firma	*we work for a large firm*
ein wichtiger Brief ist heute bei der Post gekommen	*an important letter came in the post today*
bei meiner Abfahrt	*on my departure*
bei Ihrer Ankunft	*on your arrival*
bei einem Glas Bier	*over a glass of beer*
Wollen Sie mir bei der Umschulung helfen?	*Will you help me with the training programme?*
Bei wem kaufen Sie die Ware?	*Who(m) do you buy the goods from?*
Beim Großhändler?	*From the wholesaler?*

67 Beim + infinitive

In German it is extremely easy to turn a verb into a noun. All you need to do is give it a capital letter and 'hey presto' a new noun is created! To make things easier still, all these nouns are neuter. So, to indicate that an action is happening while another one is still going on you would say: **"beim ..."**. For example:

essen *(to eat)*	→	das Essen	→	beim Essen *while eating*
nach|denken *(to ponder)*	→	das Nachdenken	→	beim Nachdenken *while reflecting*
arbeiten *(to work)*	→	das Arbeiten	→	beim Arbeiten *while working*
verhandeln *(to negotiate)*	→	das Verhandeln	→	beim Verhandeln *while negotiating*

Der Verkaufsleiter macht seine Abschlüsse beim Essen.
The sales manager conducts his business over lunch/dinner.

Der Besucher hat ihn beim Nachdenken gestört.
The visitor disturbed him while (he was) thinking.

Beim Verhandeln muß man einen klaren Kopf haben.
While negotiating, you must keep a clear head.

68 sagen ('to say'/'to tell')

Sagen is a very important verb in German and we want to give you a little more practice in using it. Note the following:

Er hat ihr die Wahrheit gesagt.
He's told her the truth.

Sie hat ihm die Öffnungszeiten gesagt.
She told him the opening times.

Sie haben mir schon gesagt, daß Sie nach Deutschland exportieren wollen.
You have already mentioned that you intend to export to Germany.

It may be as well to mention here that German and English differ slightly regarding quotation marks. At the beginning of direct speech, the quotation marks are to be found at the bottom of the line, not at the top as in English and any quote or direct speech is preceded by a colon, not a comma:

Er sagte: „Hören Sie zu!" *He said, 'Listen!'*

69 German word order (subclauses beginning daß)

Study these two sentences:

Er sagt:　　"Wir wollen nach Deutschland exportieren."
Er sagt, **daß** wir _____ nach Deutschland exportieren **wollen**.

After **daß**, the word order changes. Initially you may find it confusing to see two verbs at the end of the sentence, especially as they both end in **-en**. Now let's see how this construction works in the singular (**er** instead of **wir**):

Er sagt: "Ich will nach Deutschland exportieren."
Er **hat gesagt, daß er** _____ nach Deutschland exportieren **will**.

Note: In a **daß**-clause, the verb that shows the personal ending
goes to the very end (after an infinitive or past participle, if
there is a second verb in the sentence).

70 Asking questions ('why?'/'when?'/'where?' etc.)

The most frequently used question-words are:

warum?	*why?* (less common: **weshalb?, wieso?**)
wie?	*how?*
wann?	*when?*
womit?	*what ... with?*
was?	*what?*
wo?	*where?*
wer?	*who?*
wie lange?	*how long?*
wie viel?	*how much?*
wie viele?	*how many?*
wie schnell?	*how fast?*

Take care NOT to confuse **wo** with 'who' and **wer** with 'where'! Some
examples of the above in use:

Wie geht es Ihnen?	*How are you?*
Wann haben Sie den Brief erhalten?	*When did you receive the letter?*
Wer kommt morgen?	*Who's coming tomorrow?*
Wie lange bleibt er in Deutschland?	*How long is he staying in Germany?*

71 Indirect questions

Study the following:

Er fragt, wann die Lieferung in London ankommt.
He's asking when the consignment (will) reach London.

Sie möchte wissen, ob sie ein Hotelzimmer bestellen soll.
She would like to know if she should book a hotel room.

In German, indirect questions work the same way as in English,
except that in the 'reported' sentence the verb goes to the end.

72 Comparisons ('as dear as'/'dearer than' etc.)

In business one often has to make comparisons. Study the following:

a) er it so erfolgreich wie ich   *he's as successful as I (am)*
    so gut wie neu   *as good as new*
    so teuer wie in Rom   *as expensive as in Rome*

b) sie ist reicher als er   *she is richer than he (is)*
    billiger als in Tokio   *cheaper than in Tokyo*
    größer als je zuvor   *bigger than ever (before)*

From the above examples you'll have seen that:

a) when the items under discussion are alike, you have to use **so ... wie** ('as ... as');

b) when a comparative form is used, you have to use **als** ('than').

Both these uses appear in this Unit's dialogue ("Wenn die Mieten weiter so stark steigen wie in den letzten Jahren..." and "Das ist ... günstiger als im Zentrum").

c) **groß** ('big') but **größer** ('bigger') – why the umlaut? We mentioned in Checknote 43 that some adjectives are irregular in the comparative form. One fairly common irregularity is that, in addition to the ending **-er**, in short adjectives the vowel takes an umlaut:

arm *(poor)*   →   ärmer *(poorer)*
kurz *(short)*   →   kürzer *(shorter)*
lang *(long)*   →   länger *(longer)*

73 Wenn ..., dann ('If ..., then...')

Let's look again at the second part of the dialogue sentence given as an example in Checknote 72 (on this occasion **dann** is in brackets to indicate that its use is optional, just like its English equivalent 'then').

"Wenn die Mieten weiter so stark steigen wie in den letzten Jahren, (dann) werden auch wir eines Tages in die Außenbezirke ziehen müssen."

Here's another example:

a) Der Profit fällt. *Profit goes down.*

b) Wir müssen die Produktion einstellen. *We have to halt production.*

This is what happens when we combine these two sentences:

Wenn der Profit weiter fällt, (dann) müssen wir die Produktion einstellen.

The rule is that after a **wenn**-clause the <u>main</u> clause starts with the verb, followed by the subject. Of course, you might find it simpler to say:

Wir müssen die Produktion einstellen, wenn der Profit weiter fällt.

74 Future tense: **werden**

You have already seen that Germans often use the present tense when they refer to the future, especially in informal conversation. A future tense does, however, exist and it is formed with the verb **werden**. You'll remember that Frau Schneider said:

"Wir werden in die Außenbezirke ziehen müssen."
"We will have to move to the suburbs."

You may have spotted three verbs in that sentence: **werden**, as the second idea in the sentence (to indicate the future tense), sends the infinitive **müssen** (to indicate the necessity) to the end of the sentence, where it is placed after the main verb **ziehen** ('to move'). Rest assured that not all sentences expressing the future are as complicated as this! Here are some simpler ones:

Wir werden einen Testmarkt aussuchen.	*We'll choose a test market.*
Sie werden den Bauplatz kaufen.	*They'll buy the building plot.*
Sie werden begeistert sein!	*You'll be delighted.*

The singular forms of **werden** are: **ich werde** ('I shall'); **er/sie/es wird** ('he/she/it will'):

Ich werde einen Mechaniker bestellen.	*I'll get an engineer to come.*
Er wird morgen bestimmt kommen!	*He'll definitely come tomorrow!*

Note that when **werden** is used to indicate the future, it is followed by another verb in the infinitive.

75 man ('one', 'people')

The German equivalent of those vague, impersonal English expressions 'one', 'people', 'they', etc. is **man**. We saw in this Unit's dialogue: **Aber was soll man da tun?** ('But what ought one to do?'). **Man**, however, has other forms ... consider the following:

a) When you refer to **man** in the dative case →, you use **einem**:

Man hat keine andere Wahl. → Es bleibt einem nichts anderes übrig!
One has no other choice.   *There's nothing else one can do.*

Man muß aufpassen. → Was kann einem dann schon passieren?
One has to be vigilant.   *What can happen (to a person), then?*

b) When you refer to **man** using the accusative case →, you use **einen**:

Man hat Geldsorgen.	→ Geldsorgen können einen die ganze Nacht wach halten.
One has money problems.	*Money problems can keep someone awake all night.*

Man liest die Fachpresse.	→ Die Fachpresse kann einen in seinen Entscheidungen beeinflussen.
One reads professional magazines.	*Professional magazines can influence one in one's decisions.*

Comprehension Practice 5

This time we'd like you to <u>write</u> <u>out</u> the German answers to the questions: (You may copy your answers from the text, if you like.)

New words:

viele	*many*
in Bezug auf (acc.)	*concerning*

1 Was versichert Herr Jackson Frau Schneider?
2 Hat Excel-Equip eine Niederlassung in Frankreich?
3 Was fragt Frau Schneider in Bezug auf die französische Niederlassung?
4 Wo liegt die französische Niederlassung von Excel-Equip?
5 Warum ist das günstiger?
6 Sind die Mieten in den letzten Jahren stark gestiegen?
7 Was werden viele Firmen eines Tages tun?
8 Sind die Mieten in Paris hoch?

FLUENCY PRACTICE 19
*Solve the puzzle: **beim** or **bei der**?*

New words:

die Umschulung	*retraining programme*
die Terminplanung	*planning one's schedule*
der Abschluß, ¨-sse	*business deal/s*

Your task in the following sentences consists merely in deciding whether you have to use **bei dem/beim** or **bei der**. In other words, you have to know the gender of the noun that **bei** refers to!

1 Der Personalchef hilft seinen Mitarbeitern ... Umschulung.
2 Die Sekretärin hilft dem Chef ... Terminplanung.
3 Der Verkaufsleiter macht seine Abschlüsse ... Essen.

4 Der neue Kunde kauft seine Ware ... Großhändler.
5 Der Besucher hat ihn ... Nachdenken gestört.
6 ... Verhandeln muß man einen klaren Kopf haben.

FLUENCY PRACTICE 20
Adjectival endings

New words:

die Kantine	*canteen*
der Schreibcomputer	*(simple) word processor*
die Lieferbedingungen	*terms of delivery*

We want you to imagine that your colleague has spilled some correction fluid on one of your German texts. Would you believe, it seems to have erased all the important endings! Fill in the gaps.

1 Sagen Sie d___ neu___ Mitarbeiter, wo die Kantine ist.
2 Der Kalender gehört d___ pensioniert___ Direktor.
3 Geben Sie d___ nett___ Sekretärin ein___ neu___
   Schreibcomputer!
4 Erzählen Sie mir mehr über Ihre neu___ Expansionspläne!
5 Geben Sie d___ neu___ Kunden unser___ neu___
   Lieferbedingungen!

FLUENCY PRACTICE 21
Role-play

Play the part of Mr Jackson in this conversation with Frau Schneider:

Frau Schneider: Herr Jackson, warum wollen Sie nach Deutschland exportieren?

Mr Jackson: *We want to expand. We already have a branch in France.*

Frau Schneider: Wo befindet sich denn Ihre französische Niederlassung?

Mr Jackson: *On the outskirts of Paris.*

Frau Schneider: Unsere Büros liegen im teuren Westend von Frankfurt. Eines Tages werden wir in die Außenbezirke ziehen.

Mr Jackson: *I'm sure you know that the rents in Paris are extremely high.*

Frau Schneider: Allerdings! Aber was soll man da tun? Man muß zahlen!

FLUENCY PRACTICE 22
Traffic signs

New words:

an|halten (tr. + intr.)	*to stop*
geradeaus fahren	*to drive straight on*
parken	*to park*
tanken	*to fill the petrol tank*
die Vorfahrt	*priority*
beachten	*to comply with*
schnell(er) fahren	*to drive fast(er)*

Note: man darf nicht ('one must not'), man muß nicht ('one need not')

If you were driving in Germany (or Austria or Switzerland), you would of course come across the following traffic signs. What do they mean – in German? Underline the correct answer (you may wish to revise Checknote 56).

A1 Hier darf man parken.
  2 Hier muß man parken.
  3 Hier soll man parken.

B1 Hier soll man nicht über 60 km/h fahren.
  2 Hier kann man nicht über 60 km/h fahren.
  3 Hier darf man nicht über 60 km/h fahren.

C1 Hier muß man geradeaus fahren.
  2 Hier kann man geradeaus fahren.
  3 Hier will man geradeaus fahren.

D1 Hier darf man nicht parken.
  2 Hier muß man nicht parken.
  3 Hier soll man nicht parken.

E1 Hier soll man tanken.
  2 Hier kann man tanken.
  3 Hier darf man tanken.

F1 Hier muß man die Vorfahrt beachten.
  2 Hier will man die Vorfahrt beachten.
  3 Hier muß man anhalten.

DICTIONARY PRACTICE 2

In the following Units you'll find more and more Dictionary Practices, as it's absolutely essential that you should be able to use a German dictionary quickly and confidently. For this reason you should now study the following extract from a leaflet produced by Dresdner

Bank. Look up the words you can't guess, so as to get the gist of the text, then tick the correct answer in the multiple choice section at the end. Remember, you have only to understand the gist of the text. Gist-reading is probably what you'll be doing most of the time in your work anyway.

Wer sie nicht hat, verzichtet auf vieles.

Seit über dreißig Jahren gibt es jetzt Kreditkarten in Deutschland. Über zwei Millionen Bundesbürger benutzen sie bereits beim Einkaufen, beim Reisen, ja inzwischen sogar beim Tanken.

Weil es einfach und bequem ist. Weil man nie darauf achten muß, wieviel Geld man gerade in der Tasche hat.

Kurz: Weil es das Leben erleichtert.

Heute ist die Auswahl an Kreditkarten groß. Jetzt wird sie noch größer. Durch eine ganz besondere Kreditkarte: die Eurocard Gold der Dresdner Bank.

Wie alle Eurocards besitzt sie in Deutschland die meisten Akzeptanzstellen. Über ihre Verbindung mit dem MasterCard-Netz ist sie praktisch auf der ganzen Welt einsetzbar.

Was die Eurocard Gold darüber hinaus auszeichnet, ist ein reichhaltiges Paket wichtiger Zusatzleistungen: ...

Insgesamt bietet Ihnen diese Karte Leistungen, die nur 130 DM im Jahr kosten und Gold wert sein können.

Auch die Eurocard erhalten Sie jetzt mit dem Namen der Dresdner Bank. Mit dem bisherigen Leistungsumfang und für nur 40 DM im Jahr.

Und noch eine gute Nachricht für alle, die die vielen Vorteile einer Kreditkarte noch nicht kennen: Sie können die Eurocard Gold und die Eurocard der Dresdner Bank jetzt drei Monate lang testen. Und sollten Sie innerhalb dieser Zeit nicht von den Vorzügen überzeugt sein, geben Sie die Karte einfach zurück. Die Jahresgebühr wird Ihnen dann selbstverständlich erstattet. ...

Please tick the correct answers:

1 How long have credit cards been in use in Germany?
   a) *exactly 30 years*   b) *under 30 years*   c) *over 30 years*
2 How many citizens of the Federal Republic use them?
   a) *over three million*   b) *over four million*   c) *over two million*
3 When are credit cards used?
   a) *for shopping/travelling*   b) *for telephoning*   c) *on tankers*
4 What is the meaning of Tanken?
   a) *have a drink*   b) *fill the petrol tank*   c) *fill the fish tank*
5 What are the advantages mentioned in the text?
   a) *it's convenient*   b) *it's inexpensive*   c) *it's trendy*
6 Do credit cards make life:
   a) *more difficult?*   b) *easier?*   c) *more fun?*
7 What is said about the choice of credit cards?
   a) *it's big*   b) *it's gross*   c) *it's getting even bigger*
8 What sort of a card is the Gold card?
   a) *a normal card*   b) *a special card*   c) *a business card*
9 How much is the Gold card per year?
   a) *40 DM*   b) *130 DM*   c) *only 130 DM*
10 How much is the Eurocard per year?
   a) *130 DM*   b) *40 DM*   c) *only 40 DM*
11 How long can you try the cards out for?
   a) *3 months*   b) *5 months*   c) *13 months*
12 What happens if you return the card after a trial period?
   a) *you lose the fee paid*   b) *you lose half the fee paid*
   c) *the full fee is returned to you*

ADDITIONAL INFORMATION

If Mr Jackson had to spell out his name on the phone to a German, he'd probably not be fully understood if he pronounced the letters as we do in English ("jay eh sea kay ess oh en"). In German, it would be "yot ah tsay kah ess oh enn" - see Introduction

Or, he could use the German 'code' names for letters (which differ from the "Alpha/Bravo/Charlie/Delta" system you may be used to):

A/Anton; Ä/Ärger; B/Berta; C/Cäsar; Ch/Charlotte; D/Dora; E/Emil; F/Friedrich; G/Gustav; H/Heinrich; I/Ida; J/Julius; K/Kaufmann; L/Ludwig; M/Martha; N/Nordpol; O/Otto; ö/ökonom; P/Paris; Q/Quelle; R/Richard; S/Samuel; T/Theodor; U/Ulrich; Ü/Übermut; V/Viktor; W/Wilhelm; X/Xantippe; Y/Ypsilon; Z/Zacharias.

UNIT 6

Looking for an agent

In this Unit you will learn more about the plural of German nouns and about negatives. We take another look at the all-important modal verbs and we introduce a new tense, the pluperfect. Frau Schneider's conversation with Mr Jackson turns to the topic of the Single European Market.

Mr Jackson:	Frau Schneider, ich kann Ihnen versichern, daß unsere Produkte zuverlässig sind und unsere Preise konkurrenzfähig. Wir haben ein renomiertes Marktforschungsinstitut damit beauftragt, unsere Ausgangsposition auf dem deutschen Markt zu analysieren. Das Ergebnis war sehr ermutigend.
Frau Schneider:	Das hat Sie also ermuntert, den deutschen Markt zu erobern.
Mr Jackson:	Genau; so ist es. Der europäische Binnenmarkt ist die Chance, auf die wir gewartet haben, um hier Fuß zu fassen. Deutschland war schon immer ein sehr wichtiger Markt. Man erwartet für das neue Deutschland die höchsten Zuwachsraten in Europa.
Frau Schneider:	Da haben Sie ganz recht. Schon Ende 1990 lag das Wirtschaftswachstum in der BRD über den Schätzungen.
Mr Jackson:	Sehen Sie! Wir dürfen diesen Markt nicht ignorieren! Unser Umsatz auf dem Inlandsmarkt ist im vergangenen Jahr leider nicht gestiegen. Die schlechte Auftragslage ist wohl Schuld daran. Nur die Ausweitung unseres Verkaufsgebiets auf ganz Europa kann uns Zuwachsraten bringen.
Frau Schneider:	In einem Punkt haben Sie sicher recht: die Wirtschaft wird immer internationaler. Man darf heutzutage nicht mehr in nationalen Kategorien denken.

TRANSLATION

Mr Jackson:	Frau Schneider, I can assure (to) you that our products are reliable and that our prices are competitive. We have engaged a renowned market researcher (*lit.* 'with it entrusted'), to analyse our starting position in the German market. The result was very encouraging.
Frau Schneider:	So, that has encouraged you to conquer the German market.
Mr Jackson:	Exactly! That's right (*lit.* 'So it is'). The Single European Market is the chance we've been waiting for (in order) to take a (foot)hold here. Germany has always been a very important market. One expects for the new Germany the highest rates of economic growth in Europe.
Frau Schneider:	You are quite right there. Already by the end of 1990, the economic growth in the FRG was higher than the estimated figures (*lit.* 'lay above the estimated figures').
Mr Jackson:	You see! We mustn't ignore this market! Unfortunately, last year our turnover in the domestic market did not increase (*lit.* 'Our turnover on the home market has (is) last year unfortunately not increased'). The poor situation as regards orders is probably to blame for it (*lit.* 'the poor order situation...'). Only by expanding our sales area to the whole of Europe, can we achieve an increase in growth (*lit.* 'Only the expansion of our sales area to the whole of Europe can to us increased growth rates bring').
Frau Schneider:	You're certainly right in one respect: The economy is becoming increasingly international. Nowadays, one mustn't think in national categories any more.

Checklist 6

As in Unit 5, the plural noun endings are shown after the full singular form; if no plural is given, it either doesn't exist or isn't used in the context in which this noun appears in the dialogue.

Masculine nouns:

der Preis, -e	*price*
der Umsatz	*turnover*
der Inlandsmarkt, ¨-e	*domestic market*
der Punkt, -e	*point*

Feminine nouns:

die Position, -en	*position*
die Ausgangsposition	*initial/starting position*
die Chance, -n	*opportunity*
die Rate, -n	*rate*
die Zuwachsrate	*growth rate*
die Wirtschaft	*(national) economy*
die Lage, -n	*situation*
die Auftragslage	*the situation vis-à-vis orders*
die Ausweitung	*expansion*
die Kategorie, |*-n	*category* (|* = see Checknote 79d)

Neuter nouns:

das Produkt, -e	*product*
das Institut, -e	*institute*
das Marktforschungsinstitut	*market research organization*
das Ergebnis, -se	*result*
das Wachstum	*growth*
das Wirtschaftswachstum	*economic growth*
das Jahr, -e	*year*
das Gebiet, -e	*area*
das Verkaufsgebiet	*sales area*

Adjectives/adverbs:
(Note the example phrases shown here.)

zuverlässig	*reliable*	ein zuverlässiges Gerät
konkurrenzfähig	*competitive*	ein konkurrenzfähiger Preis
renomiert	*renowned*	ein renomiertes Institut
ermutigend	*encouraging*	ein ermutigendes Resultat
europäisch	*European*	der europäische Binnenmarkt
wichtig	*important*	ein wichtiger Markt
sehr wichtig	*very important*	ein sehr wichtiger Markt
vergangen	*past*	im vergangenen Jahr
international	*international*	der internationale Handel (*trade*)
national	*national*	eine nationale Katastrophe

Strong/irregular verbs:

fassen	*to seize*
sie faßt, sie faßte, sie hat gefaßt	
steigen (intr.)	*to rise, go up*
es steigt, es stieg, es ist gestiegen	
bringen	*to bring, take*
er bringt, er brachte, er hat gebracht	
werden	*to become*
es wird, es wurde, es ist geworden	
denken	*to think*
er denkt, er dachte, er hat gedacht	

Weak verbs:
(pp = past participle)

versichern	dat.	versichert (pp)	*to assure someone*
beauftragen	acc.(inf.)	beauftragt (pp)	*to instruct someone (to do s.th.)*
analysieren	acc.	analysiert (pp)	*to analyse*
ermutigen	acc.(inf.)	ermutigt (pp)	*to encourage someone (to do s.th.)*
ermuntern	acc.(inf.)	ermuntert (pp)	*to encourage, stimulate*
erobern	acc.	erobert (pp)	*to conquer*
warten	auf acc.	gewartet (pp)	*to wait for*
erwarten	acc.	erwartet (pp)	*to expect*
ignorieren	acc.	ignoriert (pp)	*to ignore*

Other expressions:

schuld sein	*to be at fault*
recht haben	*to be right*
heutzutage	*nowadays*

CHECKNOTES

76 Plurals of nouns

In the six Units you've studied so far you'll have noticed the great variety of plural forms which exist in German. However, you shouldn't be too distressed by this because, after all, in English we meet irregular plurals such as 'child/children', 'mouse/mice', 'goose/geese', etc.

If you have heeded the advice given in Checknote 2 and learnt the plural along with every new noun and its definite article, and if you are quite happy with your progress, you may prefer to skip Checknotes 77-82. If you are a more analytical kind of person, you will want to study these generalizations very carefully and revise them as often as you feel necessary. They will be quite helpful. In time, your 'informed guesses' about the plural forms should be spot-on!

Generally speaking, there are four different types of plural endings, in addition to the plural ending **-s** used on words of English and French origin:

1 no change - only the umlaut (¨) over a preceding vowel (a, o, u)
2 **-e** - umlaut + -e (in the lists you'll find: **¨-e**)
3 **-er** - umlaut + er (**¨-er**)
4 **-en** - or **-n**, if the noun ends in **-e**

77 Masculine nouns (plural)

Unfortunately, the plural forms of masculine nouns are not very predictable, as they can show all the above-mentioned changes, but here are some useful generalizations:

a) Monosyllabic masculine nouns add an **-e**. (If there is an **a**, **o** or **u** it may take an umlaut.) For example:

der Preis	die Preise	*price/s, prize/s*
der Brief	die Briefe	*letter/s*
der Zug	die Züge	*train/s*
der Markt	die Märkte	*market/s*

b) Masculine nouns ending in **-en**, **-el** and **-(t)er** don't take an ending, but may have an umlaut. For example:

der Wagen	die Wagen	*car/s*
der Wechsel	die Wechsel	*bill/s of exchange*
der Kalender	die Kalender	*calendar/s; diary/ies*
der Leiter	die Leiter	*head/s of dept, manager/s; leader/s*

Most names for professions and citizens of many countries are to be found in this group:

der Engländer	die Engländer	*Englishman/men*
der Techniker	die Techniker	*technician/s, engineer/s*

c) Some masculine nouns end in **-e** and simply add **-n**. Examples:

der Kunde	die Kunden	*customer/s*
der Name	die Namen	*name/s*
der Gedanke	die Gedanken	*thought/s*

78 Neuter nouns (plurals)

a) Some neuter nouns add **-er** and take an umlaut if there's an a, o or u in the stem:

das Haus	die Häuser	*house/s*
das Buch	die Bücher	*book/s*
das Amt	die Ämter	*office/s; authority/ies*
das Land	die Länder	*land; country/ies*

b) Neuter nouns which end in **-er**, **-el**, **-en** (and all the diminutive forms which end in **-chen** or **-lein**) do <u>not</u> change:

das Zimmer	die Zimmer	*room/s*
das Fenster	die Fenster	*window/s*
das Mädchen	die Mädchen	*(young) girl/s*
das Fräulein	die Fräulein	*young lady/ies, Miss/es*

c) Other neuter nouns usually add **-e**:

das Gerät	die Geräte	*machine/s; equipment*
das Programm	die Programme	*programme/s*
das Telefon	die Telefone	*telephone/s*
das Produkt	die Produkte	*product/s*

d) Neuter nouns ending in **-nis** add **-se**:

das Ergebnis	die Ergebnissen	*result/s*
das Hindernis	die Hindernisse	*obstacle/s*

79 Feminine nouns (plural)

a) A vast number of feminine nouns simply add **n** in the plural:

die Regel	die Regeln	*rule/s*
die Akte	die Akten	*file/s*
die Börse	die Börsen	*stock market/s; exchange/s*
die Ware	die Waren	*ware/s; goods*
die Reise	die Reisen	*trip/s, journey/s*

b) Many other feminine nouns, including all those ending in **-ung, -heit, -keit** and **-ion**, add **en**:

die Zeitung	die Zeitungen	*newspaper/s*
die Zahl	die Zahlen	*number/s*
die Bilanz	die Bilanzen	*balance sheet/s*
die Schwierigkeit	die Schwierigkeiten	*difficulty/ies*

c) Feminine nouns ending in **-in** add **-nen**:

die Sekretärin	die Sekretärinnen	*secretary/ies*
die Kassiererin	die Kassiererinnen	*cashier/s*
die Direktions-assistentin	die Direktions-assistentinnen	*PA to the director*

d) Feminine nouns which end in **-ie** add **-n**. Note that this changes the pronunciation; the **-ien** is sounded as two syllables, not one ('„ee-en', not 'een'). In this book we'll signal such endings by a vertical stroke, as in Checklist 6 (**Kategori|en**) and below:

die Industrie	die Industri|en	*industry/ies*
die Strategie	die Strategi|en	*strategy/ies*

80 Foreign words (plural)

a) Sometimes the final vowel or syllable is dropped from a word of foreign origin and **-en** added for the plural:

die Firma	die Firmen	*firm/s*

das Konto	die Konten	*account/s*
das Medium	die Medien	*medium/media*

b) English and French nouns which have been absorbed into the German language retain the **-s** plural:

Hotels, Restaurants, Autos, etc.

81 Nouns existing only in the singular

Just like 'information' and 'electricity' in English, quite a number of German nouns are used only in the singular. We put an* or (sing.) beside these; see Checklist 7 (**das Marketing*** etc.) and below:

das Markenimage (sing.)	*brand image*
der Maschinenbau (sing.)	*mechanical engineering*

However, some 'singular only' German nouns have English counterparts which are 'plural only' or usually plural. This singular/plural pattern is reflected in the accompanying verbs as well:

die Polizei (sing.)	*police* (pl.)
die Presse (sing.)	*press* (pl.)
die Regierung (sing.)	*government* (sing./pl.)

Die Polizei informiert die Presse.	*The police inform the press.*
Die Presse ist informiert.	*The press are informed.*
Die Regierung hat entschieden, ...	*The government have decided ... .*

Abstract nouns, in particular, are used in the singular; they take on a more descriptive, factual meaning when used in the plural:

das Geld (abstract idea = *money*)	die Gelder (concrete idea = *funds*)
die Schönheit (abstract = *beauty*)	die Schönheiten (*attractions, beautiful things in general*)

82 Nouns existing only in the plural

Like 'data' etc. in English, there are quite a number of plural nouns for which different words have to be used to express the singular:

plural	singular
die Möbel *(furniture)*	das Möbelstück *(piece of furniture)*
die Eltern *(parents)*	der Vater, die Mutter *(father, mother)*
die Ferien *(holidays)*	der freie Tag, der Urlaubstag *(day off)*
die Kosten *(costs)*	der Preis, die Rechnung *(price, bill)*

83 Simple past forms: **sein, haben**

We would like to repeat what has already been said about the past tense. In spoken German most of the conversation is conducted in the present perfect, which is interspersed with short simple past forms, particularly of **sein, haben** and other short verbs. In the dialogue of Unit 6 **war** ('was') appeared twice. The simple past of **sein** and **haben** is easily learnt, as there are only two important forms for each: **war/waren** and **hatte/hatten**. Please study the following:

ich war	*I was*	**ich hatte**	*I had*
er war	*he was*	**er hatte**	*he had*
sie war	*she was*	**sie hatte**	*she had*
wir waren	*we were*	**wir hatten**	*we had*
sie waren	*they were*	**sie hatten**	*they had*
Sie waren	*you were*	**Sie hatten**	*you had*

Ich war vorige Woche in Amsterdam, denn ich hatte noch eine Woche Urlaub.
I went to Amsterdam last week, as I still had a week's holiday.

Wir hatten zwar noch genug alte Broschüren, aber die neuen Entwürfe waren besser.
(Admittedly) we still had enough old brochures, but the new designs were better.

Sie hatten Gelegenheit unseren neuen Vertreter kennenzulernen. Waren Sie mit seinen Mustern zufrieden?
You were able (lit. 'had the opportunity') *to make the acquaintance of our new sales rep. Were you satisfied with his samples?*

Wir hatten immer schon einen guten Umsatz, aber im letzten Jahr war er hervorragend!
We've always had a good turnover, but last year it was excellent!

84 The pluperfect tense

The simple past tense forms given in the previous Checknote can also be used in conjunction with the past participles in order to express the idea of 'had sent'; 'had received'; 'had written', i.e. to form the pluperfect. For example:

Ich hatte den Brief schon geschrieben. *I had already written the letter.*
Er war schon in Urlaub gewesen. *He had already been on holiday.*

Wir hatten gesagt, daß ... *We had said that ...*
Sie waren hierhin gekommen, um ... zu... *They had come here in order to ...*
Sie hatten mir gesagt, daß ... *You had told me that ...*

To give you a couple of extended sentences:

Wir hatten gesagt, daß er nächste Woche kommen sollte.
We had said that he should come next week.

Es war gut, daß wir schon Nachschub bestellt hatten.
It was good that we had already ordered (some) new stock.

85 Simple past tense of weak and mixed verbs

So far you have learnt how to use the present perfect tense in spoken German (**ich habe gefragt** 'I have asked'). In formal statements or reports you should use the simple past (**ich fragte** 'I asked'). Refer back to Checknotes 32 and 33 – you'll remember that weak verbs form their simple past by adding **-te(n)** to the stem. Here are some more examples to refresh your memory:

to say, tell	sagen	er sagte	sie sagten
to inform	informieren	er informierte	sie informierten
to ask (a question)	fragen	sie fragte	sie fragten
to believe	glauben	er glaubte	sie glaubten
to buy	kaufen	sie kaufte	sie kauften
to think	denken	ich dachte	wir dachten
to count	zählen	ich zählte	wir zählen
to send	schicken	er schickte	sie schickten

Very often, the two tenses (present perfect and simple past) are used next to each other in spoken German, as shown in these examples:

Ich habe ihm gesagt, warum ich gestern nicht kommen konnte.
I've told him why I couldn't come yesterday.

Ich habe doch wirklich gedacht, daß er vorige Woche krank war.
I really thought that he was ill last week.

Ich habe mich gefragt, warum er immer so aggressiv war.
I asked myself, why he was always so aggressive.

Ich habe immer geglaubt, daß er recht hatte.
I've always been convinced that he was right.

86 Simple past of strong verbs

Again, just to refresh your memory, we repeat that, once you have memorized the stem vowel changes, the strong verbs are very easy to use. There are no variations on the endings of the first and third person singular and the plural forms end in **-en**, as these two verbs **fahren** *to drive, travel* and **gehen** *to go (on foot)* will demonstrate:

ich fuhr	*I travelled*	**ich ging**	*I went*
er/sie fuhr	*he/she travelled*	**er/sie ging**	*he/she went*

wir fuhren	*we travelled*	**wir gingen**	*we went*
sie fuhren	*they travelled*	**sie gingen**	*they went*
Sie fuhren	*you travelled*	**Sie gingen**	*you went*

We hope that you have started to make up your own list of strong verbs which will be helpful in the situations in which you think you will be using German. Here are some more examples:

to carry	tragen:	er trägt,	er trug,	er hat getragen (dat.) acc.
to go, walk	gehen:	sie geht,	sie ging,	sie ist gegangen (-)
to begin	beginnen:	es beginnt,	es begann,	es hat begonnen (acc.)
to leave, let	lassen:	sie läßt,	sie ließ,	sie hat gelassen (dat.) acc.
to win	gewinnen:	er gewinnt,	er gewann,	er hat gewonnen (acc.)

87 Negation of nouns: kein/e

'K' is a very important letter in German, because it drastically changes the meaning of the indefinite article to 'not a'/'not any'/'no':

k + ein = **kein**   *not a/not any* (before masc. and n. nouns)
k + eine = **keine** *not a/not any* (before fem. and all pl. nouns)

Look at these two pairs of sentences, where the first in each is positive (**einen, eine**) and the second negative (**keinen, keine**):

Ich nehme einen Kaffee.	*I'll have a coffee.*
Ich nehme keinen Zucker.	*I don't take (any) sugar.*

Ich habe eine Sekretärin.	*I have a secretary.*
Ich habe keine Sekretärin.	*I have no/I don't have a secretary.*

Here's an example of its use with a plural noun:

Wir haben keine Gardinen im Büro. *We have no curtains in the office.*

88 Negation of verbs/adjectives/adverbs

We have already met the little German word **nicht** ('not'). There are two general rules to remember about this simple negative, which is like the English 'not' except that it never needs the addition of 'do'/'does' ('I know him'/'I do not know him'):

a) **nicht** is put in front of the word it refers to.

b) when negating a whole clause, **nicht** goes to the end of that clause.

Das Problem ist nicht neu!	*The problem isn't new.*
Er kommt nicht heute, sondern morgen.	*He's not coming today, but tomorrow.*
Er kommt heute nicht.	*He is not coming today.*
Ich kenne ihn nicht.	*I don't know him.*
Ich weiß nicht, was ich tun soll.	*I don't know what to do.*

89 Nein and nichts

Nein means 'no', that's to say, it is the opposite of **ja** ('yes'). When it begins a sentence it is followed by a comma. Then comes the subject, followed by the verb. Here are two examples:

Nein, ich exportiere nicht nach Japan.
No, I don't export to Japan.

Nein, ich habe keine japanische Geschäftskontakte.
No, I don't have any Japanese business contacts.
  or: *I have no Japanese business contacts*

Note that although it may remind you of 'ein', **nein** cannot be placed in front of a noun.

Please do not confuse **nicht** ('not') with **nichts** ('nothing'). You'll remember the following sentence taken from Unit 5's dialogue:

Es bleibt einem nichts anderes übrig als zu zahlen!
One can't do anything but pay!

and similarly:

Da kann man nichts machen/tun.
(In cases like that) you can do nothing.

90 Mögen (mag/möchte)

Just as in English where 'want' can sound a little abrupt ('I want a coffee'), in German you should avoid using **wollen** when making a polite request. Use **möchte** ('would like') instead, as in the following question and answer:

Q: Möchten Sie einen Kaffee?   A: Ja, ich möchte einen Kaffee.

Möchte normally requires another verb in the clause (in the above example either **haben** or **trinken** is implied, but not actually stated):

Ich möchte ein Telegramm schicken.	*I'd like to send a telegram.*
Ich möchte ein R-Gespräch anmelden.	*I'd like to reverse the charges* (lit. 'book a reverse charge call').
Wir möchten bestellen.	*We'd like to order.* (e.g. in a restaurant)

The infinitive form of **möchte/n** as given in the dictionary is **mögen**; its present tense forms simply mean 'like':

Ich mag Mikrocomputer.	*I like micro-computers.*
Er mag bezahlte Überstunden.	*He likes paid overtime.*
Sie mag Anrufbeantworter.	*She likes answerphones.*
Wir mögen keinen Kaffee.	*We don't like coffee.*
Sie mögen keine Verzögerungen.	*You don't like delays.*
Sie mögen keine langen Lieferfristen.	*They don't like long delivery periods.*

Note: **mögen** may also express a possibility (as in 'it may be'):

Es mag ja stimmen, aber ...	*It may be true, but ...*
Er mag ja der beste Verkäufer sein, aber ...	*He may be the best salesman, but ...*

Note that **ja** doesn't mean 'yes' in the above examples; **ja** is added here for emphasis, a little like the English word 'well' in 'It may well be true, but ...'.

91 Sollen

There is one more modal verb to learn: **sollen** ('to be obliged to'):

ich soll	*I am to*	**wir sollen**	*we are to*
er soll	*he is to*	**sie sollen**	*they are to*
sie soll	*she is to*	**Sie sollen**	*you are to*

Wir sollen weitermachen.	*We are to carry on.*
Er soll einen Kredit aufnehmen.	*He is to take out a loan.*
Ich soll eine Übersetzung machen.	*I'm to do a translation.*

Note: **sollen** can also give a prognosis, or relate a fact to hearsay (in English: 'is said to ...'). For example:

Es soll ein gutes Jahr werden.	*A bumper year has been forecast.*
Es soll morgen regnen.	*Rain has been forecast.*
Er soll Konkurs angemeldet haben.	*He is said to have gone bankrupt.*

92 nicht dürfen - nicht müssen/nicht brauchen

You are already familiar with the modal verb **müssen** ('to have to', 'must'). In the negative form its use differs markedly from conventional English usage. The fact that you 'must not' do something is expressed as **nicht dürfen**, whereas 'doesn't/don't have to' is translated by **nicht müssen/nicht brauchen**. If that sounds a bit complicated, the following examples will show you how it works:

Wir sollen weitermachen. Wir dürfen nicht aufgeben!	*We are to carry on. We mustn't give up!*

Er soll einen Kredit aufnehmen. Er darf nicht Bankrott machen!	*He is to ask for a loan. He mustn't go bankrupt!*
Ich soll eine Übersetzung machen. Ich darf kein Wörterbuch benutzen!	*I am to do a translation. I mustn't use a dictionary.*
Ich muß mich sehr konzentrieren, ich darf keine Fehler machen!	*I must concentrate (on what I'm doing), I mustn't make any mistakes!*
Er braucht nicht nach Paris zu fliegen. Er kann früh nach Hause gehen.	*He needn't fly to Paris today. He can go home early.*
Wir müssen die Zollerklärungen nicht mehr ausfüllen!	*We don't have to fill in customs forms any more!*

Comprehension Practice 6

Please answer the following questions with full sentences. You may refer to the dialogue at the beginning of this Unit, if you wish.

New words:

wen? (acc.)	*who(m)?*
worauf?	*what ... for?*
sich entwickeln	*to develop*
man sollte ...	*one should ...*

1 Wie sind die Produkte von Excel-Equip?
2 Wie sind die Preise?
3 Wen haben sie beauftragt?
4 Worauf haben sie gewartet?
5 Was erwartet man für das neue Deutschland?
6 Was lag über den Schätzungen?
7 Was ist im vergangenen Jahr nicht gestiegen?
8 Wie ist die Auftragslage?
9 Wie entwickelt sich die Wirtschaft?
10 Wie sollte man heutzutage nicht mehr denken?

FLUENCY PRACTICE 23
Learning how to contradict

New words:

die Konkurrenz	*competition/competitor*
spanisch	*Spanish*
zu hoch	*too high*
einen Brief beantworten	*to reply to a letter*
spezialisiert sein auf acc.	*to specialize in*

(die) Bürotechnik	*office technology*
die Lieferbedingungen	*terms of delivery*
akzeptieren	*to accept*

Imagine you've a difference of opinion with a colleague. When he/she makes a statement, you disagree. Respond to these six statements in the same way as shown in the model:

Unsere Firma expandiert stetig.
Our firm is expanding continuously.
Nein, unsere Firma expandiert nicht stetig!
No, our firm is not expanding continuously!

1 Unsere Konkurrenz ist auf dem spanischen Markt fest etabliert.
2 Er hat recht.
3 Sie haben unseren Brief beantwortet.
4 Der Preis ist zu hoch.
5 Wir sind auf Bürotechnik spezialisiert.
6 Der Kunde hat die Lieferbedingungen akzeptiert.

FLUENCY PRACTICE 24
Indirect questions

New words:

die Briefwaage	*letter scales*
die Schere	*scissors*
die Kaffeemaschine	*coffee maker/machine*
der Bericht	*report*
die Heftmaschine	*stapler*
wem?	*(to) whom?*
der Locher	*paper punch*
gebrauchen	*to use*
bekommen	*to get*
funktionieren	*to function, work*
zuletzt (adv.)	*last*

Let's suppose one of your colleagues does not speak very clearly and you have to repeat his questions to others. For example:

Wer hat die Briefwaage gebraucht? *Who's used the letter scales?*
Er fragt, wer die Briefwaage *He's asking who's used the letter*
  gebraucht hat. *scales.*

Now continue:
1 Wo ist die Schere?
2 Wann bekommen wir einen Kaffee?
3 Wie funktioniert die Kaffeemaschine?
4 Wer hat zuletzt die Heftmaschine gebraucht?
5 Wem haben Sie den Bericht gegeben?
6 Haben Sie den Locher gesehen?

FLUENCY PRACTICE 25
Plurals after 'some/several/most'

New words:

das Textverarbeitungsgerät	*word processor*
das Sortiment	*range* (of products)
auf|nehmen (in, acc.)	*to include (in)*
wünschen	*to wish*

The firm you work for is expanding rapidly and no longer doing things in 'ones'. Please insert the following words into the corresponding sentences and put the relevant nouns into the plural:

(1)+(3) einige   *some*
(2)+(4) mehrere   *several*
(5) die meisten   *most* (not followed by 'of' in German)

1 Wir haben eine Niederlassung in Frankreich.
2 Wir haben ein Textverarbeitungsgerät gekauft.
3 Wir haben ein Faxgerät im Sortiment.
4 Wir wollen einen Mikrocomputer in unser Sortiment aufnehmen.
5 Der Kunde wünscht gute Qualität.

FLUENCY PRACTICE 26
Asking for permission

New words:

benutzen	*to use*
nach Hause gehen	*to go home*
früher	*earlier*
aus|probieren	*to try out*
vor|stellen	*to introduce*
parken	*to park*
der Eingang	*entrance*

Asking for permission, particularly when visiting someone else's office, is best done like this:

(meinen Mantel hier ablegen)   *(put down my coat here)*
Darf ich meinen Mantel hier ablegen?   *May I put down my coat here?*

This may be a purely rhetorical question but you will need to use it quite often. Ask for permission to do the following, as above:

1 (einmal Ihr Telefon benutzen)
2 (die neue Software ausprobieren)
3 (heute früher nach Hause gehen)
4 (vor dem Eingang parken)
5 (meinen Kollegen vorstellen)

FLUENCY PRACTICE 27
Granting requests (very formal style)

Now, put yourself behind the boss's desk. As all the requests seem to be reasonable, you grant them in the following way:

Darf ich meinen Mantel hier ablegen?
Ich erlaube Ihnen, Ihren Mantel hier abzulegen!

Reply to the other requests in FP 26 in the same way. Of course, you could get away with just answering **'Ja sicher!'** ('Yes, of course!'), but this easy option wouldn't help you to practise the infinitive construction using **zu**).

FLUENCY PRACTICE 28
Granting requests (very friendly style)

The above requests were granted in a very formal style. Let's now try a more informal and friendly style! Look at the model question and answer below, then grant the requests in FP 26 in the same way:

Darf ich meinen Mantel hier ablegen?
Aber natürlich dürfen Sie Ihren Mantel hier ablegen!

FLUENCY PRACTICE 29
Asking for authorization

New words:

ein|kaufen	*to buy, purchase*
der Listenpreis	*list/catalogue price*
das Zugeständnis	*concession*
die Kosten	*cost*
reparieren	*to repair*
faxen	*to fax ('faxen' is very colloquial)*

You want to know if you and your assistant should carry out the following tasks. First, look at the model, then form suitable questions:

(die Geräte nach Frankreich exportieren)
Sollen wir die Geräte nach Frankreich exportieren?
Shall we export the machines to France?

1 (das Material in England einkaufen)
2 (das Produkt unter dem Listenpreis verkaufen)
3 (für den neuen Kunden Zugeständnisse machen)
4 (die Geräte auf unsere Kosten reparieren?)
5 (den Bericht nach London faxen?)

92

PRACTICAL TASK 1
Filling in an application form

As you have now decided to apply for the Eurocard Gold, offered by the Dresdner Bank in Unit 5, you'll have to fill in the form below. First of all, make yourself familiar with the words and phrases on p.94.

EUROCARD DEUTSCHLAND

Unternehmensbereich
der GZS Gesellschaft für Zahlungssysteme mbH
Postfach 11 07 11, 6000 Frankfurt
Tel. (0 69) 79 33-0, Telex 4 170 190, Telefax (0 69) 79 33-123

KARTENANTRAG

an:

über **Dresdner Bank Aktiengesellschaft**

Den Antrag bitte entweder per Schreibmaschine oder mit Blockschrift in Großbuchstaben (bitte keine Umlaute verwenden) vollständig ausfüllen und bei der Bank einreichen. Bei Rückgabe der EUROCARD innerhalb der dreimonatigen Probezeit wird der gesamte Jahresbeitrag erstattet; dies gilt nur, wenn erstmals eine EUROCARD, unabhängig über welches Institut, ausgestellt wird. **Bei gleichzeitigem Antrag für Haupt- und Zusatzkarte bitte zwei Formulare ausfüllen.**

Ich beantrage die Ausstellung einer

☐ **EUROCARD GOLD** als Hauptkarte für mich zum Jahresbeitrag von z. Zt. DM 130,-
☐ **EUROCARD GOLD** als Zusatzkarte* gemeinsam mit nachstehend genanntem Familienmitglied auf dessen Namen zum Jahresbeitrag von z. Zt. DM 90,-

*EUROCARD GOLD als Zusatzkarte nur, wenn es sich bei der zugehörigen Hauptkarte auch um **EUROCARD GOLD** handelt.

**Persönliche Angaben dessen,
für den die Karte beantragt wird**

	KA	Karten-Nr. (wird automatisch ermittelt)				
		5	2	3	2	1

| Anredeschl.
1 = Herr
2 = Frau
3 = Fräulein
0 = ohne Anrede | Name (ggf. Titel, Vorname, Nachname) |
| Name (Fortsetzung) |

| Privatadresse,
kein Postfach | Straße und Hausnummer | | wohnhaft seit (MM JJ) |
| PLZ | Ort | Zustellbez. |

| Geburtsdatum (TT MM JJ) | Telefon (für eventuelle Rückfragen) | Staatsangehörigkeit | Schlüssel |

| Waren/sind Sie bereits EUROCARD-Inhaber? ☐ ja ☐ nein | Besitzen Sie auch andere Kreditkarten? ☐ ja ☐ nein |
| Wenn ja, Kartennummer
5 2 3 2 | Verfalldatum (MM JJ) | Wenn ja, welche? |

Korrespondenzadresse
(wenn nicht identisch mit Privatadresse)

Anredeschl.	Name
1 = Herr	
2 = Frau	Name (Fortsetzung)
3 = Fräulein	
0 = ohne Anrede	

Straße und Hausnummer/Postfach

| | | Zustellbez. |

| PLZ | Ort |

Berufliche Angaben

| Beschäftigt bei | Seit (Monat/Jahr) |

| Ausgeübter Beruf | Branche | Selbständig seit |

Bei Beantragung einer Zusatzkarte

| Name des Hauptkarteninhabers | Karten-Nr. des Hauptkarteninhabers 5 2 3 2 1 |

Einzugsermächtigung

Ich bin bis widerruflich damit einverstanden, daß alle im Zusammenhang mit der EUROCARD von mir zu entrichtenden Beträge mittels Lastschrift

☐ von meinem nachstehenden Privatkonto e ngezogen werden;

☐ von dem nachstehenden Konto des Hauptkarteninhabers eingezogen werden.

| Kontonummer | Bankleitzahl |

Turn over for the list of words and phrases attached to this Practical Task.

Kartenantrag (m.)	*application for a card*
Zusatzkarte (f.)	*additional card*
Blockschrift (f.) mit Großbuchstaben	*block capitals*
verwenden	*to use*
Karten-Nr. (wird automatisch ermittelt)	this indicates that there is no need to fill in this section (lit. 'card No. will be supplied by computer')
persönliche Angaben dessen, für den die Karte beantragt wird	*personal details of the applicant* (lit. 'person for whom card is applied for')
Anredeschl(üssel)	*key to form of address*
Fortsetzung (f.)	*continuation*
ggf. = gegebenenfalls	*in case this applies to you* (lit. 'given the case')
für evtl. Rückfragen	*in case of queries*
Staatsangehörigkeit (f.)	*nationality*
Postfach (n.)	*PO Box*
wohnhaft seit	*resident since*
TT; MM; JJ	*day/s; month/s; year/s*
PLZ	*postcode*
Zustellbez(irk) (m.)	*town district*
Korrespondenzadresse (f.)	*address to which correspondence should be sent*
berufliche Angaben	*details of employment*
bei Beantragung einer Zusatzkarte	*(fill in only) if applying for an additional card*
beschäftigt bei	*employed by*
ausgeübter Beruf	*profession practised*
selbständig	*self-employed*
Haupt-...	*main...*
Einzugsermächtigung (f.)	*authorization for direct debit*

FLUENCY PRACTICE 30
'Nicht dürfen/müssen/brauchen'

Cover up the German sentences in Checknote 92, and see how well you can reproduce them from the English translations.

Reaching agreement

In this Unit we take another look at pronouns, question-words and those prepositions which can take either the dative or the accusative case. We also study adverbs of time, and we learn about a very important aspect of the German language, namely word-building. Frau Schneider and Mr Jackson are finally reaching the crucial point in their discussions, and Mr Jackson is determined to get 'a foot in the door'.

Mr Jackson: Sie teilen also durchaus meine Meinung, daß nationalstaatliches Denken in der Welt des Handels überholt ist. Darf ich mir dann vielleicht die Frage erlauben, warum Sie nur deutsche Prudukte verkaufen?

Frau Schneider: Es stimmt, daß wir bisher ausschließlich deutsche Geräte in unserem Programm hatten. Viele unserer Kunden denken leider immer noch in traditionellen nationalen Kategorien und stellen hohe Ansprüche an die Qualität der Geräte. Außerdem glauben sie, daß nur deutsche Geräte ihren Ansprüchen genügen, besonders bei der "Hardware".

Mr Jackson: Diese ablehnende Haltung finde ich erstaunlich. Viele Deutsche kennen eine Reihe von englischen Fachwörtern. Heutzutage spricht alle Welt von "Fax", "Computer", "Marketing", "Management", "Training" und natürlich darf man bei dieser Aufzählung "Business" nicht vergessen.

Frau Schneider: *(lachend)* So gesehen haben Sie sicher recht. Unsere Alltagssprache wird immer englischer, oder sollte ich sagen: amerikanischer? *(wieder ernst)* Aber, um beim Thema zu bleiben: es ist Ihnen sicher bekannt, daß die Lohn- und Produktionskosten in der Bundesrepublik sehr hoch sind. Insbesondere im Bereich der

Forschung und Entwicklung fallen enorme Kosten an. Darum sind die deutschen Preise ins Astronomische gestiegen. Wenn wir konkurrenzfähig bleiben wollen, müssen wir uns nach einer neuen Bezugsquelle umsehen. Wir sind deshalb durchaus bereit, englische Geräte in unsere Produktpalette aufzunehmen; eventuell mit einigen technischen Änderungen.

Mr Jackson: Das freut mich zu hören. Dann darf ich Ihnen also unsere Prospekte zeigen und Ihnen dann unsere Liefer- und Zahlungsbedingungen erläutern.

TRANSLATION

Mr Jackson: So you share my opinion that the idea of the nation-state (*lit.* 'nation-state thinking') is quite outdated in the world of business. May I take the liberty, then, of asking why you only sell German products?

Frau Schneider: It is true that so far we have had exclusively German products in our range. Unfortunately, many of our customers still think in traditional national categories and have high expectations as far as the quality of the machines is concerned. Furthermore, they believe that only German equipment meets their expectations, especially as regards hardware.

Mr Jackson: I find this negative attitude astonishing. Many Germans are familiar with a number of English technical terms. Nowadays everyone talks of 'fax', 'computer', 'marketing', 'management', 'training', and, of course, 'business' must not be forgotten in this list.

Frau Schneider: (*laughing*) If you put it like that, I must say you're absolutely right! Our everyday language is getting more English by the day, or should I say more American?
(*serious again*) But, to get back to the subject of our conversation, you're surely aware that wages and production costs are very high in the Federal Republic. In the area of research and development, in particular, very high costs are incurred. Because of this, German prices have rocketed (*lit.* 'reached astronomical heights'). If we want to stay

competitive, we'll have to look for a new source of supply. We're therefore quite prepared to incorporate English equipment into our range of goods; if necessary with some technical modifications.

Mr Jackson: I'm pleased to hear that. May I then now show you our brochures and then proceed to explain our terms of delivery and conditions of payment?

Checklist 7

Masculine nouns:

der Kunde, -en	*customer*
der Anspruch, ¨-e	*demand, expectation*
der Preis, -e	*price*
der Prospekt, -e	*brochure*

Feminine nouns:

die Meinung, -en	*opinion*
die Chance, -en	*opportunity*
die Frage, -n	*question*
die 'Hardware'*	*hardware*
die Reihe, -n	*row*
die Haltung, -en	*attitude*
die Aufzählung, -en	*enumeration, list*
die Alltagssprache	*everyday language*
die Forschung	*research*
die Entwicklung	*development*
die Bezugsquelle, -n	*source; supplier*
die Änderung, -en	*modification*
die Bedingung, -en	*condition*
die Lieferbedingungen	*terms of delivery*
die Zahlungsbedingungen	*terms of payment*

Neuter nouns:

das Wort, ¨-er	*(single, individual) word*
das Fach, ¨-er	*subject, field of expertise*
das Fachwort, ¨-er	*technical term*
das Marketing*	*marketing*
das Management*	*management*
das Training*	*training*
das Business*	*business*
das Thema, die Themen	*subject, topic*

(*nouns used only in singular)

Adjectives:

nationalstaatlich	*of the nation-state*
traditionell	*traditional*
national	*national*
unsere *(pl.)*	*our*
ihr *(m. & n.)* ihre *(f., pl.)*	*their; her*
Ihr *(m. & n.)* Ihre *(f., pl.)*	your
ablehnend	*negative*
all-	*all*
viele	*many*
dieser, -e, -es	*this (one)*
enorm	*enormous*
einige	*some, several*
technisch	*technical*
hoch	*high* (before a noun: hoher, -e, -es)

Adverbs:

überholt	*outdated*
nur	*only; nothing but*
ausschließlich	*exclusively*
besonders bei	*especially with regard to ...*
erstaunlich	*astonishing*
heutzutage	*nowadays*
sicher	*certainly; surely*
recht	*right*
immer (+ comp.)	*more and more ...*
es ist bekannt	*it is well known*
insbesondere	*in particular*
deshalb	*therefore*
durchaus	*quite; absolutely*
eventuell	*possibly* (never 'eventually')
außerdem	*besides*

Strong/irregular verbs:

werden: es wird, es wurde, es ist geworden	*to become*
bleiben: er bleibt, er blieb, er ist geblieben	*to stay*
steigen *(intr.)* er steigt, er stieg, er ist gestiegen	*to rise*
sich um|sehen: er sieht sich um, er sah sich um, er hat sich umgesehen	*to look out for*
auf|nehmen: er nimmt auf, er nahm auf, er hat aufgenommen	*to incorporate*

Weak verbs:

erlauben *(dat., acc.)*: erlaubte, hat erlaubt	*to allow*
verkaufen *(dat., acc.)*: verkaufte, hat verkauft	*to sell*
glauben *(dat., acc.)*: glaubte, hat geglaubt	*to believe; feel (that)*

Other words/expressions:

so gesehen	*put (seen) like that*
eine Reihe von Wörtern	*a number of words*
alle Welt	*everyone (the whole world)*
ihren Ansprüchen genügen	*to satisfy their expectations*
in das Programm auf|nehmen	*to add to the range of goods*

CHECKNOTES

93 Prepositions linked to verbs of movement

You've now found the letter you mislaid in Checknote 65. Let's imagine you're just about to put it down again absent-mindedly:

Ich lege den Brief ...

auf den Schreibtisch	*on the desk*
hinter die Ringordner	*behind the ring-binders/files*
in die Schublade	*into the drawer*
neben das Diktiergerät	*next to the dictating machine*
über den Papierkorb	*across (the top of) the waste-paper basket*
unter die Bestellungen	*underneath the orders*
vor das Telefon	*in front of the telephone.*

Note that when the prepositions **an, auf, hinter, in, neben, über, unter, vor** and **zwischen** are used in connection with a verb which expresses movement from one place to another, the accusative case is used.

Unfortunately, the English verb 'to put' does not have just one equivalent in German; it can be translated as **legen, stellen** or **setzen**, depending on the position in which the object is put. **Legen** was chosen for the above examples, because things were placed in a lying position.

In the following examples we are going to put two objects, **der Aktenordner** ('file') and **die Kiste** ('box') in an upright position, so we'll have to use the verb **stellen**:

Ich stelle den Aktenordner ...

an die Ablage	*next to the filing tray*
hinter die Schreibmaschine	*behind the typewriter*
neben den Computer	*next to the computer*
über die Wörterbücher	*(on the shelf) on top of the dictionaries*
zwischen die Telefonbücher	*between the phone books.*

Ich setze die Kiste ...

neben den Gabelstapler	*next to the fork-lift truck*
hinter die Tür	*behind the door*
auf die Theke	*on the counter*
unter den Tisch	*under the table/desk*
zwischen die Schränke	*between the cupboards.*

Setzen is used less often, but it implies that you're placing an object on a surface:

Ich setze den neuen Monitor auf den Schreibtisch.	*I put the new monitor on the desk.*

Setzen can also be used as a reflexive verb to mean 'to sit down':

Er setzt sich auf den Stuhl.	*He sits down on the chair.*

94 da(r) + preposition

Please study these sentences:

Ich stelle die Tasche auf den Schreibtisch.
→ Die Tasche steht darauf.
I put the case on top of the desk. → *The case is standing on it.*

Ich stelle die Lampe neben den Kalender.
→ Ich stelle die Lampe daneben.
I'll put the lamp next to the calendar. → *I'll put the lamp next to it.*

Ich habe die Rechnung mit dem Kostenvoranschlag verglichen.
→ Ich habe die Rechnung damit verglichen.
I compared the invoice with the estimate. → *I compared the invoice with it.*

Ich unterhalte mich mit dem Abteilungsleiter über den Jahresabschluß.
→ Ich unterhalte mich mit dem Abteilungsleiter darüber.
I'm having a conversation with the head of department about the end-of-year results. → *I'm having a conversation about it with the head of department.*

Note: If a preposition is not followed by a noun, **da-** (or **dar-** if the preposition starts with a vowel) is put in front of it.

There are many German verbs which are always followed by a certain preposition, but it might be a different preposition from the one you were expecting. In the following list you'll find a number of such verbs + prepositions (*w* = weak, *st* = strong):

achten *(w)* **auf** + acc.	*to pay attention to*
denken - gedacht an + acc.	*to think of*
sich handeln (es..., *w*) um + acc.	*to be in connection with*

sich gewöhnen *(w)* an + acc.	*to get used to*
sich interessieren *(w)* für + acc.	*to be interested in*
sich konzentrieren *(w)* auf + acc.	*to concentrate on*
nach|denken - nachgedacht über + acc.	*to think about*
sprechen - gesprochen über + acc.	*to talk about*
sich verlassen *(st)* auf + acc.	*to depend on*
sich wundern *(w)* über + acc.	*to be astonished about*

Here are some examples of their use:

1 Haben Sie daran gedacht, den neuen Katalog anzufordern?
2 Er hat darauf geachtet, daß die Geräte in einwandfreiem Zustand waren.
3 Er hat sich daran gewöhnt, alles zu delegieren.
4 Es handelt sich nur darum, den Käufer zufriedenzustellen.
5 Sie interessiert sich (zwar) dafür, aber sie findet es zu teuer.

The translations of these numbered sentences follow; we've separated them (and others in this Unit) so that you may gain extra practice by attempting to translate either way without reference to the original.

1 Did you remember (lit. 'think of it') *to request the new catalogue?*
2 He made sure that the machines were in perfect condition.
3 He got used to delegating everything.
4 It's only a question of satisfying the customer.
5 (Admittedly) she is interested in it, but she finds it too expensive.

Now, study this second list of verbs and the prepositions used with them:

ab|hängen *(st)* von + dat.	*to depend on*
erkennen *(st)* an + dat.	*to recognize by*
sich erkundigen *(w)* nach + dat.	*to enquire about*
sprechen *(st)* von + dat.	*to talk of*
etwas zu tun haben mit + dat.	*to have something to do with*

Can you understand the following sentences?

1 Der Liefertermin hängt davon ab, welche Route der Spediteur nimmt.
2 Sie erkennen daran, daß wir unsere Verpflichtungen ernst nehmen.
3 Sie haben sich mehrmals danach erkundigt (i.e. 'dem Liefertermin').
4 Wir haben letztes Jahr schon mal davon gesprochen.
5 Was hat das damit zu tun?

Translations (just in case you didn't understand everything):

1 The delivery date depends on the route the shipping agent chooses.
2 You'll see from this that we take our responsibilities seriously.
3 They enquired several times about it (i.e. the delivery date).

4 We already spoke about it last year.
5 What has that to do with it?

Da-/dar- + preposition is frequently used in impersonal constructions , conveying a figurative meaning which is a little tricky to translate:

es kommt *(st)* **an auf** + acc.	*it depends on; the crux of the matter is*
es handelt *(w)* **sich um** + acc.	*as far as ... is concerned*
es hängt *(st)* **ab von** + dat.	*it hinges/pivots, (depends) on*
es liegt *(st)* **an** + dat.	*it lies with; the reason is that*

Now, study these sentences:

1 Es kommt darauf an, den Gewinn zu maximieren.
2 Es kommt darauf an, ob sich das Produkt gut verkaufen läßt:
3 Es handelt sich darum, eine neue Verkaufsstrategie zu entwickeln.
4 Es handelt sich darum, ob er seine Provision bekommt oder nicht.
5 Es hängt davon ab, wie viel wir umsetzen können.
6 Es hängt davon ab, ob die Bezahlung per Scheck erfolgt.
7 Es liegt daran, daß die Verwaltung zu viel kostet.

You'll notice that the English translations are quite different:

1 The important point is to maximize the profit.
2 The heart of the matter is whether the product will sell well.
3 The main task is to develop a new sales strategy.
4 The question is whether he'll get his commission or not.
5 It depends on our level of turnover.
6 The decisive factor is whether payment will be made by cheque.
7 The reason is that the administration is too costly.

95 Adverbs of time

In business it's essential to be able to say clearly whether you mean 'now', 'today', 'yesterday' or 'in the future'. Study the following:

a) Adverbs relating to the present:

heute	*today*
heutzutage	*nowadays*
jetzt	*at this moment, now*
nun	*now;* (also used for special emphasis)
gerade	*at this very moment; just a short while ago*
sofort	*at once*
augenblicklich	*immediately*
gegenwärtig	*at present*

Examples (followed by their translations):

1 Der Brief kam heute per Eilboten.
2 Heutzutage macht man die Buchhaltung nicht mehr ohne Computer.
3 Wir besitzen jetzt 25% (Prozent) der Aktien.
4 Was sollen wir nun tun?
5 Das haben wir (nun) davon!
6 Ich schreibe gerade die Rechnung.
7 Er hat gerade angerufen, um den Empfang der Sendung zu bestätigen.
8 Ich komme sofort.
9 WIr müssen den Auftrag augenblicklich stornieren.
10 Gegenwärtig sind Konsumgüter schlecht zu verkaufen.

1 *The letter arrived today by special delivery.*
2 *Nowadays the accounts aren't done (any more) without a computer.*
3 *We now own 25% of the shares.*
4 *What shall we do now?*
5 *That serves us right!* (idiomatic use)
6 *I'm just writing/typing the invoice.*
7 *He has (only) just rung to acknowledge receipt of the shipment.*
8 *I'm coming./I'm on my way.*
9 *We'll have to stop this order immediately!*
10 *At present consumer goods are difficult to sell.*

b) Adverbs relating to the past:

gestern	*yesterday*
vorgestern	*the day before yesterday*
bereits, eben, soeben	*(only) just*
vorhin	*a moment ago*
früher	*earlier, in the past*
neulich, kürzlich	*recently*
inzwischen, unterdessen	*in the meantime*
einst, ehemals	*formerly*
einmal	*once, at one time*
jemals	*ever*
seither	*since*
vorher	*before, previously*
damals	*at that time*
anfangs	*in the beginning*

Examples and translations:

1 Ich habe seine Hausmitteilung gestern bekommen.
2 Die Frist ist vorgestern abgelaufen.
3 Ich habe den Brief bereits abgeschickt.
4 Sie hat eben angerufen.
5 Wie wir soeben von unserem Klienten erfahren ...

1 *I got his memo yesterday.*
2 *The time limit expired the day before yesterday.*
3 *I've already posted the letter.*
4 *She rang just a moment ago.*
5 *As we have just learned* (lit. 'as we learn') *from our client ...*

c) Adverbs relating to the future:

morgen	*tomorrow*
übermorgen	*the day after tomorrow*
bald	*soon*
demnächst	*in the near future*
nächstens	*next time, in future*
künftig	*in future*
nachher	*afterwards*
später	*later*
danach	*after that (time/date)*

Some model sentences to give you more practice:

1 Wir wollen den Vertrag morgen Punkt für Punkt durchsprechen.
2 Übermorgen ist offizielle Geschäftseröffnung.
3 Wir werden bald mit einem neuen Produkt auf den Markt kommen.
4 Wir müssen uns demnächst einmal über die Kosten unterhalten.
5 Wir sollten nächstens eine Spezialfirma beauftragen.
6 Wir wollen künftig mehr Produkte aus Asien einführen.
7 Sollen wir ihn nachher noch einmal anrufen?
8 Das können wir später noch regeln.
9 Zum 31.12. läuft die Sonderaktion aus. Danach gelten die neuen Preise.

1 *We intend to discuss the contract tomorrow in great detail.*
2 *The shop will officially open the day after tomorrow.*
3 *We'll soon bring a new product onto the market.*
4 *We'll have to have a chat about the costs in the near future.*
5 *Next time we should engage a specialist firm.*
6 *In future we'll be importing more products from Asia.*
7 *Shall we give him another ring later?*
8 *We'll be able to arrange that later.*
9 *On 31st December the special offer/sales drive comes to an end. After that (date) the new prices come into effect.*

96 Verbs taking the dative case

You've met the verb **helfen** ('to help') and you know that it's followed by the dative case. There are other important verbs which always take the dative case. You may find it easier to remember the German construction if you study the more literal translations (but these are not necessarily given in the best of styles!):

to answer	**jemandem antworten**	'to give/send an answer to'
to meet	**jemandem begegnen**	'to run into someone'
to thank	**jemandem danken**	'to give thanks to someone'
to remember	**jemandem einfallen**	'to occur to someone'
to be short of	**jemandem fehlen**	'something is lacking to someone'
to like	**jemandem gefallen**	'to be pleasing to someone'
not to like	**jemandem mißfallen**	'to be displeasing to someone'
to own	**jemandem gehören**	'to belong to someone'
to succeed in	**jemandem gelingen**	'it succeeds to someone' (imp.)
to suffice	**jemandem genügen**	'to be sufficient to someone'

Now study the following sentences:

Er hat mir sofort geantwortet.	*He answered me immediately.*
Ich danke Ihnen für die Einladung.	*I thank you for the invitation.*
Der Name fällt mir einfach nicht ein.	*I simply cannot remember the name.*
Mir fehlen 500 Mark.	*I'm 500 marks short.*
Die Sache gefällt mir nicht!	*I don't like it!*
Die Firma gehört meinem Vater.	*My father is the owner of the firm.*
Das Design ist ihm gut gelungen.	*The/his design is a great success.*
Zwei Wochen Urlaub genügen mir.	*Two weeks holiday are enough for me.*
Der neue Vertrag hat ihm mißfallen.	*He disliked the new contract.*
Der neue Vorschlag hat den Gewerkschaftsvertretern mißfallen.	*The new proposal was disliked by the trade union representatives.*

97 Adjectival endings – dative case

You are already familiar with the most common case endings for adjectives. Please study these adjectival endings:

1 Ich gebe dem neuen Direktor meinen Bericht.
2 Ich danke der netten Dame für ihre freundliche Einladung.
3 Er ist mit einer deutschen und einer englischen Zeitung gekommen.
4 Wir gewähren guten Kunden (pl.) schon einmal einen Zahlungsaufschub.

Translations:

1 I give my report to the new director.
2 I thank the nice lady for her kind invitation.
3 He arrived with a German and an English newspaper.
4 In the case of good customers we sometimes agree to deferred payments.

The rule is quite simple, really: after the definite or indefinite article or possessive adjective ('my', 'your', 'his' etc.) and in the plural, the dative case ending on the adjective is always **-en!**

Now study these sentences:

Ich habe die neuen Maschinen mit teurem Geld gekauft.
I bought the new machinery with hard-earned money.

Wir haben die Pläne mit unserem Architekten besprochen.
We discussed the plans with our architect.

Sie haben diesen Rat von ihrer Rechtsanwältin bekommen.
They got this advice from their (female) lawyer.

You'll have noticed that it is only when the adjective stands alone (i.e. when there is no **dem/der** or **einem/einer** in front of it), that it takes the dative signal **-m/r.**

98 Position of the personal pronoun

Take another look at the first example in the previous Checknote:

Ich gebe dem neuen Direktor meinen Bericht.
I give my report to the new director.

This sentence shows the usual German word order for two nouns coming together, i.e. the indirect object comes first! Now look at the following sentences in which we've used personal pronouns:

Ich gebe ihm (dat.) meinen Bericht (acc.).
I give him my report.

Ich gebe ihn (acc.) dem neuen Direktor (dat.).
I give it to the new director.

Note that a single personal pronoun (no matter whether it is in the dative or accusative) is placed immediately behind the main verb.

Now, let's replace both nouns with personal pronouns:

Ich gebe ihn ihm (acc., dat.).
I give it to him

This may look a little puzzling: in fact it isn't used very often, as the two pronouns sound too much alike, even for German ears. However, you will often hear:

Ich gebe es ihm (acc., dat.).
I('ll) give it to him.

Let's assume now that you're giving your report to a female director:

Ich gebe der neuen Direktorin meinen Bericht.

The corresponding sentences with pronouns would then be:

Ich gebe ihr den Bericht.	*(to her)*
Ich gebe ihn der neuen Direktorin.	*(it)*
Ich gebe ihn ihr (acc., dat.).	*(it to her)*

Let's look at some more examples of verbs using a dative and an accusative object:

Er bewilligt ihr einen Überziehungskredit.	Er bewillift ihn ihr.
He grants (for) her overdraft facilities.	*He grants it to her.*
Wir bieten ihr einen neuen Vertrag an.	Wir bieten ihn ihr an.
We offer her a new contract.	*We offer it to her.*
Er beweist dem Richter seine Unschuld.	Er beweist sie ihm.
He proves his innocence to the judge.	*He proves it to him.*

99 Dieser, jener, jeder, ('this', 'that', 'every') Einer, eine, eins ('one')

Please study the following examples:

Dieser neue Computer ist sehr leistungsfähig, jener ist noch besser.
This new computer is very powerful. That one is better still.

Dieses Buch kostet DM 50, aber jenes kostet das doppelte.
This book costs DM 50, but that one costs double.

Ich kann diesen alten Schreibtisch nicht mehr sehen! - Ich kann mir aber jenen nicht leisten!
I cannot stand the sight of this old desk any more, but I cannot afford that one.

Jeder Angestellte muß über seine Ausgaben Buch führen.
Every employee has to keep a record of his/her expenses.

Ich habe jedem neuen Kunden einen Gutschein geschickt.
I sent a voucher to every new customer.

Einen kann ich mir leisten, aber nicht mehr. (referring to a masc. noun)
I can afford one, but not more.

Note that **dies-, jen-, jed-,** show the same endings as the definite articles. Adjectives coming after any of these words take the same endings as adjectives following the definite article. Here is the pattern in case you need to refer to it:

	m. sing.	f. sing.	n. sing.	m./f./n. pl.
nom.	dieser	diese	dieses	diese
	jener	jene	jenes	jene
	jeder	jede	jedes	(alle)
	einer	eine	eins	—

	m. sing.	f. sing.	n. sing.	m./f./n. pl.
acc.	diesen	diese	dieses	diese
	jenen	jene	jenes	jene
	jeden	jede	jedes	(alle)
	einen	eine	eins	—
dat.	diesem	dieser	diesem	diesen
	jenem	jener	jenem	jenen
	jedem	jeder	jedem	(allen)
	einem	einer	einem	—

100 Interrogatives ('which?', 'what ... with?', 'what ... about?', etc.)

a) Welcher, -e, -es

Welch- means 'which' and follows the same pattern as **dieser** (see previous Checknote):

n.sing.nom.	Welches Telefon hat geklingelt? *Which telephone rang?*
m.sing.dat.	Welchem Händler wollen Sie diese Aufstellung schicken? *Which dealer do you want to send this list to?*
f.pl.nom.	Welche Banken haben Filialen in London? *Which banks have branches in London?*
m.pl.dat.	Welchen Kunden wollen Sie die Broschüren schicken? *Which customers do you want to send the brochures to?*

Note that **welch-** can also be used as a relative pronoun ('who', 'whom', 'which', etc.), but this use is not very common. Here's an example:

Die Firma, welche Sie als Agenten gewählt haben, hat einen sehr guten Ruf.
The firm which you have chosen (to act) as agents has a very good reputation.

b) Wo-/wor- + preposition

If you want to express 'what ... about?', 'what ... with?', 'what ... for?' etc. in German, you use **wo-** + the preposition (or **wor-** if the preposition starts with a vowel). Here are some of the sentences from Checknote 94 turned into questions:

Womit haben Sie die Rechnung verglichen?	*What did you compare the bill with?*
Worüber unterhalten sie sich?	*What are they chatting about?*
Woran haben Sie gedacht?	*What were you thinking of?*
Woran hat er sich gewöhnt?	*What has he got used to?*
Wofür interessiert er sich?	*What is he interested in?*

Here are some more useful phrases:

Wovon spricht er?	*What is he talking about?*
Wozu dient das?	*What is that used for?*
Worum handelt es sich?	*What is it all about?*
Worauf wartet sie?	*What is she waiting for?*

101 Word detective

You'll find it very useful if you can detect familiar words in any new verb, adjective or adverb you meet. Obviously, our memories work much better if we can find a link between new words and already well-established ones.

Let's begin our detective work by making a list of verbs we already know and noting how other words are derived from them. But first study some typical suffixes that are added to adjectives/adverbs:

-bar (possibility)
-haft (of a certain nature)
-los (without)
-lich ⎫
-ig ⎬ (English: -y, -ly, -al, -ic)
-isch ⎭

Revise the verbs below before studying the examples that follow:

verb:	noun:	adjective/adverb:
teilen (*to share*)	der (or das) Teil (*part*)	teilbar (*divisible*)
denken (*to think*)	der Gedanke (*thought*)	denkbar (*conceivable*)
liefern (*to deliver*)	die Lieferung (*delivery*)	lieferbar (*available*)
sprechen (*to speak*)	die Sprache (*language*)	sprachlich (*linguistic*)
		sprachlos (*speechless*)
fragen (*to ask*)	die Frage (*question*)	fraglich (*doubtful*)
		fraglos (*undoubtedly*)
verkaufen (*to sell*)	der Verkauf (*sale*)	verkäuflich (*marketable*)
kosten (*to cost*)	die Kosten, pl. (*cost*)	kostspielig (*costly*)

102 Word-building by using suffixes

Let's continue our detective work and see how nouns are often formed in German by adding suffixes to verbs, adjectives, etc.

a) **-ung**. This is the suffix most used to coin new nouns. The basic word is normally a verb:

erklären *(to explain)*	→	die Erklärung *(explanation)*
eröffnen *(to open a shop*, etc)	→	die Eröffnung *(opening)*
anleiten *(to instruct)*	→	die Anleitung *(instruction)*

b) **-heit.** The basic word used with this common suffix is normally an adjective, or sometimes a past participle:

schön *(beautiful)*	→	die Schönheit *(beauty)*
sicher *(safe, secure)*	→	die Sicherheit *(security)*
dunkel *(dark)*	→	die Dunkelheit *(darkness)*
gegeben *(given)*	→	die Gegebenheit *(reality*, lit. 'given' fact)
beliebt *(chosen)*	→	die Beliebtheit *(popularity)*
entschlossen *(determined)*	→	die Entschlossenheit *(determination)*

c) **-keit.** This suffix is often added to adjectives/adverbs ending in **-ig, -lich, -sam:**

notwendig *(necessary)*	→	die Notwendigkeit *(necessity)*
ehrlich *(honest)*	→	die Ehrlichkeit *(honesty)*
gemeinsam *(joint, common)*	→	die Gemeinsamkeit *(community, common interest)*

d) **-igkeit.** This is a variation on **-keit:**

schnell *(fast)*	→	die Schnelligkeit *(speed)*
feucht *(damp)*	→	die Feuchtigkeit *(dampness)*

e) **-schaft.** This is often used for collective nouns:

der Arbeiter *(worker)*	→	die Arbeiterschaft *(workforce)*
wissen *(to know)*	→	die Wissenschaft *(science)*
bürgen *(to vouch for)*	→	die Bürgschaft *(bail; security)*

f) **-ion.** This forms the noun which relates to verbs ending in **-ieren:**

variieren *(to vary)*	→	die Variation *(variation)*
qualifizieren, refl. *(to qualify)*	→	die Qualifikation *(qualification)*
organisieren *(to organize)*	→	die Organisation *(organization)*

g) **-(i)tät.** This often relates to adjectives or adverbs:

aggressiv *(aggressive)*	→	die Agressivität *(agressiveness)*
normal *(normal)*	→	die Normalität *(normality)*

All the suffixes so far mentioned in this section denote feminine nouns. However, the following one signals a masculine noun and denotes things or people that habitually do something:

h) **-er.**

aufsteigen *(to go up)*	→	der Aufsteiger *(yuppy)*
blinken *(to signal)*	→	der Blinker *(direction indicator)*
anzeigen *(to indicate)*	→	der Anzeiger *(indicator; gauge)*

Comprehension Practice 7

Study the dialogue once more and then answer the following questions in German.

New words:
fast   *nearly*
lustig   *funny*

1 Was will Herr Jackson von Frau Schneider wissen?
2 Was für Geräte hatte Futura Büromaschinen ausschließlich im Programm?
3 Wie denken viele deutsche Kunden noch?
4 Woran stellen die Kunden hohe Ansprüche?
5 Was glauben sie außerdem?
6 Was findet Herr Jackson erstaunlich?
7 Welche englischen Fachwörter kennen fast alle Deutschen?
8 Was findet Frau Schneider lustig?
9 Wie sind die Lohn- und Produktionskosten?
10 Warum sind die Kosten ins Astronomische gestiegen?
11 Wonach muß sich Futura umsehen?
12 Wozu ist Futura bereit?
13 Was will Herr Jackson Frau Schneider zeigen?
14 Was will Herr Jackson Frau Schneider erläutern?

FLUENCY PRACTICE 31
Puzzle

Supply the missing letters (all the words are found in Checklist 7):

1   - reis
2   Ände - ung
3   Pr - spekt
4 Lieferbe - ingungen
5   A - fzählung
6   Prospe - t
7   En - wicklung

Which word appears in the vertical gap?

FLUENCY PRACTICE 32
Prepositions linked to verbs

New words:

die Beschwerde	*complaint*
die Diskretion	*discretion*
sich konzentrieren	*to be concentrated* (in a place)
die Höhe	*height; high amount*
die Gehaltserhöhung	*rise: salary increase*
Mailand	*Milan*

Please insert the correct preposition:

1 Es handelt sich ..... die Beschwerde aus Mailand.
2 Wir verlassen uns ..... Ihre Diskretion
3 Die Kunden interessieren sich sehr ..... die neuen Gabelstapler.
4 Wir haben oft ..... dieses Problem nachgedacht.
5 Der Verkehr konzentriert sich ..... das Stadtzentrum.
6 Der Vertreter wundert sich ..... die Höhe der Bestellung.
7 Haben Sie ..... die Fotokopien gedacht?
8 Haben Sie mit dem Chef ..... Ihre Gehaltserhöhung gesprochen?

FLUENCY PRACTICE 33
Role-play

Play the part of Mr Jackson in this conversation with Frau Schneider, putting his words into German.

Mr Jackson:	*May I ask you why you only sell German products?*
Frau Schneider:	Viele unserer Kunden glauben leider, daß nur deutsche Geräte ihren Ansprüchen genügen.
Mr Jackson:	*I find this negative attitude astonishing. Nowadays, many Germans are familiar with a number of English technical terms. Everyone talks of 'fax', 'computer', and so on.*
Frau Schneider:	Sie haben sicher recht. Wir sind jetzt durchaus bereit englische Geräte in unsere Produktpalette aufzunehmen.
Mr Jackson:	*I'm pleased to hear that. May I show you our brochures? We can then talk about conditions of payment and terms of delivery.*

DICTIONARY PRACTICE 3

With the help of your dictionary, study this authentic German text and then answer in English the questions that follow.

Bald bleibt der Koffer zu

Wenn der EG Ministerrat
dem Gesetz zustimmt, wird es ab
1993 auf Flug- und Schiffsreisen
innerhalb der Gemeinschaft
keine Gepäckkontrollen mehr
geben. Davon ausgenommen
bleiben natürlich Reisende, die
von entfernteren Zielen kommen
und lediglich das letzte Teilstück
innerhalb der EG-Grenzen
zurücklegen.

['Check-In': Nov./Dez. 1990]

Please tick the correct answers:

1 What is the EC Council expected to do?
   a) accept the proposed new law
   b) reject the proposed new law
   c) change the proposed new law

2 What may be abolished in 1993?
   a) travel by air and ship inside Europe
   b) travel by air and ship outside Europe
   c) baggage checks

3 Which group of people will not be covered by this proposal?
   a) intercontinental travellers
   b) international travellers
   c) travellers from outside the EC

Letter writing

In this Unit you will learn how to write German business letters and you will be introduced to the ordinal numbers and the genitive case.

Mr Jackson is now back in London. He has returned with a trial order from Frau Schneider of Futura Büromaschinen who, if the English goods sell well on the German market, may act as agents for Excel-Equip. Frau Schneider writes to confirm her order, prices, delivery dates, conditions and terms of payment, etc. Here is her letter:

FUTURA BÜROMASCHINEN
Feuerbachstr. 105/7
6000 Frankfurt 1

Mr
P. Jackson, Sales Manager
Excel-Equip
400 Regent Street
London W1R 6XZ   Frankfurt, den 3.Mai 1992

Bestellung   Unser Zeichen: FS/ST

Sehr geehrter Herr Jackson,

im Anschluß an das mit Ihnen im April geführte Gespräch möchte ich unsere Bestellung und die von uns vereinbarten Konditionen schriftlich bestätigen.

16	tragbare Textcomputer, incl. Drucker	Typ TKD 2000
24	elektronische Schreibmaschinen	Typ EX 4000
50	Telefonbeantworter	Typ TB 1800
50	Diktiergeräte	Typ DK 5000

Die Lieferung erfolgt frei Haus Anfang/Mitte Juni an unser Lager durch eine von Ihnen beauftragte Spedition. Wie vereinbart, räumen Sie uns für diese Probelieferung 50% Rabatt auf die derzeit gültigen Preise ein. Zahlung ohne weitere Skonti binnen 21 Tage.

Wir hoffen im beiderseitigen Interesse, daß der von uns anvisierte Kundenkreis positiv auf Ihre Produkte ansprechen wird. In diesem Fall werden wir uns gerne mit Ihnen über eine Tätigkeit als Agent für Excel-Equip in Deutschland unterhalten.

In der Hoffnung auf gute Geschäftsbeziehungen,

Mit freundlichen Grüßen,

F. Schneider

F. Schneider
Einkaufsleiter

TRANSLATION

3rd May, 1992

Order   Our ref: FS/ST

Dear Mr Jackson,

Following our meeting in April, I would like to confirm in writing our order and the conditions we agreed upon.

16	portable word processors (inclusive of printers)	type TKD 2000
24	electronic typewriters	type EX 4000
50	telephone answering machines	type TB 1800
50	dictating machines	type DK 5000

Delivery to our warehouse will take place early or mid-June by shipping agents, instructed and paid by you. As agreed, you will grant us a discount of 50% on current prices for this trial order. Payment without further discounts within 21 days.

We hope that, in our mutual business interests, our potential customers will react positively to your products. In that case, we would like to discuss acting as agents for Excel-Equip in Germany.

We look forward to a good business relationship.

Yours sincerely,

F. Schneider
Purchasing Manager

Checklist 8

Masculine nouns:

der Anschluß, ¨-sse	connection
der Telefonbeantworter, -	answerphone
der Anfang, ¨-e	start, beginning
(der) Juni	June
der Rabatt, -e	discount
der Tag, -e	day
der Fall, ¨-e	case
der Kundenkreis	customers, clientele

Feminine nouns:

die Bestellung, -en	order
die Konditionen	(commercial) terms and conditions
die Lieferung, -en	delivery; order
die Probelieferung, -en	trial order
die Mitte, -n	middle
die Spedition, -en	shipping agent
die Zahlung, -en	payment
die Tätigkeit, -en	activity, function, occupation
die Hoffnung, -en	hope
die Beziehung, -en	connection, relationship
die Geschäftsbeziehungen	business contacts, business relations

Neuter nouns:

das Gespräch, -e	talk, meeting
das Diktiergerät, -e	dictating machine
das Lager, -	warehouse
das/der Skonto, die Skonti	discount (on cash payments)
das Interesse, -n	interest

Adjectives/Adverbs:

geehrt-	honoured
geführt (pp.)	held; conducted
vereinbart (pp.)	agreed (upon)
schriftlich	in writing
tragbar	portable
elektronisch	electronic
derzeit	currently, at present
gültig	correct, valid
weiter	further
beiderseitig	mutual (lit. 'on both sides')
positiv	positive, favourable
freundlich	friendly

Weak verbs:

führen acc.	to lead
bestätigen acc. dat.	to confirm
erfolgen	to happen, take place
anvisieren, pp. anvisiert	to aim at
vereinbaren acc.	to arrange, agree to
Konditionen vereinbaren	to agree on terms and conditions
beauftragen acc. + inf.	to instruct
ein|räumen acc.	to concede
hoffen acc.	to hope

Other words/expressions:

ein Gespräch führen	to conduct a conversation
frei Haus	free delivery, carriage free (a commercial term)
ohne acc.	without
binnen gen.	within, inside
positiv an|sprechen auf + acc.	to react positively to

CHECKNOTES

103 Ordinal numbers

When you read the letter, did you notice the dot after the first number of the date (**3.Mai**)? It's easy to miss, but it's quite important. It changes a cardinal number (1, 2, 3, 4, etc.) into an ordinal number (1st, 2nd, 3rd, 4th, etc.).

When giving the date you put **der** in front of the number, and for the numbers 2 to 19 you add **-te**, (also for 102-119; 1002-1019; etc.) and for higher numbers you add **-ste**.

In the following examples the names of the days of the week and months have been used, so that you can become more familiar with them:

(Monday)	Montag, der 1. Januar	=	der erste Januar
(Tuesday)	Dienstag, der 2. Februar	=	der zweite Februar
(Wednesday)	Mittwoch, der 3. März	=	der dritte März
(Thursday)	Donnerstag, der 4. April	=	der vierte April
(Friday)	Freitag, der 5. Mai	=	der fünfte Mai
(Saturday)	Samstag, der 6. Juni	=	der sechste Juni
(Sat., regional)	Sonnabend, der 7. Juli	=	der siebte Juli
(Sunday)	Sonntag, der 8. August	=	der achte August

Note the irregularities in the numbers 1, 3, 7, and 8.

As in English, a figure is sometimes used to represent the month, but when you read it aloud, always say the name of the month, e.g.:

15.	9.	der fünfzehnte September
20.	10.	der zwanzigste Oktober
21.	11.	der einundzwanzigste November
31.	12.	der einunddreißigste Dezember

Going beyond the numbers on the calendar:

der fünfundsechzigste Geburtstag	*65th birthday*
die hundertste Lieferung	*100th delivery*
die tausendste Sendung	*1000th broadcast*

Note also that ordinal numbers are used like ordinary adjectives and that they take the normal adjectival endings:

Ich komme am dritten Mai.	*I'll be coming on the 3rd May.*
Weihnachten ist am fünfundzwanzigsten Dezember.	*Christmas falls on the 25th December.*
Er bleibt vom ersten bis zum sechsten Mai.	*He'll stay from the 1st to the 6th May.*

104 Dates on German letters

You will normally find the date on the right hand side of letters, but this custom seems to be changing with the increasing use of word processors etc. When writing a letter in German it is usual to name the place where the letter is written, alongside the date. For example: **London, den 15.Januar 1992.**

The definite article **den** in the previous line is no misprint, as indications of time take the accusative. But along with the name of the town where the letter is written, this convention is gradually disappearing.

105 Salutations in German business letters

You address a letter to a company in the following manner: **Sehr geehrte Damen und Herren, ...**

When you know the person, you put: **Sehr geehrter Herr Götz, ...** or **Sehr geehrte Frau Haupt, ...**

You never use initials in the salutation, but you *do* include a title: **Sehr geehrter Herr Dr. Metzger, ...**

When you write to a friend you address him/her as: **Lieber Hans, ...** or **Liebe Mathilde, ...**

In business correspondence it is becoming quite common to use: **Lieber Herr Köhnen, ..., Liebe Frau Warnke, ...**

These days, a comma follows at the end of the salutation and, unlike the English convention, the next line starts with a lower case letter. A more traditional style of salutation uses an exclamation mark, in which case, as you might have expected, the following word starts with an upper case letter.

106 Complimentary close in business letters

Thankfully, the old-fashioned complimentary close **Hochachtungsvoll** ('with our highest esteem') is gradually dying out, along with bowing to the customer and lifting one's hat to greet acquaintances in the street. (Who wears a hat these days? Certainly very few people in Germany.) German business people would only use this phrase to express a certain aloofness, i.e. in the third or fourth reminder for an unpaid bill. It has to be stressed, however, that you may prefer to use it, if you are providing a service, like running a hotel (where the porter and bellboys still have to bow!).

These days, most letters close with **mit freundlichem Gruß** (sing.) or **mit freundlichen Grüßen** (pl.), i.e. 'friendly greetings'. Unfortunately, both versions use specific German letters which are not to be found on an ordinary English keyboard, but most word processors and PCs provide them with their extra key combinations.

Note: **Mit freundlichem (-en) Gruß (Grüßen)** is the equivalent of 'Yours sincerely'/'Yours faithfully'. Unlike the English complimentary close 'With kind regards', it can be used in a letter to someone you have not yet met. The abbreviation **mfG** is frequently used at the end of a telex.

107 Body of the letter

Here are some expressions that you will find useful when writing your letter:

1	*in respoot of*	**wegen** (gen./dat.)
2	*with regard to*	**in Bezug auf** (acc.); **über** (acc.); **zu** (dat.)
3	*in order to*	**um ... zu**
4	*by, through*	**durch** (acc.): **mit** (dat.)
5	*considering, in view of*	**angesichts** (gen.)
6	*despite*	**trotz** (gen./dat.)

Here are those expressions in sentences:

1 Ich bitte um Rücksprache wegen den neuen Preisen.
2a Zu den neuen Verträgen müssen wir folgendes feststellen: ...
2b Über die neuen Verträge kann man folgendes sagen: ...

2c In Bezug auf die neuen Verträge kann man folgendes sagen: ...
3 Wir sollten uns Ende des Monats treffen, um die Einzelheiten zu besprechen.
4a Durch den neuen Dienstplan gab es weniger Ausfall.
4b Mit einem konkurrenzfähigen Angebot können wir den Kunden für uns gewinnen.
5 Angesichts der* steigenden Preise ist das Käuferverhalten abwartend.
(*see Checknote 110)
6 Trotz den steigenden Kosten konnten wir die Preise auf dem Vorjahresniveau halten.

The English translations that follow may sound slightly more traditional than the German original, as conventions regarding the way you write letters differ considerably from one language to another. Indeed, they even differ from one country to another where the same language is spoken (e.g. an Austrian letter will be different in style from a German one.) Here are the translations:

1 *I would like to have a discussion regarding the new prices.*
2 *With regard to the new contracts, we have to state the following: ...*
3 *We should meet at the end of the month to discuss the details.*
4a *Due to the new rota there was less wastage.*
4b *With a competitive offer, we will be able to win the customer over.*
5 *In view of rising prices, consumer behaviour is hesitant.*
6 *Despite rising costs, we were able to keep prices at the previous year's level.*

108 Extended adjectives

We hope that you are now beginning to accept German word order and the long compound nouns as 'normal'. Unfortunately, the Germans have some other bad habits, too, and one of them is to replace subclauses on occasion by so-called extended adjectives.

There are two instances of this in the letter given at the beginning of this Unit where you may have found the adjectives puzzling:

1) **das mit Ihnen im April geführte Gespräch**
the -with you in April held- talk
instead of:
das Gespräch, das ich mit Ihnen im April geführt habe, ...
the talk we had (lit. 'which I conducted with you') *in April*

2) **die derzeit gültigen Preise**
the currently valid prices
instead of:
die Preise, die zur Zeit gültig sind
the prices that are valid at the moment

Now study the following long adjectives, which use three new suffixes:

ein einsatzfähiger Lastwagen	*a lorry that is ready for use* (or: *a lorry that is in good working order*)
ein einsatzwilliger Mitarbeiter	*an employee who is always willing to do his best*
ein schadenersatzpflichtiger Arbeitgeber	*an employer who is liable for compensation*

Note that -**fähig** expresses ability (**die Fähigkeit**), -**willig** expresses willingness (**die Willigkeit**) and -**pflichtig** expresses duty (**die Pflicht**). Very often, these long adjectives also have to be translated as subclauses.

109 Avoiding very formal vocabulary

There are quite a number of German words which you will be tempted to use because of their similarity to English words, but do be careful – they might have an unexpected effect on your German business associates, as these words can sound formal, unfriendly, and even pompous.

too formal:	normal:	meaning:
(attestieren)	bescheinigen, beglaubigen	*to certify, testify*
(basieren)	beruhen (auf + dat.)	*to be based on*
(die Direktiven)	die Richtlinien	*directives, guidelines*
(effektiv)	tatsächlich, wirkungsvoll	*effective, actual*
(exakt)	genau	*exact*
(der Experte)	der Fachmann	*expert*
(die Intention)	die Absicht	*intention*
(der Kontrakt)	der Vertrag	*contract*
(modifizieren)	verändern	*to modify*
(die Periode)	die Zeitspanne	*period*
(die Prosperität)	der Aufschwung/Wohlstand	*prosperity*
(die Quantität)	die Menge	*quantity*
(revidieren)	überarbeiten	*to revise, redraft*
(spezifizieren)	genau angeben	*to specify*

This is how some of these words ('normal' version) are used in practice:

Die tatsächlichen Zinsen belaufen sich auf ...
The actual interest rate stands at ...

Er hat seine Werbemittel wirkungsvoll eingesetzt.
He has used the various advertising media to great advantage.

Er ist wirklich ein Fachmann auf seinem Gebiet.
He really is an expert in his field.

Wir müssen die Konstruktion verändern.
We'll have to modify the construction/design.

110 Genitive case

There is one more case to get used to, namely the genitive case. The fact that you have met it only once in the dialogues indicates that it is not as often used in the spoken language as the other cases. However, it is widely used in written communication and it is therefore quite important to be familiar with it, as it denotes possession. Please study the following examples:

das Geschäft des Vaters	*the father's business*	der → des
die Investitionen der Mutter	*the mother's investment*	die → der
das Sparbuch des Kindes	*the child's savings book*	das → des

Other examples:

die Laufzeit des Sparvertrags	*the duration of the savings contract*
der Umsatz der Firma	*the turnover of the company*
die Steigerung des Gehalts	*the increase in (of) salary*

Note: There are two genitive forms in the singular: **des** for masculine and neuter nouns and **der** for feminine nouns. Note also the genitive **-s** ending which is added to many masculine and neuter nouns!

If you weren't convinced before of the necessity of always learning the definite article at the same time as learning the noun, it must be clear to you now that you'd miss important pointers in a text and get very confused, if you were unsure about German genders.

As you know, Germans like using compound nouns. They talk about **die Vertragslaufzeit** ('duration of the contract'), **die Gehalts-steigerung** ('salary increase'), **die Marktchancen** ('opportunities in the market place'), **Wirtschaftswissenschaften** ('economics'), **die Kontenauflösung** ('closure of a bank account/s'), but - believe it or not - there are limits to what even the Germans find acceptable as a compound noun.

Where they feel that creating a compound noun isn't possible (thank goodness), they use the genitive case. Here are some examples:

Wir müssen die Chancen des Europäischen Marktes nutzen.
We must seize the opportunities of the Single Market.

Er wies auf die Gefahren der freien Marktwirtschaft hin.
He pointed out the dangers/pitfalls of the free market economy.

Die Auflösung des gemeinsamen Bankkontos ist beschlossen.
The closure of the joint bank account is/has been agreed upon.

Now, study the plural forms:

die Laufzeiten der Sparverträge	*the term/duration of the savings contracts*
die Öffnungszeiten der Geschäfte	*the opening times of the shops*
die Verlegung der Termine	*the change of the appointments/ dates*
die Anmietung der Fabrikhallen	*the renting of the factory units*
die Steigerung der Gehälter	*the increase in salaries*
die Auflösung der Bankkonten	*the closure of the bank accounts*

You will have been pleased to see that, in the plural, there is only one form to learn: **der.**

Before going on, you may find it useful to test yourself by covering up first the right-hand column of the previous examples and then the left-hand one.

Here now are three complete sentences showing the use of the genitive plural:

Die Öffnungszeiten der Geschäfte sind gesetzlich festgelegt.
The shop opening times are regulated by law.

Die Verlegung der Termine war leider unvermeidlich.
Unfortunately, it was not possible to avoid a change of dates.

Die Steigerung der Gehälter hielt mit der Inflation Schritt.
The increase in wages was in step/line with inflation.

111 Prepositions taking the genitive case

There is quite a large group of prepositions, used mostly in writing, which take the genitive case. Unfortunately, these are widely used in written instructions, and a passive knowledge is therefore desirable. This means that you have to be able to understand these constructions, but you don't have to use them, if you don't want to!

There are three groups of prepositions taking the genitive case, given in this long Checknote. At the end of each section you'll find simpler and more common alternatives to using the genitive case.

1) - those giving an indication of time:

anläßlich des Jubiläums	*on the occasion of the jubilee*
außerhalb der Bürostunden	*outside office hours*
binnen 30 Tagen	*within 30 days*
innerhalb dieser Frist	*within this time limit*
während meines Besuches	*during my visit*
zeit seines Lebens	*during his lifetime*

Alternatives:

> zu + dat.: zum Jubiläum
> wenn das Büro geschlossen ist
> binnen/innerhalb von 30 Tagen
> während ich ihn/die Firma besuchte
> sein Leben lang (indication of time in the acc. case)

2) – those giving an indication of place:

abseits der Autobahn	*off the motorway*
außerhalb des Grundstücks	*outside the plot (of land)*
beiderseits der Grenze	*on both sides of the border*
diesseits des Kanals	*on this side of the canal*
innerhalb des Gebäudes	*within the building*
längs der Kante	*along the rim/edge*
oberhalb der Steuergrenze	*above the tax threshold*
unterhalb der Steuergrenze	*below the tax threshold*
seitens seiner Vorgesetzten	*from/on the part of his bosses*
unweit der Stadt	*close to the town*

Alternatives:

> in der Nähe von (+ dat.) der Autobahn
> neben (= dat.) dem Grundstück
> auf beiden Seiten von (+ dat.) der Grenze
> auf dieser Seite vom Kanal
> in (+ dat.) dem = im Gebäude
> die Kante entlang (acc.)
> über/unter (+ dat.) der Steuergrenze
> von (dat.) seinen Vorgesetzten aus
> nicht weit von (+ dat.) der Stadt

3) – those giving a causal connection/reasons

angesichts der Verluste	*in view of the losses*
aufgrund der Kursschwankungen	*due to/because of fluctuations in the exchange rate*
der Bequemlichkeit halber*	*for reasons of convenience*
infolge eines Rechenfehlers	*because of an arithmetical mistake*
laut §1 der Verordnung	*in accordance with §1 of the regulation*
mangels Nachfrage	*due to the lack of demand*
zugunsten des Angeklagten	*in favour of the accused*
wegen der Reparaturarbeiten	*due to repair work*

*Some prepositions, e.g. **halber**, are placed after the noun.

May we remind you that these prepositions taking the genitive case need only form part of your passive vocabulary; the alternatives that follow are much less formal:

Alternatives:

wegen (+ dat.) seinen Verlusten
wegen den Kursschwankungen
aus (+ dat.) Bequemlichkeit
wegen einem Rechenfehler
entsprechend dem Paragraph(en) 1
or: dem Paragraph(en) 1 der Verordnung entsprechend
wegen der geringen Nachfrage (gen., but more common)
zugunsten von (+ dat.) dem Angeklagten
or: dem Angeklagten zugunsten
wegen (+ dat.) (den) Reparaturarbeiten

If you enjoy a challenge (and perhaps with your dictionary by your side), you might like to work out the meaning of the following five sentences in which we've used prepositions with the genitive case. Their translations follow after.

1 Außerhalb der Bürostunden ist der Kundendienst nicht besetzt.
2 Während meines letzten Besuches habe ich die neue Produktionsanlage besichtigt.
3 Aufgrund der Kursschwankungen können wir keine Festpreise angeben.
4 Mangels Nachfrage haben wir die Produktion dieses Artikels eingestellt.
5 Der Bequemlichkeit halber verlegte er das Konstruktionsbüro ins Hauptgebäude.

1 The customer service department is not manned outside office hours.
2 During my last visit I had a look at the new production line.
3 Due to the fluctuations in the exchange rates, we cannot give fixed prices.
4 Due to lack of demand, we discontinued the production of this item.
5 For reasons of convenience he moved the construction department to the main building.

How good were your guesses? (Very often, of course, you will be able to guess the meaning of an unknown word from its context, which is easier in a report or letter than in unconnected sentences.)

Let's do it again! This time we'll use the less formal alternatives and you should find the German sentences easier to understand:

1 Nach Dienstschluß ist der Kundendienst nicht besetzt.
2 Bei meinem letzten Besuch habe ich die neue Produktionsanlage besichtigt.
3 Wegen Kursschwankungen können wir keine festen Preise festlegen.

4 Weil die Nachfrage gesunken ist, haben wir die Produktion dieses Artikels eingestellt.
5 Aus Bequemlichkeitsgründen verlegte er das Konstruktionsbüro ins Hauptgebäude.

1 After office hours the customer service department is not manned.
2 On my last visit I had a look at the new production line.
3 Owing to the fluctuations in the rate of exchange, we cannot give fixed prices
4 We have discontinued production of this article, because demand has fallen.
5 He moved his construction department for reasons of convenience to the main building.

112 Adjectival endings (genitive case)

As you might have expected, adjectives have genitive case endings, too. Please study the following examples:

aufgrund des unerwarteten Erfolgs	*due to the unexpected success*
wegen der großen Nachfrage	*because of the great demand*
während des letzten Besuches	*during the last visit*
angesichts der großen Verluste	*in view of the heavy losses*
aufgrund eines großen Schocks	*due to a great shock*
wegen einer plötzlichen Flaute	*because of a sudden recession*
während eines starken Aufschwungs	*during a strong upturn*

Note: The adjectival ending in the genitive case after the definite article (singular and plural) and the indefinite article is always **-en**!

Here now are examples of the above adjectival endings in complete sentences (with translations):

1 Aufgrund des unerwarteten Geschäftserfolgs konnten sie schneller expandieren als geplant.
2 Wegen einer plötzlichen Flaute auf dem Immobilienmarkt konnten sie für ihre neue Fabrikhalle keinen Käufer finden.
3 Angesichts der großen Verluste mußte er einige Filialen schließen.

1 Due to the unexpected business success, they were able to expand faster than planned.
2 Because of a sudden lull (recession) in the property market, they could not find a buyer for their factory unit.
3 In view of the heavy losses he had to close down some branches.

113 Complete table of adjectival endings
(FOR REFERENCE ONLY)

When composing your own letters you may wish to consult the following tables occasionally to check up on adjectival endings:

a) After **der, die, das; dieser; jener; jeder; welcher:**

	masc. sing.	*fem. sing.*	*neut. sing.*
nom.	der neue Mitarbeiter	die neue Regelung	das neue Gebäude
acc.	den neuen Mitarbeiter	die neue Regelung	das neue Gebäude
dat.	dem neuen Mitarbeiter	der neuen Regelung	dem neuen Gebäude
gen.	des neuen Mitarbeiters	der neuen Regelung	des neuen Gebäudes

	masc. pl.	*fem. pl.*	*neut. pl.*
nom.	die neuen Mitarbeiter	die neuen Regelungen	die neuen Gebäude
acc.	die neuen Mitarbeiter	die neuen Regelungen	die neuen Gebäude
dat.	den neuen Mitarbeitern	den neuen Regelungen	den neuen Gebäuden
gen.	der neuen Mitarbeiter	der neuen Regelungen	der neuen Gebäude

b) After **ein/eine:**

	masc. sing.	*fem. sing.*	*neut. sing.*
nom.	ein neuer Mitarbeiter	eine neue Regelung	ein neues Gebäude
acc.	einen neuen Mitarbelter	eine neue Regelung	ein neues Gebäude
dat.	einem neuen Mitarbeiter	einer neuen Regelung	einem neuen Gebäude
gen.	eines neuen Mitarbeiters	einer neuen Regelung	eines neuen Gebäudes

	masc. pl.	*fem. pl.*	*neut. pl.*
nom.	neue Mitarbeiter	neue Regelungen	neue Gebäude
acc.	neue Mitarbeiter	neue Regelungen	neue Gebäude
dat.	neuen Mitarbeitern	neuen Regelungen	neuen Gebäuden
gen.	neuer Mitarbeiter	neuer Regelungen	neuer Gebäude

c) Adjectival endings without preceding article:

	masc. sing.	*fem. sing.*	*neut. sing.*
nom.	guter Kontakt	gute Arbeit	gutes Material
acc.	guten Kontakt	gute Arbeit	gutes Material
dat.	gutem Kontakt	guter Arbeit	gutom Material
gen.	guten Kontakts	guter Arbeit	guten Materials

	masc. pl.	*fem. pl.*	*neut. pl.*
nom.	gute Kontakte	gute Arbeiten	gute Materialien
acc.	gute Kontakte	gute Arbeiten	gute Materialien
dat.	guten Kontakten	guten Arbeiten	guten Materialien
gen.	guter Kontakte	guter Arbeiten	guter Materialien

Don't be disheartened by the variety you find in these lists. In practice you'll be using just a few of them most of the time and, of course, you'll have an opportunity to practise the most frequently used ones in the Fluency Practices of the next few Units.

Comprehension Practice 8

The following questions are based on Frau Schneider's letter to Mr Jackson:

1 Wann war das Gespräch zwischen Frau Schneider und Herrn Jackson?
2 Welches Datum hat der Brief?
3 Wieviele Textcomputer hat Frau Schneider bestellt?
4 Wieviele Anrufbeantworter hat sie bestellt?
5 Wann erfolgt die Lieferung?
6 Wieviel Rabatt haben sie vereinbart?
7 Wann muß die Rechnung bezahlt sein?
8 Was soll der anvisierte Kundenkreis tun?
9 Worüber will sie sich mit Herrn Jackson unterhalten?
10 Worauf hofft Frau Schneider?

FLUENCY PRACTICE 34
*The genitive case: **des** or **der**?*

New words:

die Eröffnung	*opening*
die Zulieferfirma	*firm supplying components*
die Beleuchtung	*lighting*
die Montagehalle	*assembly shop*
die Buchhaltung	*accountancy; accounts department*
das Geschäftskonto	*business bank account*
das Ersatzteil	*spare part*

Please insert the correct form of the definite article:

1 Die Lieferung d__ Ersatzteile
2 Die Eröffnung d__ Geschäftskontos
3 Anfang d__ Monats
4 Ende d__ Jahres
5 Die Direktoren d__ Zulieferfirma
6 Die Computer d__ Buchhaltung
7 Die Beleuchtung d__ Montagehallen
8 Der Fahrer d__ englischen Spedition

PRACTICAL TASK 2
Replying to a letter of complaint

Please study the following letter from a company your firm has been dealing with for many years. You will need your dictionary:

Hans Josef
SCHWEIGERT
Kaiserhof 35, D 8000 München 1

Extrawear
387 High Street
London EC14 6XZ   München, den 1.3.1992

Betr.: Transportschaden
Bezug: WW/ad 1190

Lieber Herr Johnson,

Ihre Sendung traf heute bei uns ein, aber leider nicht unversehrt. Alle Kartons waren beschädigt und der Inhalt ist verschmutzt. Da es sich um teure Strickwaren handelt, ist ein Weiterverkauf ausgeschlossen. Teilen Sie uns bitte mit, wie Sie diese Angelegenheit regeln wollen.

Mit freundlichen Grüßen,

W. Wildu

(W. Wildemann, Leiter des Einkaufs)

Please prepare a reply, using these words and expressions:

Es tut uns leid, daß ...	*We are sorry to hear that ...*
natürlich	*naturally*
zurück|nehmen	*to take back*
sich bemühen	*to endeavour*
in Zukunft	*in future*
Sie können sicher sein, daß ...	*Please rest assured that ...*
sorgfältiger verpacken	*to wrap more carefully*
wir möchten uns entschuldigen	*we wish to apologize*
nochmals	*again*
weitere erfolgreiche Zusammenarbeit	*further successful co-operation*

FLUENCY PRACTICE 35
Story without adjectival endings

New words:

der Rückflug	*return flight*
die Verspätung	*delay*
der Bestseller	*best seller*
der Umschlag	*cover*
die Aufmerksamkeit	*attention*
der Hundertmarkschein	*hundred mark note*
das Wechselgeld	*change (money)*

ziemlich	*fairly*
dick	*thick; fat*
unbequem	*awkward*
genau	*exact, correct*
anscheinend	*apparently*
trotzdem	*all the same*
sich ärgern	*to get angry*

Please insert the missing endings:

1 Herr Jackson hatte ein-__ ziemlich gut-__ Rückflug nach London.
2 Die Maschine hatte ein-__ klein-__ Verspätung.
3 Am Flughafen kaufte er ein-__ dick-__ Bestseller.
4 Der Umschlag dies-__ Buch-__ hatte seine Aufmerksamkeit erregt.
5 Er gab d-__ Verkäuferin ein-__ neu-__ Hundertmarkschein.
6 Sie ärgerte sich anscheinend über d-__ unbequem-__ Kunden.
7 Sie gab ihm aber trotzdem d-__ genau-__ Wechselgeld (heraus).

DICTIONARY PRACTICE 4
Matching sentences

Please match the German sentences with the correct English translations given afterwards.

1 Anläßlich des 50. Jubiläums gewähren wir unseren Kunden 10% Rabatt.
2 Wir erwarten die Lieferung binnen/innerhalb dieser Woche.
3 Während der Umbauarbeiten bleiben unsere Geschäftsräume geöffnet.
4 Angesichts der hohen Kosten sehen wir uns gezwungen, ...
5 Infolge eines Rechenfehlers wurden ihm DM 300, – mehr ausgezahlt.
6 Er zog sich zugunsten seines Schwiegersohns aus dem Geschäft zurück.

A *On the occasion of the firm's fiftieth anniversary we will grant our customers ten percent discount.*
B *We expect delivery sometime this week.*
C *He retired from the business in favour of his son-in-law.*
D *Our premises will remain open while building work is in progress.*
E *Owing to/Faced with high costs, we are obliged to ...*
F *Because of a miscalculation he was overpaid by three hundred marks.*

DICTIONARY PRACTICE 5
The revolutionary world of advertising

Find the German equivalents in the following advertisement:

1) in fifty-two steps
2) the realisation
3) of a revolutionary idea
4) the idea to create a watch
5) almost diamond-hard
6) for example
7) costly production stages
8) one of the secrets
9) to be based on the same consistency
10) utmost perfection
11) unique quality of the material
12) expensive treatment
13) uncompromising aesthetics
14) (can be bought) at
15) MRP

«In 52 Schritten zur ewigen Schönheit.»

Eine Rado ist die faszinierende Verwirklichung einer revolutionären Idee.

Der Idee, eine Uhr zu schaffen, die ewig schön ist. Allein für die sphärische

Wölbung des nahezu diamantharten Saphirglases der «La Coupole»

beispielsweise benötigen wir 52 aufwendige Arbeitsschritte. Aber dies ist

nur eines der Geheimnisse, die die «La Coupole» so kostbar machen. Denn

jedes Detail einer Rado beruht auf der gleichen Konsequenz: Höchste

Vollendung durch einzigartige Materialqualität, aufwendige Verarbeitung

und kompromißlose Ästhetik. Die Rado «La Coupole». Bei Ihrem Rado

Fachhändler. DM 790.- (unverbindliche Preisempfehlung).

Switzerland

UNIT 9

On the telephone

In this Unit we teach you all the words and phrases you'll need when speaking German on the telephone. You will also learn how to use the informal modes of address and the passive voice, and we introduce you to the important verb **lassen**.

The office equipment ordered by Frau Schneider has now been delivered to Futura Büromaschinen, but there are some problems with the packaging. Frau Schneider decides to telephone Mr Jackson in London. As the office is closed, she hears a message on the answerphone, but can't understand it as it is spoken rather too quickly.

Frau Schneider: Da ist en Anrufbeantworter, Sabine. Ich versteh' kein Wort! Wähl doch bitte noch einmal und sag mir dann, ob du die Nachricht verstehen kannst.

A few moments later:

Sekretärin: Da ist schon Dienstschluß. Wir möchten bitte unsere Telefonnummer und unsere Nachricht auf Band sprechen.

Frau Schneider: Ach, das war alles? - Ich werde also langsam und deutlich sprechen, damit Herr Jackson mich versteht. Ich habe ja eben selbst gemerkt, wie schwierig es ist, eine telefonische Nachricht in einer Fremdsprache zu verstehen.

Frau Schneider redials and speaks after the answerphone pips.

Frau Schneider: Guten Tag. Hier Schneider von der Firma Futura Büromaschinen. Ich möchte Herrn Jackson für die schnelle Zustellung der bestellten Ware danken. - Leider gab es ein paar Probleme mit dieser Lieferung. Hm. Ich möchte Herrn Jackson bitten, mich morgen Vormittag, das heißt also am Mittwoch, zwischen zehn und zwölf Uhr anzurufen. Vielen Dank. Auf Wiederhören.

Wednesday, 11 a.m. Mr Jackson rings Futura Büromaschinen.

Frau S.:   Tag, Herr Jackson. Nett von Ihnen, daß Sie sich so schnell gemeldet haben.

Mr J.:   Das ist doch selbstverständlich. Ich habe Ihre Nachricht heute morgen bekommen. Was ist denn schiefgegangen?

Frau S.:   Es ist nicht dramatisch, aber ich wollte es Sie so schnell wie möglich wissen lassen; auf jeden Fall bevor die nächste Sendung verpackt wird.

Mr J.:   Wenn ich Sie also richtig verstanden habe, gab es Probleme mit der Verpackung. Sind die Geräte denn durch den Transport beschädigt worden?

Frau S.:   Nein, nicht alle Herr Jackson, nur eins. Aber die Verpackungen von drei Geräten waren schwer beschädigt.

Mr J.:   Waren die Geräte denn nicht in Styropor verpackt?

Frau S.:   Doch, aber nur an den Enden. Die Kartons darum waren aufgerissen, die waren zu dünn.

Mr J.:   Frau Schneider, Sie können sich darauf verlassen, daß das nicht noch einmal passiert. Ich werde gleich der Versandabteilung eine Hausmitteilung schicken und eine sachgemäßere Verpackung für unsere Auslandssendungen veranlassen. - Was ist denn beim Transport beschädigt worden?

Frau S.:   Einer der Drucker ist defekt. Er macht einen ohrenbetäubenden Lärm.

Mr J.:   Am besten schicken Sie uns das defekte Gerät zurück. Wir lassen es dann in unserer Workstatt auf Herz und Nieren prüfen.

Frau S.:   Wollen Sie damit sagen, daß wir auf die Reparatur dieses Druckers warten müssen?

Mr J.:   Aber nein, natürlich nicht! Wir tauschen ihn gegen einen neuen aus. Ich werde noch heute ein fabrikneues Gerät losschicken, aber diesmal per Paketpost. Innerhalb dieser Woche haben Sie den neuen! Gibt es sonst noch Reklamationen?

Frau S.:   Tja, wenn Sie schon fragen: Die Gebrauchsanleitung ist nicht so ganz gelungen. Das Lay-out und der Druck sind einwandfrei, aber die Übersetzung ist sehr umständlich und – schwer zu verstehen.

Mr J.:   Wirklich? – Na, ja. Ich habe die hier im Haus übersetzen lassen. Aber wenn die Übersetzung so schlecht ist, dann muß die natürlich neu gemacht werden. Aber diesmal machen wir die nicht selbst; wir lassen sie von einem Fachmann machen. Natürlich haben Sie da recht, Frau Schneider, Übersetzungen von technischen Anweisungen müssen klar und leicht verständlich sein. Ich werde gleich eine Aktennotiz machen und das notieren. Das ist doch nur eine Kleinigkeit, Frau Schneider. Das läßt sich leicht ändern. Sobald wir die neuen Übersetzungen bekommen haben, werde ich sie Ihnen faxen. Vielleicht könnten Sie so nett sein, sie zu überprüfen, bevor sie neu gedruckt werden.

Frau S.:   Aber sicher, Herr Jackson. Kein Problem. Das ist doch auch in unserem Interesse, und natürlich dem unserer Kunden. Freut mich, daß wir uns in allen Punkten so schnell geeinigt haben.

Mr J.:   Wir geben uns die größte Mühe, unsere Kunden im In- und Ausland zufriedenzustellen. Rufen Sie mich bitte sofort an, falls noch andere Probleme auftauchen sollten. Wir versuchen immer, alles schnell und unbürokratisch zu regeln.

Frau S.:   Vielen Dank, Mr Jackson. Auf Wiederhören.

Mr J.:   Auf Wiederhören, Frau Schneider.

TRANSLATION:

Frau S.:   Sabine, there's an answerphone. I can't understand a word. Could you please redial and tell me (then), if you can understand the message.

A few moments later:

Secretary: The office is (already) closed. We're asked to leave (*lit.* 'speak') our telephone number and our message on(to) the tape.

Frau S.: Oh, is that all it was? I'll speak slowly and clearly, so that Mr Jackson can understand me. I've just found out myself how difficult it is to understand a telephone message in a foreign language. (*After the answerphone pips*) Hello. This is Frau Schneider of Futura Büromaschinen. I would like to thank Mr Jackson for the prompt delivery of the goods (we) ordered. Unfortunately, there are (were) a few problems with this delivery. Hm... I would like to ask Mr Jackson to phone me tomorrow morning, that is to say Wednesday, between ten and twelve. Thank you (very much). Goodbye.

Wednesday, 11 a.m.:

Frau S.: Hello, Mr Jackson. (It's) nice of you to get back to me so promptly.

Mr J.: That's the least I could do (*lit.* 'that goes without saying'). I got your message this morning. Tell me, what has gone wrong?

Frau S.: Nothing very dramatic, really, but I wanted to bring it to your attention as quickly as possible. Certainly before the next consignment is packed.

Mr J.: (Let me see) if I understand you correctly, there were problems with the packaging. Have the machines been damaged in transit?

Frau S.: No, not all (of them), Mr. Jackson, only one. But the packaging of three machines was badly damaged.

Mr J.: Weren't they packed in polystyrene, then?

Frau S.: Yes, they were, but only at the ends. The cardboard boxes around them were torn open, they were too flimsy.

Mr J.: Frau Schneider, you can rest assured that this will not happen again. I'll be sending an internal memo to our despatch department immediately and I'll make arrangements for more suitable packaging for shipments going abroad. Tell me, what has been damaged in transit?

Frau S.: One of the printers is faulty. It makes a deafening noise.

Mr J.: It would be best if you sent the faulty machine back to us. We'll have it thoroughly checked in our workshop.

Frau S.: Do you mean to say that we will have to wait for this printer to be repaired?

Mr J.: Oh no, of course not! We('ll) exchange it for a new (one). In the course of the day I'll be sending out a brand-new machine, but this time by Parcel Force. You'll get it by the end of the week! Are there any other problems (*lit.* 'complaints')?

Frau S.: Well, as you're asking (there is one): the manual for the answerphone hasn't turned out very well. Layout and printing are perfect, but the translation is very long-winded and quite difficult to understand.

Mr J.: Really? Well, you see, I had it translated here, in our firm. But if the translation is so bad, it'll have to be done again. This time we won't do it ourselves: we'll have it done by an expert. Of course you're right there, Frau Schneider, translations of technical instructions have to be clear and easy to understand. I'll write a memo (for my files) and note this down straight away. But that's a mere trifle, Frau Schneider. That's easily put right. As soon as we have received the new translations I'll fax them to you. Maybe you would be so kind as to check them before they are reprinted.

Frau S.: But of course, Mr Jackson. No problem. It's also in our interests and, of course, our clients', too. I'm pleased that we have agreed on all points so quickly.

Mr J.: We are very anxious to satisfy our customers at home and abroad. Please call me immediately, if any more problems (should) crop up. We always try to put things right, quickly and without red tape (unbureaucratically).

Frau S.: Thank you, Mr Jackson, Goodbye.

Mr J.: Goodbye, Frau Schneider.

Checklist 9

Masculine nouns:

der Dienstschluß	*end of the working day*
der Transport, -e	*transport, shipment*
der Lärm (no pl.)	*noise*
der Druck	*print*
der Punkt, -e	*point*
der Übersetzungsdienst	*translation service*

Feminine nouns:

die Nachricht, -en	*message; news*
die Telefonnummer, -n	*telephone number*
die Fremdsprache, -n	*foreign language*
die Zustellung, -en	*delivery*
die Lieferung, -en	*shipment, delivery*
die Kleinigkeit, -en	*trifle, minor problem*
die Sendung, -en	*shipment*
die Verpackung, -en	*packaging*
die Versandabteilung	*despatch department*

die Hausmitteilung, -en	*internal memo*
die Auslandssendung	*shipment going abroad*
die Werkstatt, ¨-en	*workshop*
die Niere, -n	*kidney*
die Reparatur, -en	*repair*
die Paketpost	*parcel post*
die Möglichkeit, -en	*possibility*
die Reklamatlon, -en	*complaint; letter of complaint*
die Gebrauchsanleitung	*users' manual*
die Anweisung, -en	*instruction*
die Mühe, -n	*effort*

Neuter nouns:

das Band, ¨-er	*tape*
das Problem, -e	*problem*
das Ende, -n	*end*
das Styropor	*polystyrene*
das Herz, -en	*heart*
das Lay-out	*layout*

Adverbs/adjectives :

langsam	*slowly*
deutlich	*well-articulated*
schwierig	*difficult*
telefonisch	*by phone*
schnell	*quick, fast*
bestellt	*ordered*
beschädigt	*damaged*
dünn	*thin*
defekt	*damaged, broken, not working*
ohrenbetäubend	*deafening*
fabrikneu	*brand-new*
gelungen	*well done, successful*
einwandfrei	*without fault, perfect*
umständlich	*awkward*
schwer	*difficult: heavy*
schlecht	*bad, of bad quality*
technisch	*technical*
klar	*clear*
leicht	*easy; light*

Verbs - strong verbs are identified by *(st)*, irregular verbs by *(irr)*:

verstehen *(st)*	*to understand*
wählen acc.	*to dial; to choose; to elect*
merken acc.	*to notice*
danken dat. (für)	*to thank someone (for)*
sich melden (bei + dat.)	*to get in touch (with someone); report back (to)*
bekommen *(st)* acc.	*to get, receive*

schief|gehen *(st)*	*to go wrong*
wissen lassen *(irr)* acc.	*to let someone know*
verpacken acc.	*to pack; wrap*
werden, wird, wurde, ist ... worden	auxiliary verb used to form the passive
es wird verpackt	*it is/gets packed*
ist beschädigt worden	*has been damaged*
auf|reißen *(st)* acc.	*to tear open*
sich verlassen *(irr)* auf	*to rely on*
passieren	*to happen* (used colloquially)
was ist passiert?	*what has happened?*
schicken (dat) acc.	*to send*
veranlassen *(irr)* (dat.) acc.	*to initiate something*
machen acc.	*to make, do*
neu machen	*to do again*
prüfen acc.	*to examine; check*
warten (auf acc.)	*to wait (for)*
aus|tauschen (gegen acc.)	*to exchange (for)*
los|schicken acc.	*to send off*
gelingen *(st)* (imp.)	*to succeed*
es ist (nicht) gelungen	*it was (not) successful*
übersetzen acc.	*to translate*
(verb) + lassen	*to have s.th. done*
etw. prüfen lassen	*to have s.th. examined*
etw. übersetzen lassen	*to have s.th. translated*
etw. (neu) machen lassen	*to have s.th. done (again)*
notieren	*to make a note, write down*
ändern acc.	*to change*
faxen (pp. = gefaxt)	*to fax* (coll. in German)
überprüfen acc.	*to check out, go over*
neu drucken acc.	*to reprint*
sich einigen	*to agree*
zufrieden|stellen acc.	*to satisfy*
auf|tauchen	*to come up unexpectedly*

Other phrases/expressions:

noch einmal	*once more*
das nächste Mal	*next time*
es gab (pres: es gibt)	*there was/were*
das ist selbstverständlich	*understood, it goes without saying*
am besten (adv.)	*it would be best*
auf Herz und Nieren prüfen	*to check/examine thoroughly* (lit: 'check the heart and kidneys')
wollen Sie damit sagen...?	*do you mean to say ...?*
natürlich nicht	*of course not*
diesmal	*this time*
den neuen [+noun implied]	*the new (one)*
gibt es sonst noch ...	*are there any other ...*

tja	*well, you know* [before a pause to heighten the impact]
wenn Sie schon fragen	*as you are asking*
nicht so ganz	*not quite*
schwer/leicht zu verstehen	*difficult/easy to understand*
schwer/leicht verständlich	*difficult/easy to understand*
wirklich	*really*
na, ja	*well, yes (admittedly, ...)*
hier im Haus	*in our firm/business* [a colloquialism]
das läßt sich leicht ändern	*that's easy to change/put right*
sobald wir ... bekommen haben, werden wir ...	*as soon as we have received ..., we'll ...*
umgehend	*as soon as possible; by return of post*
der (m.), die (f.), die (pl.)	In addition to their meaning of 'the', these words are often used in place of er (m.), sie (f.) and sie (pl.).

CHECKNOTES

114 Informal address **du/ihr**

Did you notice the informal way in which Frau Schneider addressed her secretary? Here it is once more:

"..., ob du die Nachricht verstehen kannst"

You may recall that the **du**-form was mentioned in Unit 1 (see Checknote 9), but as business people have few opportunities to use it, we haven't practised this form until now. There will be many occasions, though, when you will hear it being used. From the situation given in the dialogue, we can assume that the secretary is either a young girl who does not like to be addressed with the formal form **Sie**, or alternatively, the two ladies have built up a close relationship, working side by side for many years.

Please don't assume that you are to use the informal **du** when speaking to younger employees. It is safest to wait for the other party to invite you to do so. Any number of best friends and close business associates go on addressing each other as **Sie** and never change over to **du**. You can imagine that this changeover can cause problems as well; if one is used to calling someone **Sie**, one easily slips back into this old habit and this in itself can be embarrassing.

Only when you are on informal terms with your counterpart, can you use the comprehensive form **wir**, as the secretary does:

"Wir möchten bitte unsere Telefonnummer und unsere Nachricht auf Band sprechen."

Normally you would have to use the slightly awkward construction **Sie und ich** to avoid stepping on someone's toes!

Now study the following examples:

> du kaufst/ du bezahlst/ du bestellst/ du telefonierst/ du unterschreibst
> ihr kauft / ihr bezahlt / ihr bestellt / ihr telefoniert / ihr unterschreibt

You'll have noticed that the **du**-form ends in **-st** and the **ihr**-form in **-t**. (An **-e-** is inserted, if the stem ends in **d/t: du bittest/ihr bittet**.)

Imagine hearing the following instructions given to the office junior:

> "Weißt du was, du gehst jetzt mal in die Kantine und kaufst dir ein Mittagsmenü. Nach dem Essen trinkst du einen Kaffee und dann gehst du eine Viertelstunde im Park spazieren. Dann hast du sicher keine Kopfschmerzen mehr!"
>
> *Listen, why don't you go to the canteen now and buy yourself a lunch. After the meal, you have a coffee and then you go for a quarter of an hour's walk. Then you certainly won't have a headache any more!*

The instructions were quite easy to understand, weren't they? Unfortunately not all **du**-forms are regular, as you will see from the list below (we also give the **er-** form for reference):

to give	geben:	*you give*	du gibst	*he gives*	er gibt
to take	nehmen:	*you take*	du nimmst	*he takes*	er nimmt
to help	helfen:	*you help*	du hilfst	*he helps*	er hilft
to read	lesen:	*you read*	du liest	*he reads*	er liest
to measure	messen:	*you measure*	du mißt	*he measures*	er mißt
to eat	essen:	*you eat*	du ißt	*he eats*	er ißt
to see	sehen:	*you see*	du siehst	*he sees*	er sieht
to sleep	schlafen:	*you sleep*	du schläfst	*he sleeps*	er schläft
to let	lassen:	*you let*	du läßt	*he lets*	er läßt
to drive	fahren:	*you drive*	du fährst	*he drives*	er fährt

Note: In the **du-** and **er**-form, there may be a change in the stem vowel of irregular verbs!

Sometimes the ending of the verb stem influences the spelling, e.g.:

> *to sit* sitzen: ich sitze,   du sitzt,   er sitzt
> *to measure* messen: ich messe, du mißt,   er mißt
> *to eat* essen: ich esse,   du ißt,   er ißt

As we're on the topic of irregular verbs, we must mention a very important one which shows considerable irregularities:

> *to know (a fact)* wissen: ich weiß,   du weißt,   er weiß
>   wir wissen, ihr wißt,   sie wissen

115 Informal address (sein, haben)

There are just four slightly irregular forms to learn:

sein: **du bist, ihr seid**
haben: **du hast, ihr habt**

As you know, these two verbs are used to make up the past tense:

Du bist zu schnell gefahren!	*You drove too fast!*
Du hast zu viel gesehen!	*You saw too much!*
Ihr seid zu früh gegangen!	*You left too early!*
Ihr habt zu viele bekommen!	*You received too many!*

116 Informal address (imperative)

Do you remember the instructions Frau Schneider gave to the secretary?

"<u>Wähl</u> doch bitte noch einmal und <u>sag</u> mir ..."

You've probably guessed that the underlined words are the informal imperative forms (singular) of the verbs **wählen** ('to dial') and **sagen** ('to say'). Now compare the following **du-** and **ihr-**forms of some very useful verbs with their informal imperatives (singular and plural):

to come kommen	du kommst → komm! *come!*	ihr kommt → kommt! *come!*
to go gehen:	du gehst → geh! *go!*	ihr geht → geht! *go!*
to take nehmen:	du nimmst → nimm! *take!*	ihr nehmt → nehmt! *take!*
to make machen:	du machst → mach! *make!*	ihr macht → macht! *make!*
to do tun:	du tust → tu! *do!*	ihr tut → tut! *make!*
to say sagen:	du sagst → sag! *say!*	ihr sagt → sagt! *say!*
to give geben:	du gibst → gib! *give!*	ihr gebt → gebt! *give!*
to pay bezahlen:	du bezahlst → bezahl! *pay!*	ihr bezahlt → bezahlt! *pay!*

You'll have noticed from the above that:

a) the imperative (singular) is formed by dropping the **du** and the **-st** ending;
b) the imperative (plural) is formed by dropping the **ihr**.

There are some old-fashioned imperatives which still show the former **-e** ending. In the spoken language they have disappeared completely, but you may still find the odd written sample: **Sage das nicht!** ('Don't say that!').

Nevertheless, this traditional **-e** ending is kept on all those verbs which Germans would find difficult to pronounce, i.e. when the stem of a verb ends in **-t/-d/-ig** or **-n**. Some examples in the singular:

Rechne alles zusammen.   *Add it all up.*

Öffne die Tür.	*Open the door.*
Bitte ihn herein.	*Ask him (to come) in.*

Finally, let's look at some short sentences, using informal imperatives to ask people to refrain from doing certain things:

Sing.	Schreib nicht so undeutlich.	*Don't write so illegibly.*
	Kauf nicht so viel.	*Don't buy so much.*
	Rauch nicht so viel.	*Don't smoke so much.*
Pl.	Habt keine Angst!	*Don't be afraid!*
	Fahrt nicht so schnell.	*Don't drive so fast.*
	Seid nicht so nervös!	*Don't be so nervous!*

Note: Remember that, whilst the <u>formal</u> imperative (**kommen Sie, bezahlen Sie**, etc.) is the same for both singular and plural, you must distinguish between singular and plural in the <u>informal</u> imperative.

117 The passive voice (**werden**)

Before we begin to discuss the passive, can we just remind you that the verb **werden** + infinitive is used to form the future tense in German. Here are three examples of this use taken from the dialogue:

Ich werde also langsam und deutlich sprechen, ...
I'll speak slowly and clearly ...

Ich werde noch heute ein fabrikneues Gerät losschicken.
I'll send off a brand-new machine straight away.

Sobald ..., werde ich sie Ihnen faxen.
As soon as ... I'll fax them to you.

You would have thought that was straightforward enough. Unfortunately the Germans have to complicate things by using the same word to express quite a different function. Here's a different use of **werden**, also taken from the dialogue:

... bevor die nächste Sendung verpackt wird.
... before the next consignment is packed.

... dann muß die naturlich neu gemacht werden.
... of course it'll have to be done again.

... bevor sie neu gedruckt werden.
... before they're reprinted.

Here, as you can see, the verb **werden** has been used together with the past participles **verpackt**, **gemacht** and **gedruckt** and the result is the German passive voice.

Please compare the following sets of sentences:

active voice:	passive voice:
Ich bezahle die Rechnung bar.	Die Rechnung wird bar bezahlt.
I'll pay the bill with cash.	*The bill is paid with cash.*
Wir schicken die Briefe per Boten.	Die Briefe werden per Boten geschickt.
We'll send the letters by messenger.	*The letters are sent by messenger.*
Wir prüfen das defekte Gerät.	Das defekte Gerät wird geprüft.
We'll check the faulty machine.	*The faulty machine is (being) checked.*

Important note: Only those verbs taking a direct object (i.e. transitive verbs) can be used to form the passive voice.

When handling a passive construction you'll often need to mention the person by whom the action is carried out. This is done by using **von** + dative:

Die Rechnung wird von unserem Angestellten bar bezahlt. *(by our employee)*
Das defekte Gerät wird von unserem Kundendienstleiter überprüft. *(by the head of our customer service department)*

However, when giving the reason for the action, as opposed to naming a person, we use **durch** in place of **von**. Here are some examples:

Viele Geräte werden durch unsachgemäße Behandlung beschädigt. *Many machines are damaged by/through incorrect handling.*

Lebensmittel werden durch verzögerte Abfertigung an der Grenze verdorben. *Foodstuffs get spoilt by delayed checking procedures at the frontier.*

In the dialogue the passive voice was also used in the infinitive form:

Die Übersetzung muß neu gemacht werden.	*The translation has to be done again.*

Here are four more examples:

Die defekten Kabel müssen zurückgeschickt werden.	*The faulty cables have to be returned.*
Die neuen Entwürfe können ausgestellt werden.	*The new designs can be exhibited.*
Die neuen Sessel dürfen benutzt werden.	*The new armchairs may be used.*
Diese Verträge sollen geändert werden.	*These contracts have to be changed.*

In each of the above examples there were three verbs following each other, but rest assured that this is the maximum number of verbs a normal person would use. Even the Germans would get themselves into a tangle if they tried to use more than three verbs at any one time!

Now study the two past tense forms of the passive.

1. When writing about what happened yesterday we use the simple past:

Das defekte Gerät wurde geprüft.   *The faulty machine was checked.*
Die Briefe wurden geschickt.   *The letters were sent.*

Note: in the simple past the auxiliary **wird/werden** changes to **wurde/n**.

2. When talking about what happened yesterday the present perfect is used:

Das defekte Gerät ist geprüft   *The faulty machine was checked.*
worden.
Die Briefe sind geschickt worden.   *The letters were sent.*

Note: In the present perfect the construction is:
ist/sind + past participle + **worden**.

Also note that any past participle following another past participle loses its **ge-** prefix, which explains the use of **worden** instead of **geworden** in the last two examples.

In the dialogue there were two examples of the present perfect construction:

Sind die Geräte durch den Transport beschädigt worden?
Was ist denn beim Transport beschädigt worden?

As this Unit's dialogue represents a 'conversation' there are, of course, no examples of the German simple past.

118 Additional passive constructions

There is one feature of the German passive voice that will look familiar to native speakers of English. Please study these examples, based on the dialogue:

Die Geräte waren schwer   *The machines were badly*
beschädigt.   *damaged.*
Waren die Geräte denn nicht in   *Weren't the machines packed in*
Styropor verpackt?   *polystyrene, then?*
Die Kartons ... waren aufgerissen.   *The cardboard boxes ... were torn*
    open.

When an action is completed, the final result is described by using **sein** plus the past participle of the verb. Study the following:

This is happening now:	This is the completed action:
Das Geschäft wird geschlossen. *The shop is being closed.*	Das Geschäft ist geschlossen. *The shop is closed.*
Der Chef wird benachrichtigt. *The boss is being informed.*	Der Chef ist benachrichtigt. *The boss is informed.*
Die Visitenkarten werden gedruckt. *The visiting cards are being printed.*	Die Visitenkarten sind gedruckt. *The visiting cards are printed.*

Now some examples of the past tense:

Die Kunden wurden benachrichtigt. *The customers were (being) informed.*	Die Kunden waren benachrichtigt. *The customers were informed.*
Das Büro wurde frisch gestrichen. *The office was (being) repainted.*	Das Büro war frisch gestrichen. *The office was repainted.*
Der Anwalt wurde eingeladen. *The lawyer was (being) invited.*	Der Anwalt war eingeladen. *The lawyer was invited.*

As you can see from the last set of examples, the English language does not normally differentiate between these two meanings. For practical purposes, it is better to concentrate on the **wird/werden** forms to express the passive voice in German (if you want to use it). Try to resist the temptation to use the various forms of 'to be' all the time.

You'll be pleased to learn that there are ways and means of avoiding the passive voice, and the following Checknotes will show you how.

119 Man ('they', 'one')

One way of avoiding the passive voice in spoken German is to use the impersonal pronoun **man**. Study the following; instead of sentence (a) you could say sentence (b):

(a) Die Zeichnungen wurden per Boten geschickt.
The sketches were sent by messenger.
(b) Man hat die Zeichnungen per Boten geschickt.
They sent the sketches by messenger.

(a) Das defekte Gerät wurde in der Werkstatt geprüft.
The faulty machine was checked in the workshop.
(b) Man hat das defekte Gerät in der Werkstatt geprüft.
They checked the faulty machine in the workshop.

(a) Schlechtes Wetter wird vorausgesagt.
   Bad weather is forecast.
(b) Man sagt schlechtes Wetter voraus.
   They forecast bad weather.

(a) Das gestohlene Auto ist wiedergefunden worden.
   The stolen car was found.
(b) Man hat das gestohlene Auto wiedergefunden.
   They have found the stolen car.

120 Lassen ('to let')

Another way of avoiding the passive voice is to use the reflexive form of the irregular verb **lassen (er läßt, er ließ, er hat gelassen)**. In fact, near the end of the dialogue you met **das läßt sich leicht ändern** ('that can be changed easily') instead of **das kann geändert werden** (passive voice). Please compare these pairs of sentences:

Das kann man aufschieben. = Das läßt sich aufschieben.
Das kann man nachprüfen. = Das läßt sich nachprüfen.
Das kann man nicht reparieren. = Das läßt sich nicht reparieren.

You would use the constructions above to express that something 'can be postponed', 'verified' or 'not changed'. Here are some other useful examples:

Das läßt sich einrichten.	*That can be fitted in/done.*
Das läßt sich machen.	*That can be done.*
Das läßt sich nicht vermeiden.	*That can't be avoided.*
Das läßt sich nicht umgehen.	*That can't be circumvented.*

You would certainly impress your German contacts or colleagues, if you were to say:

Dieses Resultat kann sich sehen lassen! (= will stand up to close scrutiny)	*This result is rather splendid!*
Der Termin muß sich doch aufschieben lassen!	*There has to be a way to extend this deadline!*
Das wird sich wohl einrichten lassen!	*We'll find a way of doing it!*

When not used as a reflexive verb, **lassen** is used in four different ways. It can mean:

1) 'to leave' a thing/person in a place:

Ich habe meine Kreditkarten im Hotel gelassen.	*I've left my credit cards in the hotel.*
Sie haben den Aktenordner auf meinem Schreibtisch gelassen.	*You left the file on my desk.*

2) 'to let/allow' someone to do something:

Lassen Sie mich das (für Sie) tragen!   *Allow me to carry this (for you).*
Lassen Sie uns erst mal die   *Allow us to get on with the*
    Entwürfe machen!   *drafts/proposals.*

3) 'to have' or 'to get' someone to do something for you (which you wouldn't consider doing yourself or can't do):

Ich lasse den Brief neu schreiben.   *I'm having the letter retyped.*
Wir lassen alle Fahrzeuge über-   *We're having all vehicles*
    prüfen.   *checked.*

4) Used with the dative case it can mean that you are agreeable to something:

Ich lasse ihm den Vortritt.   *I let him pass in front of me.*
Wir lassen unseren Abteilungs-   *We're giving our managers a*
    leitern freie Hand bei den Dienst-   *free hand with the work*
    plänen.   *schedules.*

Examples of **lassen** used in this Unit's dialogue are:

Ich wollte es Sie so schnell wie möglich wissen lassen.
Wir lassen es dann in unserer Werkstatt auf Herz und Nieren prüfen.
Wir lassen es von einem technischen Übersetzungsdienst machen.

121 selbst ('myself', 'yourself', 'himself' etc.)

Do you remember the following phrase from the dialogue?

Aber diesmal machen wir sie nicht selbst!
But this time we won't do it ourselves!

For once German is less specific about the person who does things than English because **selbst** takes no personal endings!

Here are some more examples:

Ich entwerfe die Werbekampagne selbst.
I('ll) plan the advertising campaign myself.

Er macht alle Reparaturarbeiten selbst.
He does his own repair work/jobs.

Wir müssen die Modellplanung selbst machen.
We must do the planning for the new models ourselves.

Mal sehen, ob sie selbst auf die Idee kommen, das Geld zu investieren.
Let's see if they think of investing the money themselves.

In conversational German, **selbst** is sometimes replaced by **selber**:

Wir machen das immer selber.
We always do that ourselves.

Comprehension Practice 9

Study the dialogue once more and then answer the following questions (in German, of course!):

New words:
zunächst — *at first*
das Austauschgerät — *the replacement machine*
bekommen — *to get, receive*

1 Warum kann Frau Schneider zunächst nicht mit Herrn Jackson sprechen?
2 Worauf wird die Nachricht gesprochen?
3 Was findet Frau Schneider nett?
4 Wann hat Herr Jackson die Nachricht bekommen?
5 Warum wollte Frau S. Herrn J. so schnell sprechen?
6 Welche Probleme gab es mit der Sendung?
7 Sind viele Geräte beschädigt worden?
8 Warum waren die Kartons aufgerissen?
9 Worauf kann sich Frau Schneider verlassen?
10 Was will Herr Jackson gleich tun?
11 Was wird Herr Jackson veranlassen?
12 Was ist mit dem Drucker nicht in Ordnung?
13 Was soll Frau Schneider mit dem defekten Drucker tun?
14 Was macht Excel-Equip dann mit dem Gerät?
15 Muß Frau Schneider auf die Reparatur warten?
16 Was für ein Austauschgerät wird sie bekommen?
17 Womit ist Frau Schneider nicht ganz zufrieden?
18 Von wem wird die neue Übersetzung gemacht?
19 Was wird Herr Jackson mit den neuen Übersetzungen machen?
20 Wobei gibt sich Excel-Equip die größte Mühe?

FLUENCY PRACTICE 36
Listening/Reading Comprehension

Study the new words, listen to the telephone conversation on the cassette (or read the transcript at the end of this Unit) several times and then answer the questions. You'll find a translation of this conversation in the Key at the back of the book.

New words:
der Anruf, -e — *call*
der Apparat, -e — *telephone; machine*
die Verbindung, -en — *connection*
die Leitung, -en — *line*
das Signal, -e — *signal*

verbinden	*to connect*
(verband, verbunden)	
an|nehmen	*to assume*
(nimmt, nahm an, angenommen)	
an|rufen	*to telephone*
(rief an, angerufen)	
wiederholen	*to repeat*
buchstabieren	*to spell out*
dauern	*to last*
oder	*or; aren't you? isn't he/she? etc.*

1 Who is the first person Mr Jackson speaks to?
2 Is the line good or bad?
3 Why can't he speak to Frau Schneider right away?
4 What assumption does the telephonist make?
5 What does she suggest?
6 Does Mr Jackson decide to hold on or to ring later?
7 What does Frau Schneider say to Mr Jackson?

FLUENCY PRACTICE 37
A successful phone call

New words:

der (Telefon)hörer	*telephone receiver*
ab|nehmen	*to lift* (the receiver)
das Klingelzeichen	*ringing tone*
auf|legen	*to put down* (the receiver)
ein Gespräch führen	*to hold a telephone conversation*
das Gespräch beenden	*to finish the telephone conversation*

Please put the following in the right sequence - we've done the
first one for you:

A)	jemand antwortet	1)	E
B)	die Nummer wählen	2)	....
C)	sich verabschieden	3)	....
D)	Klingelzeichen hören	4)	....
E)	den Telefonhörer abnehmen	5)	....
F)	den Hörer auflegen	6)	....
G)	ein Telefongespräch führen	7)	....
H)	das Gespräch beenden	8)	....

FLUENCY PRACTICE 38
An unsuccessful phone call

New words:

besetzt	*engaged*
das Besetztzeichen	*engaged signal*

150

die Gabel	(here) *receiver rest*
den Hörer auf die Gabel hauen	*to slam down the receiver*
(very colloquial German)	
neu wählen	*to redial*
durch|kommen	*to get through*
"Kein Anschluß unter dieser Nummer"	*'The number doesn't exist'*

Now put these in the right sequence:

A) die Nummer wählen   1) . . . .
B) den Hörer abnehmen   2) . . . .
C) den Hörer auflegen   3) . . . .
D) den Hörer auf die Gabel hauen   4) . . . .
E) neu wählen   5) . . . .
F) das Besetztzeichen hören   6) . . . .
G) nicht durchkommen   7) . . . .
H) "Kein Anschluß unter dieser Nummer!   8) . . . .

DICTIONARY PRACTICE 6
Brief messages received on the telephone

Here, in German, are eight reasons why you may have difficulty in calling a particular number or person. Match these against their correct English translations (write out the German each time):

Falsch verbunden! - Kein Anschluß unter dieser Nummer! - Auskunft! - Der Name ist nicht aufgeführt! - Die Rufnummer hat sich geändert! - Bitte notieren Sie die neue Nummer! - Hier gibt es keinen Meier! Die Vorwahlnummer hat sich geändert!

1 The number doesn't exist.
2 There is no Mr Meier here.
3 Please note the new number.
4 Directory enquiries.
5 Wrong number.
6 The name is not listed.
7 The area code number has changed.
8 The number has been changed.

DICTIONARY PRACTICE 7
Excuses and apologies on the telephone

There are plenty of possible reasons why people will be unavailable on the telephone; of course, you'll want to know why. Please match the following pairs:

1 Der Chef ist gerade in einer Besprechung. Können Sie später noch einmal zurückrufen?

2 Frau Weiß ist zur Zeit auf Geschäftsreise.. Möchten Sie ihr eine Nachricht hinterlassen?
3 Mein Kollege ist in Urlaub. Kann ich Ihnen vielleicht helfen?
4 Meine Mitarbeiter sind gerade bei Tisch. Rufen Sie bitte in einer halben Stunde noch einmal an!
5 Der Sachbearbeiter ist leider erkrankt. Hat die Angelegenheit bis nächste Woche Zeit?
6 Herr Winter führt gerade ein Auslandsgespräch. Können Sie am Apparat bleiben?
7 Ich verbinde! - Tut mir leid, der Platz ist zur Zeit nicht besetzt.
8 Wie war der Name? ... Tut mir leid, ich habe keine Nachricht für Sie!

A I'm putting you through! - Sorry, the desk is temporarily unoccupied.
B The boss is in a meeting. Can you ring back later?
C Unfortunately the clerk you normally deal with has fallen ill. Can the matter wait until next week?
D My employees are out at lunch at the moment. Please ring back in half an hour.
E Frau Weiß is away on business. Would you like to leave a message?
F My colleague is on holiday. Can I help you?
G What was the name? Sorry, I don't have a message for you.
H Herr Winter is just taking an international call. Will you hold the line?

FLUENCY PRACTICE 39
Practising the passive voice

New words:

rufen *(st)*	to call, shout
übersetzen	to translate
der Übersetzer	translator
dolmetschen	to interpret
der Dolmetscher	interpreter
her|stellen	to produce, manufacture
der Hersteller, -	producer, manufacturer
der Pförtner	porter

Please change the following sentences into the passive voice, as in this example:

Der Pförtner öffnet die Tür. → **Die Tür wird geöffnet.**

1 Die Sekretärin ruft den Chef. Der Chef ... ...
2 Die Sekretärin bestellt den Wein. Der Wein ... ...
3 Der Mechaniker repariert das Auto. Das Auto ... ...

4 Der Übersetzer übersetzt die Anweisungen. Die
  Anweisungen ... ...
5 Der Dolmetscher dolmetscht die Konferenz. Die Konferenz ... ...
6 Die Hersteller zeigen die neuen Modelle. Die neuen Modelle ... ...

FLUENCY PRACTICE 40
Having things done for you

New words:

der Besucher, -	*visitor*
der Film, -e	*film*
die Zahl, -en	*number, figure*
das Werbefoto, -s	*advertising photograph*
berichtigen	*to correct*
stornieren	*to cancel*
entwickeln	*to develop*
ab|ziehen	*to reprint*
(zog ab, abgezogen)	
ab|holen	*to fetch, meet*
vergrößern	*to enlarge*
in Ordnung bringen	*to put right*

Ask your assistant to make sure the following tasks are carried out
– for example:

den Bericht fotokopieren → **Lassen Sie den Bericht fotokopieren!**

1 die Zahlen berichtigen
2 die Heizung in Ordnung bringen
3 den Scheck vom Direktor unterschreiben
4 den Flug nach Zürich stornieren
5 meine Filme entwickeln
6 den englischen Besucher vom Flughafen abholen
7 die Werbefotos noch einmal abziehen/vergrößern

TRANSCRIPT OF FLUENCY PRACTICE 36
(Listening/reading comprehension)

Switchboard:	Futura Büromaschinen. Guten Tag. Wen möchten Sie sprechen?
Mr Jackson:	Guten Tag. Verbinden Sie mich bitte mit Frau Schneider im Einkauf.
Switchboard:	Ihr Name bitte.
Mr Jackson:	Jackson, von der Firma Excel-Equip in London.
Switchboard:	Die Verbindung ist leider sehr schlecht. Könnten Sie bitte Ihren Namen wiederholen?

Mr Jackson:	Jackson. Ich buchstabiere: J-A-C-K-S-O-N.
Switchboard:	Einen Augenblick bitte, ich verbinde.
Mr Jackson:	Vielen Dank.

(After a little delay)

Switchboard:	Frau Schneider spricht gerade auf der anderen Leitung. Möchten Sie einen Augenblick warten?
Mr Jackson:	Dauert es lange?
Switchboard:	Ich nehme an, Sie rufen aus dem Ausland an, oder? Ich gebe Frau Schneider ein Signal, dann weiß sie, daß der nächste Anruf auf sie wartet.
Mr Jackson:	Das ist sehr freundlich. Ich bleibe am Apparat.

(Music playing in the background)

Frau Schneider:	Guten Tag, Herr Jackson, Ich hoffe, Sie haben nicht lange gewartet!

Planning an advertising campaign

> *In this Unit you will learn about affective words, the idiomatic use of some basic German verbs and how to determine your clients' precise requirements. On this occasion, the dialogue adopts a Bavarian flavour.*
>
> *After a few hiccups in the initial stages, Futura Büromaschinen is set to act as agents for Excel-Equip. On instructions from London, they now plan an advertising campaign to promote sales of the portable word processor which is very competitively priced. As Frau Schneider is in Munich on business, she has made an appointment with Herr Mittermair in the Munich branch of an international advertising agency to discuss strategies to be used.*

Herr M.: Grüß Gott, Frau Schneider. Darf ich mich vorstellen: Mittermair. Sie kommen von Futura Büromaschinen, gell?

Frau S.: Ja, ganz recht. Ich leite die Einkaufsabteilung. Wir beziehen seit einiger Zeit einen großen Teil unserer Geräte aus England, von einer Firma namens Excel-Equip. Wir glauben, daß nun der Zeitpunkt gekommen ist, um unseren Umsatz durch eine Werbekampagne zu steigern. Es trifft sich gut, daß Excel-Equip gerade einen neuen Artikel auf den Markt gebracht hat: einen extrem einfach zu bedienenden, tragbaren Textcomputer.

Herr M.: Das hört sich ja vielversprechend an. Darf ich Ihnen erst einmal ein paar Fragen stellen um zu sehen, welche Vorstellungen Sie haben. Frage eins: welche Form der Werbung haben Sie ins Auge gefaßt: Postwurfsendungen, Broschüren und Displays für Ihre Verkaufsabteilung, Radio- und Fernsehwerbung, Anzeigen in Zeitungen und Zeitschriften – oder nur in der Fachpresse – oder eine gezielte Werbeaktion mit Briefen an etablierte oder potientielle Kunden?

Frau S.: Wir denken da an eine drei- bis vierwöchige Zeitungs- und Zeitschriftenkampagne.

Herr M.: Welche Zielgruppe wollen S' denn ansprechen?

Frau S.: Die Anzeigen sollen speziell kleinere Firmen ansprechen die sich gerade selbständig gemacht haben, und auch die Kunden, die bisher aus Kostengründen keine Textcomputer angeschafft haben, die aber jetzt, wo die Preise gefallen sind, ihre Büroausstattung quasi auf den neusten Stand bringen wollen.

Herr M.: Meine nächste Frage zielt auf den Umfang der Kampagne: soll sie regional oder national durchgeführt werden?

Frau S.: Beides. Die Anzeigen sollen in regionalen und überregionalen Zeitungen und Zeitschriften erscheinen, und auch in der Fachpresse.

Herr M.: Außerdem bleibt zu klären, ob Sie schon irgendwelche konkreten Vorstellungen haben.

Frau S.: Excel-Equip hat uns unfangreiches Werbematerial zugeschickt. Ich habe Ihnen ein paar Handzettel und Poster mitgebracht, aber natürlich keine großen, auf Karton aufgezogenen Plakate.

Herr M.: *(inspecting the advertising material)* Hm. Ah, das ist gut. – Und das hier ist recht komisch! – Ja, Frau Schneider, wie ich schon gedacht habe, ist das zwar gut gemachte Werbung, aber in der Werbebranche haben wir halt die Erfahrung gemacht, daß sich Reklame aus einem Land nicht einfach in einem anderen europäischen Land einsetzen läßt. Die Konventionen in der Werbung und die Denkmuster der Kunden sind halt zu verschieden. Die englische Werbung benutzt, wie Sie hier sehen, viele Wortspiele und ist sehr locker. Der deutsche Verbraucher erwartet halt mehr sachliche Produktinformation, wenn er von der Überlegenheit und Qualität eines neuen Produkts überzeugt werden soll.

Frau S.: Auf diesem Gebiet sind Sie der Spezialist. Deshalb bin ich ja zu Ihnen gekommen. Wir haben in der Vergangenheit immer erfolgreich zusammen gearbeitet, und das wird sicher auch diesmal wieder so sein. Was meinen Sie, wann können Sie uns Ihre Entwürfe vorstellen?

Herr M.: Darf ich vielleicht eine Gegenfrage stellen: wann wollen Sie die Anzeigenkampagne starten? In Bayern sagt man: "Ma soll nie hudln!", oder wie Sie sagen: "gut Ding will Weile haben", aber speziell in unserer Branche sind wir d'ran gewöhnt, unter Zeitdruck zu arbeiten.

Frau S.: Ich muß die Termine noch mit meinen Kollegen koordinieren. Ich melde mich in ein paar Tagen wieder bei Ihnen. Dann können wir die Einzelheiten besprechen.

Herr M.: Gut. In der Zwischenzeit werde ich unsere Auftragslage überprüfen und dann kann ich Ihnen meinerseits Terminvorschläge machen. Ich erwarte Ihren Anruf also Ende der Woche. Auf Wiederschaun!

TRANSLATION

Herr M.: Hello, Frau Schneider. May I introduce myself: Mittermair. You're from Futura Büromaschinen, aren't you?

Frau S.: Yes, that's right. I'm in charge of the purchasing department. For quite a while now, we've been getting a major part of our machines from England, from a firm called Excel-Equip. We feel that now the right moment has come to increase our turnover by means of an advertising campaign. By a lucky coincidence, Excel-Equip has just brought out a new product, a portable word processor which is extremely simple to use.

Herr M.: That sounds very promising indeed! May I just put some questions to you in order to find out what your ideas are. First question: which kind of advertising do you have in mind? Mail shots, brochures and displays for your sales team, radio and TV commercials, ads in newspapers and magazines, or just in the specialist trade press, or direct mail shots to your existing or potential customers?

Frau S.: We were thinking in terms of a three to four-week advertising campaign in newspapers and magazines.

Herr M.: Which group do you want to target?

Frau S.: The advertisements should be targeted specifically at smaller firms which have just been set up and also at customers, who have not yet invested in word processors for financial reasons, but who want to update (*lit.* 'bring up to the latest level, so to speak') their office machines, now that prices have fallen.

Herr M.: My next question refers to (*lit.* 'aims at') the size of the campaign. Do you wish it to be run on a regional or national level?

Frau S.: Both. The advertisements are to run in regional and national newspapers and magazines, and also in the trade press.

Herr M.: Also, I'd like to find out if you already have some concrete ideas.

Frau S.: Excel-Equip has sent us extensive advertising material. I've brought along some pamphlets and posters, but naturally I haven't brought the big, cardboard mounted posters.

Herr M.: *(inspecting the advertising material)* Hm. That's good! ... And this one is quite amusing ... . Well, Frau Schneider, just as I thought. This is very good advertising material; however, in the advertising industry our experience is that ads from one country cannot simply be used in another European country. The style of advertising and, of course, the mental attitudes of the customers are simply too diverse. As you can see here, English advertisements play a lot on words and are very light-hearted. The German consumer expects more factual information about the product, if he is to be convinced of the superiority and quality of a new product.

Frau S.: In this field, you're the expert! That's why I've come to you. We have always worked together successfully in the past, and I'm sure that will also be the case this time. When do you think you can submit your drafts?

Herr M.: May I answer with another question? When do you wish to start the advertising campaign? In Bavaria we say, "One mustn't rush things!" or as you'd say, "Good things take time!", but in our industry, in particular, we are used to working under great stress (*lit.* 'pressure of time').

Frau S.: I'll have to co-ordinate the dates with my colleagues. I'll get in touch with you in a few days; then we'll be able to discuss the details.

Herr M.: Very well. In the meantime, I'll be assessing our work-load and then I'll be able to give you my suggestions regarding the timescale. So, I'll be expecting your call at the end of the week. Goodbye.

Checklist 10

Masculine nouns:

(der) Gott	*God*
der Zeitpunkt	*moment; point in time*
der Umsatz	*turnover*
der Artikel, -	*article, item; product*
der Markt, ¨-e	*market*
der Umfang	*extent; scope*
der Handzettel, -	*advertising leaflet*
der Zettel, -	*small piece of paper*
(der) Karton	*cardboard*
der Karton, -s	*cardboard box*
der Verbraucher, -	*consumer*
der Zeitdruck	*stress, pressure* (of time)
der Terminvorschlag, ¨-e	*suggested time or date*

Feminine nouns:

die Werbung	*advertising*
die Fernsehwerbung	*TV advertising*
die Radiowerbung	*radio advertising*
die Postwurfsendung, -en	*mail shot*
die Broschüre, -n	*brochure*
die Anzeige, -n	*advertisement*
die Werbeaktion, -en	*advertising campaign*
(die) Reklame	*advertising*
die Reklame, -n	*advertisement*
die Presse	*the press*
die Fachpresse	*specialist/trade magazines*
die Zeitung, -en	*newspaper*
die Zeitschrift, -en	*magazine*
die Zielgruppe, -n	*target group*
die Kampagne, -n	*campaign*
die Vorstellung, -en	here: *idea*
die Erfahrung, -en	*experience*
die Konvention, -en	*convention*
die Produktinformation	*product information*
die Überlegenheit	*superiority*
die Qualität	*quality*
die Weile	*a few moments; leisure*
die Branche	here: *industry*
die Einzelheit, -en	*detail*

Neuter nouns:

das Display	*display*
das Werbematerial	*advertising material*
das Poster, -	*advertising poster*
das Plakat, -e	*poster*

| das Gebiet, -e | area; here: *field* |
| das Denkmuster | *mental attitude; way of thinking* |

Adjectives/adverbs:

extrem	*extremely*
tragbar	*portable*
vielversprechend	*promising* (lit. 'promising a lot')
erst (ein)mal	*for a start*
gezielt- (pp)	*targeted at; aimed at*
dreiwöchig/vierwöchig	*lasting three weeks/four weeks*
klein(er)	*small(er)*
selbständig	*independent; self-employed*
etabliert	*well-established*
potentiell	*possible; potential*
nächst-	*next*
regional	*regional*
überregional	*national* (lit. 'supra-regional')
irgendwelch-	*any (kind of)*
konkret	*concrete, detailed*
umfangreich	*extensive; a lot of*
aufgezogen- (pp)	*mounted*
verschieden	*different, diverse*
sachlich	*factual*
erfolgreich	*successful*

Other word/expressions:

Grüß Gott!	standard Bavarian greeting
ganz recht	*quite right*
speziell (=besonders)	*especially*
gegen	*towards*
Es trifft sich gut, ...	*It's a lucky coincidence ...*
einfach zu bedienen	*easy to operate*
aus Kostengründen	*for economic* (lit. 'cost') *reasons*
jetzt wo	*now that*
quasi	*so to speak*
beides	*both (facts/things mentioned before)*
außerdem	*also; besides*
es läßt sich (nicht) einsetzen	*it can(not) be used*
sie sind halt zu verschieden	*they are simply too different*
was meinen Sie, wann ...?	*when were you thinking of ...?*
eine Anzeigenkampagne starten	*to start an advertising campaign*
unter Zeitdruck arbeiten	*to work under stress, pressure*
einen Vorschlag machen	*to make a suggestion*
einen Terminvorschlag machen	*to suggest a date*
Ende der Woche	*at the end of the week*
Darf ich Ihnen ein paar Fragen stellen, um ... zu ...	*May I ask you some questions in order to ...?*
Darf ich eine Gegenfrage stellen?	*May I answer with another question?*

160

Verbs:

sich etwas an|schaffen (coll.)	*to buy something for oneself*
zielen auf acc.	*to target, aim at*
durch|führen acc.	*to conduct, carry out*
erscheinen (impers.)	*to be published;* (lit. 'appear')
zu|schicken dat. acc.	*to send to*
benutzen acc.	*to make use of; utilize*
erwarten acc.	*to expect*
starten acc.	*to begin, start*

Bavarian variants:

haben S' ...?	= haben Sie?	mei'	= meine
wollen S' ...?	= wollen Sie?	a'mol	= einmal
wolle'	= wollen	"hudln" (dialect)	= *to use unnecessary*
halt	(see Checknote 124)		*haste* (and thus
gell	(see Checknote 122)		mess things up!)

Auf Wiederschaun. *Goodbye.*

CHECKNOTES

122 Regional accents and dialects

When listening to the tapes which accompany this course you hear the standard pronunciation of German, which is in fact called "Hochdeutsch". It's just like the so-called "BBC English" and not every native speaker will speak like this. Quite a number of regional accents can be heard across the country and lots of jokes feed on a particular accent, e.g. Schwäbisch, Bayrisch or Sächsisch.

In the dialogue at the beginning of this Unit a moderate Bavarian accent is used, which means that quite a few endings are swallowed. The formal **Sie** is shortened to **S'**, and the middle **-e-** in adjectival endings is omitted. There's no need to worry, though, you won't be taught the Bavarian dialect, you're just exposed to a sample of a regional accent!

A distinctive feature of spoken German is the question tag which, unlike its English equivalent ('isn't it?', 'don't they?', 'weren't you?' etc.) is limited to **nicht wahr** (often shortened to **ne**) or **oder**. In southern Germany you will hear **gell(e)**. In the following Checknotes we discuss some interesting features of standard spoken German.

123 Revision of certain conjunctions and adverbs

You have already met most of the following words. Before learning about the special way in which these are used in standard spoken German, let's recall their literal meaning:

1	**aber**	*but*	6 **eigentlich**	*actually*
2	**auch**	*also, too*	7 **etwa**	*approximately*
3	**denn**	*because, as*	8 **ja**	*yes*
4	**doch**	affirmative reply	9 **(ein)mal**	*once*
		to a negative	10 **noch**	*still*
		question	11 **nur**	*only*
5	**eben**	*just (now)*	12 **schon**	*already*

Here, these little words are used in their literal meanings:

1 Wir können die Pakete als Eilpost schicken, aber das ist sehr teuer!
   We can send the parcels by express post, but that's very expensive!
2 Unser Unternehmen hat auch gute Kontakte zu osteuropäischen Firmen.
   Our firm also has good contacts with Eastern European firms.
3 Ich stelle einen neuen Fahrer ein, denn der alte hat gekündigt.
   I'll be hiring a new delivery driver, because the last one resigned.
4 Haben Sie keinen Dienstwagen? Doch, aber der ist in der Werkstatt.
   Don't you have a company car? I do, but it's gone in for a service.
5 Das Telex ist eben angekommen.
   The telex has just arrived.
6 Eigentlich wollte ich heute früher nach Hause gehen, aber ...
   Originally I wanted to go home earlier, but ...
7 Der Restposten besteht aus etwa 5000 Stück.
   The stock clearance consists of about 5000 items.
8 Haben Sie den Auftrag schon storniert? – Ja, vorgestern.
   Have you already cancelled the order? – Yes, the day before yesterday.
9 Wir hatten (ein)mal einen englischen Mechaniker.
   We once employed an English mechanic.
10 Wir haben noch 1000 Wagen auf Lager.
   We still have 1000 cars in stock.
11 Wir haben nur mit 100 Arbeitsstunden gerechnet.
   We only calculated for 100 man-hours.
12 Ich habe die Angelegenheit schon telefonisch geregelt.
   I've already settled the matter over the phone.

The above-mentioned words are frequently used in a different, more idiomatic way which will not be found in every dictionary! If you want to understand fully what is being said by native speakers, you have to be aware of this extra dimension of standard spoken German.

124 Affective words

In the various dialogues the little words mentioned in the previous Checknote were used in a way which is sometimes very difficult to translate into English. These words add a personal comment on the situation and are called 'affective words'. It will probably take quite a while and a lot of exposure to spoken German, before you feel sufficiently confident to use them yourself.

Generally speaking, people have a tendency to use a particular word quite often, as you can see from Mr Mittermair, who frequently uses the southern variant **halt**. It has the same meaning as the northern **eben**:

> Die Denkmuster der Kunden sind halt zu verschieden.
> *The mental attitudes of the customers are simply too diverse.*

When learning German, **denn** is normally the first affective word people try out. It works just like the colloquial English 'then' at the end of a question and is used in a very similar way:

> *"What do you think about that, then?*   "Was hälst du denn davon?"
> *"Is he coming, then?"*   "Kommt er denn?"

As you have no doubt noticed, Mr Jackson freely used **denn** in his conversations with Frau Schneider.

In Unit 9 Mr Jackson asked:

> "Waren die Geräte denn nicht in Styropor verpackt?"
> *"Weren't the machines packed in polystyrene, then?"*

Frau Schneider began her reply with "**Doch** ..." which expresses a strong contradiction to a negative statement or question, whereas both speakers use the same little word later to persuade and pacify.

It is important to bear in mind that these words (which can be used in a variety of combinations) are freely used in conversation. In fact, the more personal and private the conversation, the more affective words are used.

Now let's take a look at some of the uses of these affective words:

aber/aber auch → to express surprise, criticism:
> Das hat aber lange gedauert!   *That took a long time.*
> Das war aber auch Zeit!   *It was long overdue.*

denn → indicates mild surprise, urgency for an answer:
> Ist das Flugzeug denn verspätet   *Did the plane arrive late?*
> gelandet?

doch → used to persuade, pacify:
> Das ist doch nur eine Kleinigkeit!   *That's a mere trifle.*

eben/halt → signals acceptance, acquiescence:
> Da kann man eben (*or* halt) nichts   *You can't do a thing about it!*
> machen!

eigentlich → makes a general statement sound less direct; changes the topic of conversation:

Was haben Sie sich eigentlich dabei gedacht?

Whatever were you thinking of (when you did that)?

Haben Sie eigentlich die neusten Modelle schon gesehen?

[changing the subject] Have you already seen the latest models?

etwa → often expresses disbelief:

Sie wollen doch nicht etwa mit dem Bus fahren?

You're not serious about going by bus, are you?

ja → can be used for surprise, incredulity; it acknowledges the possibility of bad news:

Das hört sich ja vielversprechend an!

That sounds very promising indeed!

Das kann ja heiter werden! (coll.)

We're in for a rough ride (fig.)

mal/einmal → softens orders and requests; awakens curiosity:

Mach mal schnell!

Hurry up, will you!

Komm mal her. Das mußt du dir unbedingt mal ansehen!
(Kommen Sie mal. Das müssen Sie sich unbedingt mal ansehen!)

Come here. Just have a look at this!

noch → indicates irritation:

Was wollen Sie denn noch wissen?

What else do you want to know?

nur → expresses anger; wishful thinking:

Wo steckt der Lehrling denn nur?

Wherever has the apprentice got to?

Wenn ich nur genug Geld hätte!

If only I had enough money!

schon → expresses impatience:

Nun kommen Sie schon!

Why aren't you coming?

überhaupt → makes questions (to which the answer will be 'yes' or 'no') a little less direct:

Haben Sie denn überhaupt Handelsvertretungen im Ausland?

(I hope you don't mind my asking) do you actually have agencies in other countries?

Other examples of the use of these affective words seen in Units 9 and 10 are:

(9) Ich habe ja eben selbst gemerkt ...
     Das ist doch auch in unserem Interesse ...
(10) Die Denkmuster der Kunden sind halt zu verschieden.
     Deshalb bin ich ja zu Ihnen gekommen.

In some instances it is very difficult to decide whether a word is being used in its basic meaning or in an affective sense. The position in the sentence is often the only clue, as the affective words tend to be put after the verb. All the affective words discussed in this Checknote can have other idiomatic uses, but it would be beyond the scope of this course to pursue this interesting aspect of the German language further.

125 Further uses of some basic German verbs

Please study these examples:

Erfolg haben	*to be successful*
recht haben	*to be right*
etwas falsch machen	*to do something wrong*
sich (dat.) Sorgen machen über (acc.)	*to be worried about*
etwas gut machen	*to do something well*
(jemandem) leid tun nom.	*to feel sorry for*
es tut mir leid (um)	*I am sorry (for) ...*

You'll have noticed that in these examples the verb **haben** is not translated as 'to have', **machen** is not translated as 'to make' and **tun** is not translated as 'to do'.

Now study these short sentences which will show you how the above expressions are used:

Er hatte Erfolg mit seiner neuen Marketingstrategie.
His new marketing strategy was successful.

Er hat die Aufstellung falsch gemacht.
His list is quite wrong.

Der neue Sachbearbeiter tut ihr leid.
She's sorry for the new clerk.

Ich mache mir Sorgen über unsere Schulden.
I'm worried about our debts.

Sie hat die Übersetzung wirklich gut gemacht!
She did this translation really well!

126 Expressions with **haben**

There are many important expressions in English based on the verb 'to be' which, in German, are formed with **haben**:

a) **haben** + adverb

es eilig haben	*to be in a hurry*
es gut haben	*to be lucky* (implication of envy)

es leicht haben	*to be in a favourable position* (lit. 'to have it easy')
es nötig haben	*to be in need of something*
es schwer haben	*to be in a difficult position*

Here are some examples:

Er hatte es sehr eilig mit seinen Briefen, denn er wollte sie noch am selben Tag abschicken.
He was in a hurry to get his letters done, because he wanted to post them on the same day.

Er hatte es schwer mit einem Boss, dem man es nie recht machen konnte.
He had a difficult boss whom one could never please/satisfy.

Der hat's wohl nötig! Uns die Kunden vor der Nase wegzuschnappen!
He must be desperate to steal our customers from under our nose!

Here are two more important expressions with haben:

recht haben	*to be right*
unrecht haben	*to be wrong*

Ich hatte recht mit der Annahme, daß er heute kommt!
I was right to assume that he was coming today.

Er hat unrecht, wenn er meint, daß der neue Vertrag schlechter ist.
He is wrong in thinking that the new contract is worse.

b) **haben + noun**

The following expressions are heard frequently in German and should be learnt as soon as possible. An effective way to do this is by covering alternately the right-hand and left-hand columns and testing yourself:

Angst haben (daß)	*to be afraid; fear that; be worried*
Chancen (pl.!) **haben**	*to be in with a good chance*
Durst/Hunger haben	*to be thirsty/hungry*
Geduld haben (mit)	*to be patient (with)*
Glück/Pech haben	*to be lucky/unlucky*
Lust haben auf/zu + inf.	*to feel like having/doing something*
Mut haben	*to be courageous*

The following sentences will give you a chance to get used to them:

Ich habe Angst, daß mir der Vertrag durch die Finger rutscht!
I fear that the contract will slip through my fingers.

Wir hatten Pech mit der letzten Ladung; sie ist unterwegs verrutscht.
We were unlucky with the last consignment; it shifted in transit.

Ich habe Lust auf ein Glas Bier.
I feel like having a beer.

Ich habe Lust, ihm einmal meine Meinung zu sagen!
I feel like giving him a piece of my mind!

Ich habe Glück gehabt! Der Zug hatte Verspätung, und ich habe ihn doch noch erreicht.
I was lucky! The train was running late and I managed to catch it.

127 Expressions with **machen**

The verb **machen** appears in many useful expressions:

a) **machen** + adverbs

etwas richtig/falsch machen	*to do something right/wrong*
etwas gut/schlecht machen	*to do something well/badly*
etwas nötig machen	*to make something necessary; to necessitate*
etwas unnötig machen	*to do something unnecessarily, in vain*
etwas schön machen	*to make something look beautiful, execute a task well*
sich bemerkbar machen	*to get oneself noticed, attract attention*
jemanden lächerlich machen	*to make someone look ridiculous*

This is how they work in practice:

Meine Krankheit machte die Verschiebung meiner Reise nötig.
My illness made it necessary to postpone my trip.

Ich habe die Übersetzung völlig unnötig gemacht!
I did the translation completely in vain!

Sie machte sich bei der Verkäuferin bemerkbar, um bedient zu werden.
She attracted the sales assistant's eye in order to get served.

b) **machen**

Arbeit machen / Mühe machen	*to be laborious*
Freude machen	*to give pleasure*
Lärm machen / Krach machen	*to be noisy*
Spaß machen	*to be fun/enjoyable*

and also:

sich Gedanken machen über + acc.	*to be worried about something/someone*
sich Mühe machen	*to take extra care*
sich Sorgen machen über + acc.	*to be worried about*

Other useful combinations are:

jemandem Angst machen	*to get someone worried*
jemandem Schwierigkeiten machen	*to create problems for someone*
jemandem Hoffnung machen	*to build up someone's hopes*
jemandem Mut machen	*to encourage someone*
jemandem Platz machen	*to make space for someone*

Here are some examples to show you how they are used in practice:

Dieser Kunde macht uns immer die größten Schwierigkeiten.
This customer always creates the biggest problems for us.

Der Chef macht mir Hoffnung auf eine Beförderung.
The boss builds up my hopes for advancement.

Ich habe ihm auf dem Schreibtisch Platz gemacht, damit er seinen Laptop/Kompaktcomputer abstellen konnte.
I created some desk space so that he could put down his laptop computer.

128 Expressions with **tun**

There are considerably fewer combinations with **tun** differing in use from their English equivalents, but the following two standard phrases are worth remembering:

freundlich tun	*to appear/pretend to be friendly*
überrascht tun	*to appear/pretend to be surprised*

This is how they work:

Seinen Kunden gegenüber tat er immer sehr freundlich.
He always put on a friendly act for his customers.

Sie tat überrascht als sie die leere Geldkassette öffnete.
She pretended to be surprised when she opened the empty cash box.

Note that when **tun** is used with nouns which derive from adverbs or adjectives, the noun takes a capital letter:

richtig	→ das Richtige tun	*to do the right thing*
falsch	→ das Falsche tun	*to do the wrong thing*

129 **Wo** used as relative pronoun

A fairly rare use of **wo** can be found in this Unit's dialogue: **jetzt, wo die Preise gefallen sind** ('now that prices have dropped'). To give you another example where **wo** is used when referring to <u>time</u>:

In den letzten Jahren, wo es der Wirtschaft gut ging, haben wir stetig expandiert.
In the last few years, when the economy was booming, we kept expanding.

Some people might prefer to say or would write: **In den letzten Jahren, als es ... .** Similarly, **wo** is often used as a relative pronoun, giving a <u>location</u>:

In dem Haus, wo ich früher gewohnt habe, ...
In the house where I used to live ...

instead of:

In dem Haus, in dem ich früher gewohnt habe, ...
In the house in which I used to live ...

Comprehension Practice 10

The following questions require only short answers:

New words:

das Treffen	*meeting*
statt|finden	*to take place*
an|sprechen	*to target; to address*
bezwecken	*to try and achieve*
zielen auf + acc.	*to aim at*

1 Wer stellt sich vor?
2 Wo findet das Treffen statt?
3 Welcher Zeitpunkt ist für Futura gekommen?
4 Was wollen sie mit einer Werbekampagne bezwecken?
5 Was hat Excel-Equip auf den Markt gebracht?
6 Warum will Herr Mittermair ein paar Fragen stellen?
7 Was ist seine erste Frage?
8 An welche Kunden könnte man Werbebriefe schicken?
9 Worauf zielt seine zweite Frage?
10 Welchen Kundenkreis sollen die Anzeigen ansprechen?
11 Warum haben viele Firmen sich noch keinen Textcomputer gekauft?
12 Warum wollen sie ihre Ausstattung auf den neusten Stand bringen?
13 Soll die Werbekampagne regional durchgeführt werden?
14 Wo sollen die Anzeigen erscheinen?
15 Welche Erfahrung hat Herr Mittermair gemacht?
16 Was erwartet der deutsche Verbraucher?
17 Woran ist Herr Mittermair gewöhnt?
18 Was will Herr Mittermair bis Ende der Woche tun?

FLUENCY PRACTICE 41
Questions using denn, etwa, eigentlich

New words:

der Tippfehler, -	*typing error*
der Briefumschlag, ¨-e	*envelope*
der Terminkalender, -	*appointments diary*
die Unterschrift, -en	*signature*
vergessen acc.	*to forget* (vergißt, vergaß, vergessen)
ab|schicken acc.	*to send off*
hin|legen acc.	*to put down*
halten von + dat.	*to think of* (hält, hielt, gehalten)
verbessern	*to correct; improve*

Even when taking note of the intended meaning given in brackets, there may be more than one possibility: **etwa** expresses strong astonishment, whereas **denn** (used in questions to which the answer is 'yes' or 'no') expresses surprise and **eigentlich** just gives the conversation a new twist or a friendly tone. In the following questions put by the boss to his new secretary (who seems to be having some problems) you have to fill in the gaps:

1 Haben Sie _____ die Tippfehler noch nicht verbessert?
(slightly annoyed)
2 Haben Sie den Brief _____ ohne Unterschrift abgeschickt?
(very annoyed)
3 Haben Sie _____ schon meinen Stellvertreter kennengelernt?
(friendly conversation)
4 Haben Sie _____ vergessen, den Scheck in den Briefumschlag zu stecken?
(quite contrary to his expectation)
5 Haben Sie _____ keinen Hunger?
(he's just noticed that she hasn't taken a lunch break)
6 Wo haben Sie _____ die Entwürfe für die Zeitungsanzeigen hingelegt?
(in a friendly manner)
7 Was halten Sie _____ von den englischen Anzeigen?
(drawing her into the conversation)
8 Sprechen Sie _____ auch Niederländisch?
(he wasn't aware of it!)
9 Wo haben Sie _____ den Terminkalender hingelegt?
(as he enters her office, looking for it)
10 Haben Sie _____ Angst vor mir?
(contrary to his expectation)

FLUENCY PRACTICE 42
Firing questions at a business associate

New words:

der Generalvertreter, -	*main (national) agent*
der Expansionsplan ¨-e	*plan to expand*
eine Zusage halten	*to keep a promise/undertaking/one's word*
Die Zeitplanungsmethode, -n	*time management system*
besprechen acc.	*to talk something over*
in Ruhe	*in peace and quiet*

Complete the following with one of these question words:

welche?
wann und wo?
wie?
wie lange?
warum?
seit wann?
wer?
was für einen? *(what kind of?)*

1) _____ können wir das einmal in Ruhe besprechen?
2) _____ ist der neue Generalvertreter für Deutschland?
3) _____ finden Sie unsere Expansionspläne?
4) _____ bleiben Sie in München?
5) _____ glauben Sie, daß wir unsere Zusage nicht halten?
6) _____ Zeitplanungsmethode benutzen Sie?
7) _____ Drucker wollen Sie kaufen?
8) _____ sind Sie schon in Frankfurt?

FLUENCY PRACTICE 43
Haben / machen / tun

New words:

der Chef (coll.)	*boss*
die Voraussage, -n	*prediction*
der Devisenkauf, ¨-e	*purchase of foreign currencies*
die Exportbeschränkung, -en	*restriction on exports*

Please insert the correct verb (haben, machen or tun) into the gap:

1 Die neue Sekretärin _____ mir leid!
2 Die Exportbeschränkungen _____ uns große Schwierigkeiten.
3 Wir _____ *(past)* großes Glück mit unseren Devisenkäufen.
4 Der junge Mann _____ der alten Dame Platz.
5 Der Chef _____ recht mit seiner Voraussage.
6 *(Present perfect)* Ich hoffe, wir _____ das Richtige _____ !

DICTIONARY PRACTICE 8
Telemarketing

Please study the visual aid below, then complete the following list
with one of these verbs: A anrufen; B aufgeben; C ermitteln;
D fragen; E einholen; F machen; G aussprechen;
H auffordern; I ankurbeln; J richten an + dat; K vereinbaren;
L führen

Telemarketing

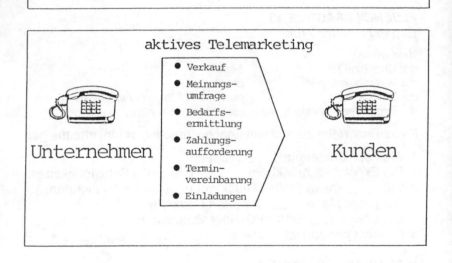

passives Telemarketing

Kunden

- Anfrage
- Bestellung
- Reklamation
- Information einholen über 0130

Unternehmen

aktives Telemarketing

Unternehmen

- Verkauf
- Meinungs- umfrage
- Bedarfs- ermittlung
- Zahlungs- aufforderung
- Termin- vereinbarung
- Einladungen

Kunden

1 Telefongespräche ____
2 eine Bestellung ____
3 eine Reklamation ____
4 eine Information ____
5 den Verkauf ____
6 nach einer Meinung ____

7 den Bedarf ____
8 eine Einladung ____
9 zur Zahlung ____
10 einen Kunden ____
11 einen Termin ____
12 eine Anfrage ____

Visit to a trade fair

> In this Unit you will learn about the different kinds of conjunctions in German and the special verb forms required for reported speech.
>
> As the advertising campaign is about to be launched, Mr Jackson has returned to Germany. He and Frau Schneider take this opportunity to visit CeBIT, the Hannover specialist fair for office equipment. They discuss what they have seen and what future developments are likely in their industry. We join them as they are summing up their impressions of the day.

Frau S.: Wie ist Ihr Eindruck von der Messe, Herr Jackson?

Mr J.: Ich bin überrascht über die Besucherzahlen. Solchen Andrang gibt es bei uns höchst selten.

Frau S.: Früher gab es hier einen wahren Massenandrang, aber vor einigen Jahren ist die traditionelle Hannover Messe auf zwei Veranstaltungen aufgeteilt worden. Jetzt ist es wieder einigermaßen erträglich.

Mr J.: Ich war übrigens sehr überrascht über die perfekte Gestaltung der Verkaufsstände. Die sind ja wirklich mit allen technischen Finessen ausgestattet! Die Kosten sind sicher enorm hoch.

Frau S.: Das schon, aber ob sich dieser Aufwand in den Auftragsbüchern niederschlägt, das steht auf einem anderen Blatt!

Mr J.: Wie ich feststellen konnte, haben Sie sich die Stände der Konkurrenz besonders genau unter die Lupe genommen. Haben Sie irgendwelche Neuentwicklungen erspäht, die wir noch nicht im Programm haben?

Frau S.: Nicht direkt. Aber das Verkaufspersonal berichtete von interessanten Neuentwicklungen. Es wird intensiv an sogenannten intelligenten Rechnern gearbeitet. Außerdem soll die nächste Computergeneration auf Sprache reagieren. Welche technischen Umwälzungen das mit sich bringen wird, ist gar nicht auszudenken!

Mr J.: Es ist immer problematisch für uns, wenn die "Riesen" in unserer Branche einen großen Sprung vorwärts machen. Wir brauchen immer ein paar Jahre, um diesen Technologievorsprung wieder einzuholen. Auf der anderen Seite haben wir natürlich längst nicht so hohe Entwicklungskosten und unsere Preise liegen deshalb entsprechend niedrig!

Frau S.: Gehe ich richtig in der Annahme, daß Sie diese Neuentwicklungen genauestens verfolgen?

Mr J.: Aber gewiß doch! Wir arbeiten momentan an mehrsprachigen Übersetzungscomputern. Die Finanz- und Geschäftswelt wird immer internationaler und die geschäftliche Kommunikation darf nicht durch bloße Sprachprobleme behindert werden. Bisher haben nur wenige Geschäftsleute und leitende Angestellte gute Fremdsprachenkenntnisse, von Bürokräften und Verkäufern ganz zu schweigen.

Frau S.: Ich habe erst gestern wieder in der Zeitung gelesen, daß es im Hinblick auf die Veränderungen in Europa wichtig sei, daß alle Unternehmen, und zwar nicht nur die Multis, sondern auch mittelständische Betriebe, mehr in die sprachliche Ausbildung investieren. Im letzten Jahrzehnt habe sich in dieser Hinsicht zwar schon einiges getan, aber längst noch nicht genug!

Mr J.: Nun, für's erste ist das ein lukrativer Markt, den wir uns erschließen müssen! Bis die Firmen ihre Sprachprogramme durchgezogen haben, können wir ihnen eine Menge Übersetzungscomputer verkaufen! Ich wollte mich heute in erster Linie mit dem Angebot auf dem deutschen Markt vertraut machen. Die Hannover Messe und neuerdings natürlich auch CeBIT sind nun mal weltbekannt und ein wichtiger Treffpunkt für Hersteller und Käufer.

Frau S.: Haben Sie denn in absehbarer Zukunft vor, auch auf deutschen Messen und Ausstellungen vertreten zu sein?

Mr J.: Aber ja doch! Es muß ja nicht gleich CeBIT sein. Wir sollten uns vielleicht einmal den Messe- und Ausstellungskalender ansehen, und uns überlegen, welche Möglichkeiten es für den Einstieg gibt.

Frau S.:	Wir könnten uns auch mit unserer PR Abteilung zusammensetzen und sehen, was für Pläne die haben.
Mr J.:	Eine Kooperation auf diesem Gebiet wäre sicher für beide Seiten vorteilhaft, besonders was das Standpersonal betrifft und die ganze Organisation. So was läßt sich vor Ort doch wesentlich leichter in die Wege leiten, als wenn man alles aus der Ferne regeln muß.
Frau S.:	Auf diesem Gebiet verfügen wir ja mittlerweile über einschlägige Erfahrungen. Bei der Planung der Werbekampagne haben wir ja schon erfolgreich zusammen gearbeitet. Ich sehe da für andere Projekte keine prinzipiellen Schwierigkeiten.
Mr J.:	Das ist wirklich ein ausgezeichneter Vorschlag. Diesen Gedanken müssen wir unbedingt weiter verfolgen. Wie weit im voraus plant man solche Dinge denn bei Ihnen, Frau Schneider?
Frau S.:	Das kommt ganz drauf an, um welche Messe oder Ausstellung es sich handelt. Wie wir eben gesehen haben, wird dem Publikum einiges geboten, und wenn man da nicht mithält, wird man glatt(weg) ignoriert! Aber das werden wir schon zu verhindern wissen!
Mr J.:	Davon bin ich überzeugt! Wenn es Ihnen recht ist, können wir morgen früh unser Gespräch fortsetzen, wenn wir uns von diesem anstrengenden Messebesuch erholt haben.
Frau S.:	Mit Vergnügen, Herr Jackson.

TRANSLATION

Frau S.:	What is your impression of the fair, Mr Jackson?
Mr J.:	I'm surprised by the number of visitors. Such a crush is very rare at home.
Frau S.:	In the past such large crowds attended that, a few years ago, the traditional Hannover Fair was split into two separate events. Now it has become quite tolerable again.
Mr J.:	I was astonished by the superb presentation of the stands. Some of them were equipped with all the technical gadgets imaginable. The cost must be exorbitant!

Frau S.: True, but whether this high level of spending is reflected in their order books is a different matter altogether!

Mr J.: I couldn't help noticing that you took a particularly close look at the stands of our competitors. Have you spotted any new developments which we can't offer yet?

Frau S.: Not exactly. But the sales staff talked about interesting new developments. They are working hard on so-called intelligent computers. What's more, the next generation of computers is said to react to speech. One can't begin to imagine what sort of technical innovations that will bring with it!

Mr J.: It's always problematical (for us), when the 'giants' in our industry take a big leap forward. It always takes us (*lit.* 'we always need') a few years to catch up with this technological lead. On the other hand, we don't incur the same level of development costs, and consequently our prices are correspondingly lower.

Frau S.: Am I right in assuming that you watch these new developments very closely?

Mr J.: Most certainly! At the moment we are working on multi-lingual translating machines. The world of finance and business is becoming increasingly international and business communication must not be hindered by mere translation problems. Up to now few business people or executives have had a knowledge of foreign languages, not to mention office workers and sales staff.

Frau S.: I was reading in the newspaper only yesterday that in view of the changes in Europe, it was important that all businesses, not just the multinationals but also the medium-sized firms, put more money into language training. It was said that a lot had already been done in the last decade, but that it was nowhere near enough.

Mr J.: Well, for the time being that's a very lucrative market which we must corner for our own purposes! Until such time when the firms have completed their language development programmes, we'll be able to sell them a lot of translating machines. Today, my prime objective was to get to know what is on offer in the German market place. Without any doubt, the Hannover Fair and more recently CeBIT are world-famous and a very important meeting point for manufacturers and buyers.

Frau S.: Are you planning to be represented at German fairs and exhibitions in the near future, (then)?

Mr J.: But of course! It won't have to be CeBIT straight away. But perhaps we should consult the calendar of fairs and exhibitions and consider what possibilities exist for entering the (German) scene.

Frau S.:   We could get together with our PR department and find out what their plans are.

Mr J.:   Co-operation in that area would most certainly be beneficial for both sides, especially with regard to manning the stand and the overall planning. Something like that is much easier to arrange on the spot than having to organize everything from a distance.

Frau S.:   In this area we've already gained some valuable experience. After all, during the planning of the advertising campaign, we have already co-operated most successfuly. In principle, I don't foresee any problems with new ventures.

Mr J.:   That is really an excellent suggestion. We definitely must pursue this idea further. How far ahead do you normally plan these things, Frau Schneider?

Frau S.:   That depends which fair or exhibition you have in mind. As we've seen today, many attractions are offered to the public and if one doesn't keep up, one gets ignored completely. But we'll know how to stop that from happening!

Mr J.:   I'm quite sure about that! If it's all right by you, we'll continue this discussion tomorrow morning, when we have recovered from this strenuous visit.

Frau S.:   With pleasure, Mr Jackson.

Checklist 11

Masculine nouns:

der Eindruck , ¨-e	*impression*
der Besucher, -	*visitor*
der Andrang	*crowd, crush*
der Massenandrang	*masses of people*
der Hersteller, -	*producer, manufacturer*
der (Messe-)Stand, ¨-e	*stand at a fair*
der Aufwand	*high spending, extravagance*
der (Elektronen-)Rechner	*(electronic) computer*
der Riese, -n	*giant*
der Sprung, ¨-e	*jump; leap*
der Vorsprung, ¨-e	*advantage, lead*
der Technologievorsprung	*technological lead* (over competitors)
Geschäftsleute (pl.)	*business people*
der Angestellte, -	*employee (male)*
der Käufer, -	*buyer, customer*
der Verkäufer, -	*sales assistant*
der Punkt, -e	*dot; point; full stop*

der Treffpunkt, -e	*meeting point*
der Messekalender	*calendar of fairs*
der Einstieg	*entry; starting point*
der Vorschlag, ¨-e	*proposal*
der Messebesuch, -e	*visit to a fair*

Feminine nouns:

die Zahl, -en	*figure, number*
die Besucherzahl, -en	*number of visitors*
die Veranstaltung, -en	*event; venue*
die Neuentwicklung, -en	*new development*
die Gestaltung, -en	*layout*
die Sprache, -n	*language*
die Fremdsprache, -n	*foreign language*
Fremdsprachen-kenntnisse (pl.)	*knowledge of foreign languages*
die Umwälzung, -en	*change; upheaval*
die Entwicklung, -en	*development*
Entwicklungskosten (pl.)	*development costs*
die Welt, -en	*world*
die Angestellte, -n	*employee (female)*
die Bürokraft, ¨-e	*office worker (m./f.)*
die Ausbildung	*training; education*
die Messe, -n	*fair*
die Ausstellung, -en	*exhibition*
die Möglichkeit, -en	*possibility*
die Verbindung, -en	*connection*
die Organisation	*organization*
die Planung	*planning*
die Schwierigkeit, -en	*difficulty*
die Veränderung, -en	*change*

Neuter nouns:

das Publikum	*public*
das Personal	*personnel, staff*
das Standpersonal	*staff working on a stand*
das Blatt, ¨-er (Papier)	*sheet (of paper)*
das Angebot, -e	*offer*
das Vergnügen, -	*pleasure*

Adjectives/adverbs:

breit	*broad; wide*
überrascht	*surprised*
besonders	*especially*
irgendwelch-?	*any (at all)?*
sogenannt-	*so-called*
nächst-	*next*
mehrsprachig	*multi-lingual*

bloß	*mere; only*
erträglich	*tolerable*
wesentlich	*considerable*
entsprechend	*corresponding*
einigermaßen	*fairly*
mittlerweile	*in the meantime*
leitend	*leading; guiding; senior*
ganz	*complete/ly, whole*
wichtig	*important*
lukrativ	*lucrative; worthwhile*
weltbekannt	*world-famous*
absehbar	*foreseeable*
vertreten (pp)	*represented*
vorteilhaft	*advantageous*
einschlägig	*relevant*
erfolgreich	*successful*
prinzipiell	*in principle*
ausgezeichnet	*excellent*
solch- ˙	*such*
ziemlich	*quite, considerably*
ignoriert (pp)	*ignored*
genauestens	*very meticulously*
wieder	*again*
momentan	*at the moment, for the time being*

Verbs:

sich niederschlagen in dat.	*to manifest itself*
erspähen acc. (coll.)	*to spy*
reagieren (auf acc.)	*to react*
mit sich bringen	*to carry/bring with it*
ein|holen acc.	*to catch up*
hoch / niedrig liegen	*to stay/be at a high / low level*
immer (+comparative of adj.) werden	*to become more and more ...*
behindern acc.	*to hinder; impede*
schweigen	*to say nothing; remain silent*
Investieren in acc.	*to invest in*
sich vertraut machen mit	*to make oneself familiar with*
vor|haben etwas zu tun	*to intend to do something*
verfolgen acc.	*to pursue*
sich etwas aus|denken	*to imagine something*
verhindern acc.	*to prevent*
aus|statten	*to equip*
fort|setzen	*to continue*
fest|stellen	*to ascertain*
berichten	*to report*
regeln	*to organize*
durch|ziehen (coll.)	*to complete, carry out*

Other expressions:

das breite Publikum	*the general public*
das schon, aber	*that may be the case, but*
Das steht auf einem anderen Blatt!	*That's a different matter altogether!*
unter die Lupe nehmen	*to scrutinize*
(das) ist gar nicht auszudenken!	*(that's) impossible to imagine!*
einen Sprung vorwärts machen	*to take a jump (forward)*
längst nicht so	*nowhere near*
Gehe ich richtig in der Annahme, ...?	*Am I right in assuming ...?*
Aber gewiß doch! Aber ja doch!	*Most certainly. But (yes) of course!*
von ... ganz zu schweigen	*to say nothing of ...*
im Hinblick auf	*in view of; in respect of ...*
es sei wichtig	*it was (said to be) important*
es habe ... gegeben	*there had been*
in dieser Hinsicht	*in this respect*
für's erste	*for the time being*
einen Markt erschließen	*to open up a market*
leitende Angestellte (pl.)	*managers; senior employees*
neuerdings	*lately; in recent years*
in absehbarer Zukunft	*in the near/foreseeable future*
unbedingt	*definitely*
weiter	*further*
so was	*something like that*
das läßt sich in die Wege leiten	*this/that can be initiated*
als wenn man .... muß	*than having to ...*
wie weit im voraus?	*how far ahead (of time)?*
das kommt ganz drauf an!	*it all depends!*
wenn man da nicht mithält. ...	*if one doesn't keep up, ...*
glatt(weg) (coll.)	*simply, just*
Aber das werden wir zu verhindern wissen!	*We'll know how to avoid that!*

CHECKNOTES

130 The conjunctions **denn, weil, da** ('because', 'as')

Frau Schneider mentioned that it was important that the general public should be able to attend trade fairs. She used the words in sentence 1) below. She could also have said 2) or 3):

1) ..., denn das breite Publikum ist für Hersteller und Handel wichtig.
2) ..., weil das breite Publikum für Hersteller und Handel wichtig ist.
3) ..., da das breite Publikum für Hersteller und handel wichtig ist.

All three conjunctions give reasons, but after **denn** the word order is not changed, whereas **weil** and **da** send the verb to the final position in the clause. Initially, you may find it easier to use **denn**, as you won't have to worry about the word order.

Weil is used more often in oral communication than **da**, but some people prefer to use **da** when writing. So, please remember:

a) after **denn**, a co-ordinating conjunction, the word order does NOT change.
b) after **weil, da**, subordinating conjunctions, the word order DOES change.

131 Co-ordinating conjunctions

Und, oder, aber, doch are other co-ordinating conjunctions which work in the same way as **denn**. Please study the following two sentences and the way in which they are then linked by the conjunction **aber** ('but'):

Früher gab es einen wahren Massenandrang. Seit einigen Jahren gibt es sogenannte Händlertage.
In the past there used to be a veritable crush. For a few years now there have been 'trade only' days.

→ Früher gab es einen wahren Massenandrang, aber seit einigen Jahren gibt es sogenannte Händlertage.

Just as you can alternate 'but' and 'however' in English, you can replace **aber** with **doch** or **jedoch**:

→ Früher gab es einen wahren Massenandrang, doch seit einigen Jahren gibt es sogenannte Händlertage.
→ Früher gab es einen wahren Massenandrang, seit einigen Jahren gibt es jedoch sogenannte Händlertage.

132 Subordinating conjunctions

In German the majority of conjunctions are subordinating conjunctions which, as you now know, send the verb to the end of the clause. You have already been introduced to **daß** (cf. Checknote 69). Here are some others:

damit	*so that* (different persons acting)
so daß	*so that* (same person acting)
falls	*in case, if*
wenn	*if*
(immer/jedesmal) wenn	*every time; whenever*
obwohl (obgleich, obschon)	*although*
als	*at the time/moment when*
während	*while*
ehe, bevor	*before*
nachdem	*after*
als ob	*as if*

Now study the following examples:

Er versteckte den Mahnbrief unter der Geschäftskorrespondenz, damit sein Chef ihn nicht sehen konnte.
He hid the reminder under the business correspondence, so that his boss couldn't see it.

Er war total verkatert, so daß er nicht wußte, wo er war.
He had such a hangover that he didn't know where he was.

Falls der Klient nicht pünktlich kommt, müssen Sie meinen nächsten Termin absagen.
If the client doesn't arrive on time, you'll have to cancel my next meeting.

Wenn sie wollen, kann ich Sie im Hotel absetzen.
I'll drop you at your hotel, if you like.

(Immer) Wenn er nach Bonn kommt, wohnt er in einem Fünf-Sterne Hotel.
Whenever he comes to Bonn, he stays in a five-star hotel.

Er läßt seine Broschüren in Holland drucken, obwohl es auch bei uns gute Druckereien gibt.
He has his brochures printed in Holland, although there are good printing firms here, too.

Als ich von meinem Chef genug gelernt hatte, habe ich mich selbständig gemacht.
When I had learned enough from my boss, I started my own business.

Während er (mit ihm) telefonierte, blätterte er in seinen Unterlagen.
While he was speaking (to him) on the phone, he glanced through his file/s.

Melden Sie sich doch noch mal bei mir, bevor Sie nach Hause fliegen!
Why don't you give me another ring before you fly home?

Nachdem er den Laptop gekauft hatte, fragte er sich, ob das richtig war.
After he had bought the laptop computer, he asked himself, if he'd done the right thing.

It would be a useful exercise to remove the subordinating conjunction in each sentence to see where the verb is normally to be found, e.g.:

Er versteckte den Mahnbrief unter der Geschäftskorrespondenz. Sein Chef konnte ihn nicht sehen.

133 How to translate 'when'

You must be careful when translating 'when', as it can be expressed in three different ways in German:

1) when? = **wann**?
This is used in direct and indirect questions:

  a) Wann sind die Entwürfe für die Werbekampagne fertig?
  When will the drafts for the advertising campaign be ready?

  b) Er möchte wissen, wann Sie die Entwürfe fertig haben.
  He'd like to know when you'll have the drafts ready.

2) when (whenever) = **(immer) wenn**
When talking about a repetitive action in general or a single action in the present or future, you use **wenn**:

  (Immer) Wenn ich nach München fahre, gehe ich ins Hofbräuhaus.
  When I go to Munich. I always go to the Hofbräuhaus.

  Wenn Herr Müller zurückkommt, sagen Sie ihm bitte, daß ich hier war.
  When Mr Müller comes back, please tell him that I called.

3) when = **als**
This is used for a single, non-repetitive action in the past:

  Als ich von der Auslandsreise zurückkam, wartete ein Postberg auf mich.
  When I returned from my trip abroad, a mountain of mail was waiting for me.

134 The use of **dann**

1) When talking about consecutive events, **dann** = 'then':

  Erst fielen die Aktienkurse über Nacht, dann stiegen sie langsam wieder an.
  First, share prices tumbled overnight, then they slowly recovered.

2) When linking two sentences, of which the first one starts with **wenn**, 'if' (cf. Checknote 73) - "**wenn ..., dann...**":

  Wenn es Neuigkeiten gibt, dann möchte ich sofort davon erfahren.
  If there's any news, I want to hear (lit. 'of') *it immediately.*

A word of warning: Don't confuse **dann** with the English word 'than' which, as you know, is expressed in German comparisons by **als**:

  Meine Ausgaben sind höher als mein Einkommen.
  My expenses are greater than my income.

Don't mix up **denn** and **dann**. (Go back to Checknote 130 if you do!)

135 **Zu** – 'to'/'too'

Let's revise some of the different functions of **zu**:

1a) **zu** + infinitive = 'to'. In Unit 10, Herr Mittermair said:

In unserer Branche sind wir daran gewöhnt, unter Zeitdruck zu arbeiten.
We are used to working under great stress.

1b) Extended infinitive: **um ... zu** + infinitive:

Wir kaufen unser Material im Ausland, um Kosten zu sparen.
We buy our material/s abroad in order to save costs.

2) **zu** + adjective or adverb = 'too'. Back to Herr Mittermair:

Die Konventionen ... sind zu verschieden.
Practices ... are too diverse.

Note that both meanings can appear in the same sentence:

Er ist zu jung, um das zu wissen.
He's too young to know that.

Die Anzeigen sind zu modisch, um beim breiten Publikum
anzukommen.
The ads are too trendy to be accepted by the general public.

3) **zu** as a preposition:

Ich fahre morgen zu unserer französischen Niederlassung.
I'll be travelling to our French branch tomorrow.

Wir gratulieren ihm zu seiner Beförderung.
We congratulate him on his promotion.

Ich bringe meine Gedanken zu Papier.
I put my thoughts/ideas down on paper.

136 **Viel/viele** – 'much'/'many'

Viel(e) can be used as an adjective:

Mein Chef hat nicht viel Geduld.
My boss doesn't have much patience.

Viele englische Anzeigen sind sehr humorvoll gemacht.
Many English advertisements are very amusing.

Viel is also used as an adverb:

Ich habe nicht viel verkauft, aber doch genug, um ohne Gewinn oder
Verlust abzuschließen.
I haven't sold much, but enough to break even (lit. 'not to make any
gain or loss').

It's used in good wishes such as **Viel Vergnügen!/Viel Spaß!** ('Have fun!') and **Viel Glück!** ('Good luck!')

137 Noun + verb combinations

When you studied Checknote 101 ("word detective"), you learnt how to detect familiar words 'hidden' in other words. Now we'd like to take you a step further and ask you to be wary, on occasions, of words you think you know. For example, **sich verabschieden** is 'to take one's leave' and **ein Gesetz** means 'a law', but **ein Gesetz verabschieden** clearly does not mean 'to take one's leave of the law', as that would make no sense. In fact, it translates as 'to pass a law'. You'd also be wrong to think in terms of cleaning, were you to hear **eine Angelegenheit bereinigen** (**bereinigen** acc. = 'to clean up') - it means 'to settle a matter'.

Study these combinations (transitive verbs + nouns); they will be a useful addition to your business vocabulary:

masc. nouns (acc.)

to place an order	einen Auftrag erteilen
to make an appointment	einen Termin vereinbaren
to make a loss/gain	einen Verlust/Gewinn machen

fem. nouns (acc.)

to order goods	eine Bestellung aufgeben
to cancel goods	(eine)Ware abbestellen
to have an idea for an ad/to draft an advertisement	eine Anzeige entwerfen

neut. nouns (acc.)

to put out to tender	ein Angebot einholen
to offer goods/services cheaper	ein Angebot unterschreiten
to transfer one's business	sein Geschäft verlegen
to have a trade mark registered	das Warenzeichen patentieren lassen
to do a good business deal	ein gutes Geschäft machen (coll)

plural nouns

to initiate changes	Änderungen vornehmen
to attract customers	Kunden werben
to arrange business contacts	Geschäftskontakte vermitteln

You'll impress your business associates tremendously by using these combinations of nouns and verbs, but please bear in mind that they are mostly used in written communication and a simpler version, using a simpler verb, would normally be used in oral communication.

One point to bear in mind is that these nouns can be replaced by personal pronouns. For example:

Das Parlament soll ein neues Gesetz verabschieden.
→ Das Parlament hat es wie geplant verabschiedet.
Parliament is to pass a new law.
→ *Parliament has passed it as (they had) planned.*

Haben Sie die Angelegenheit bereinigt? → - Ja, ich habe sie bereinigt.
Did you settle this matter? → *- Yes, I've settled it!*

We mention this because, in other instances, these noun-verb combinations are inseparable from each other and the noun cannot be replaced by a personal pronoun (cf. Checknote 142).

Again, you could make up your own list of noun-verb combinations which will be relevant to your own business situation, by mentally going through the various aspects of your work. For example:

die Briefe öffnen	*to open (your) letters*
die Briefe beantworten	*to answer the letters*
die Briefe/Post aufgeben	*to post the letters/correspondence*
einen Termin machen	*to make an appointment*
einen Termin ändern	*to change an appointment*
einen Termin verschieben	*to postpone an appointment*
einen Termin absagen	*to cancel an appointment*
ein Telefonat führen	*to make a phone call*
ein Telefonat anmelden	*to book a call*
ein Telefonat beenden	*to finish a phone call*
einen Anruf weiterleiten	*to redirect/re-route a call*
einen Anruf entgegennehmen	*to take a call*
einen Plan aufstellen	*to draw up a plan*
einen Plan ausführen	*to realize/execute a plan*
einen Plan verwerfen	*to reject a plan*

A good dictionary would be of invaluable help in this sort of exercise. Bearing in mind that you will remember things much better when you have to work them out for yourself, it is time well spent!

138 Reported speech – present subjunctive

In this Unit, when Frau Schneider mentioned what she had read in the newspaper, she said:

> "Ich habe erst gestern wieder in der Zeitung gelesen, daß es im Hinblick auf die Veränderungen in Europa wichtig <u>sei</u>, daß alle Unternehmen ... mehr in die sprachliche Ausbildung investieren. Im letzten Jahrzehnt <u>habe</u> sich in dieser Hinsicht zwar schon einiges getan, aber längst noch nicht genug!"

You may have been puzzled by the unfamiliar-looking endings of the third person singular **sei** and **habe**. The explanation is that certain other German verb forms are used when formally reporting statements, namely the 'subjunctive'. Not all Germans are keen on using the subjunctive and there are alternatives which are more popular, so it's fairly easy to avoid. We'll come to that in a moment. Here are the irregular verbs **haben** ('to have') and **sein** ('to be') in the present indicative (which you're used to) and the present subjunctive:

haben	haben	sein	sein
pres.indic.	*pres.subj.*	*pres.indic.*	*pres.subj.*
ich habe	ich habe	ich bin	ich sei
du hast	du habest	du bist	du seist
er hat	er habe	er ist	er sei
sie hat	sie habe	sie ist	sie sei
es hat	es habe	es ist	es sei
wir haben	wir haben	wir sind	wir seien
ihr habt	ihr habet	ihr seid	ihr seiet
sie haben	sie haben	sie sind	sie seien
Sie haben	Sie haben	Sie sind	Sie seien

You will have noticed a lot of "e"'s in the subjunctive endings and the most striking one is the -e ending in the third person singular. Let's study now the regular forms of the present subjunctive. We'll take as our model the verb **kaufen** ('to buy'):

pres.indic.		*pres.subj.*	
ich kaufe	wir kaufen	ich kaufe	wir kaufen
du kaufst	ihr kauft	du kaufest	ihr kaufet
er kauft	sie kaufen	er kaufe	sie kaufen
sie kauft	Sie kaufen	sie kaufe	Sie kaufen
es kauft		es kaufe	

Here are two complete sentences showing the subjunctive used in practice:

Er oagt, er kaute immer auf Vorrat.
He says he always buys/bought in bulk.

Sie entgegnete, sie gehe lieber zur Konkurrenz!
She replied, she preferred to go to our competitor!

Modals (**wollen, sollen, können, dürfen, müssen**) follow the same pattern in the present subjunctive:

ich wolle	solle	könne	dürfe	müsse
du wollest	sollest	könnest	dürfest	müssest
er/sie/es wolle	solle	könne	dürfe	müsse

wir wollen	sollen	können	dürfen	müssen
ihr wollet	sollet	könnet	dürfet	müßet
sie/Sie wollen	sollen	können	dürfen	müssen

The most frequently used form is the third person singular:

Er sagt, er wolle morgen nachmittag um 5 Uhr wiederkommen.
He says he wants to come back at 5 o'clock tomorrow afternoon.

Der Chef meint, sie solle keine Überstunden mehr machen.
The boss thinks that she ought not to work overtime any more.

Er läßt Ihnen ausrichten, es tue ihm leid, Sie heute nicht mehr empfangen zu können.
He wishes you to know that he's sorry he can't see you any more today.

Er meint, man könne das wieder zurechtbiegen.
He thinks one ought to be able to put things right again.

Note: Only when the reported speech is <u>not</u> introduced by **daß** must you use the present subjunctive.

All the above examples could have used **daß**:

Er sagt, daß er morgen nachmittag um 5 Uhr wiederkommen wolle.
Der Chef meint, daß sie keine Überstunden mehr machen solle. (etc.)

You will be relieved to hear that the following version (which most probably you would have used from the start) is equally acceptable:

Er sagt, daß er morgen nachmittag um 5 Uhr wiederkommen will.
Der Chef meint, daß sie keine Überstunden mehr machen soll. (etc.)

139 Demonstrative pronouns

The German definite articles can also be used to express 'this one' or 'that one', but they have to reflect the case, number and gender of the noun they refer to. Here are some examples, using **Zeitplaner** (m.), **Zeitschrift** (f.), **Notizbuch** (n.), **Maschinen** (pl.):

(Sie betrachten eine Auswahl an Zeitplanern:) "Ich nehme den da!"
(You're inspecting a selection of time-planning systems:) "I'll have that one!"

(Sie haben eine Zeitschrift ausgewählt:) "Die hier, bitte!"
(You've chosen a magazine:) "This one, please!"

(Sie wählen ein neues Notizbuch:) "Ich kaufe das hier!"
(You're choosing a new notebook:) "I'll buy this one!"

(Sie bestellen 2 neue Maschinen:) "Ich entscheide mich für die hier!"
(You're ordering two new machines:) "I've decided on these!"

Comprehension Practice 11

Richtig oder falsch?

New words:

eine neue Technologie entwickeln	*to develop a new technology*
in der Vergangenheit	*in the past*
in Zukunft	*In future*
getrennte Wege gehen	*to go separate ways*
die Durchführung	*carrying out*
gut ausgeruht	*well rested*
ein Thema zur Sprache bringen	*to mention a topic*

1 Herr Jackson ist überrascht über die vielen Messebesucher.
2 Auf englischen Messen gibt es immer einen solchen Andrang.
3 Die traditionelle Hannover Messe ist in diesem Jahr auf zwei Veranstaltungen aufgeteilt worden.
4 Die Verkaufsstände sind mit allen technischen Finessen ausgestattet.
5 Die Kosten für die Messestände sind enorm niedrig!
6 Dieser Aufwand schlägt sich auf jeden Fall in den Auftragsbüchern nieder.
7 Es ist immer problematisch für kleinere Firmen, wenn die Großen eine neue Technologie entwickeln.
8 Die Preise der kleineren Hersteller liegen niedriger, weil sie keine hohen Entwicklungskosten haben.
9 Die internationale geschäftliche Kommunikation wird nicht durch Sprachprobleme behindert.
10 Alle Unternehmen sollen mehr in die Fremdsprachenausbildung investieren.
11 In den letzten Jahren ist zu viel in die sprachliche Ausbildung investiert worden.
12 Futura und Excel-Equip wollen in Zukunft wieder getrennte Wege gehen.
13 Bei der Planung und Durchführung der Werbekampagne haben sie nicht erfolgreich zusammengearbeitet.
14 Frau Schneider sieht prinzipielle Schwierigkeit für die weitere Zusammenarbeit.
15 Sie wollen das Thema am nächsten Tag nicht wieder zur Sprache bringen.
16 Frau Sch. und Herr J. sind am Abend gut ausgeruht.

FLUENCY PRACTICE 44
Newspaper report

New words:

der Sprecher	*spokesperson*
das Ministerium	*ministry*
die Bundesregierung	*Federal Government*
stabilisieren	*to stabilize*
die Sitzung leiten	*to chair the meeting*
ab|warten	*to wait and see*
entwickeln	*to develop*
die Stimme	*voice*
optimistisch	*optimistic*
eine Krise verhindern	*to avoid a crisis*
erneut	*new, renewed*

The English journalist who wrote this report in German wasn't very sure about the verb forms. Please edit the following text, crossing out the incorrect forms:

Der Sprecher aus dem Ministerium ist der Meinung, daß die Bundesregierung definitiv alle nötigen Schritte unternommen (hatten / habe / haben), um die DM zu stabilisieren. Der Kanzler (habe / hätte / hat) persönlich die Sitzung geleitet. Er sagte, es (bleibe / bliebe / bleibt) abzuwarten, wie sich die internationale Situation (entwickelte / entwickle / entwickelt). Die Stimmen aus dem Ausland (würden / wären / seien) optimistisch, daß er das Richtige (tue / täte / getan habe), um eine erneute Krise zu verhindern.

FLUENCY PRACTICE 45
Matching clauses

New words:

niedrig	*low*
führend	*leading*
(noch) gar nicht	*not at all; not yet*
ein Dutzend	*a dozen*
verlagern	*to move, shift*
jüngst-	*latest*
das Marktforschungsergebnis	*results of market research*
hauptsächlich	*mainly*
durch|führen	*to carry out*
sich wenden an	*to address*
beeinflussen	*to influence*
das Kaufverhalten	*purchasing behaviour*
besichtigen	*to visit, inspect*
persönlich	*personally*

der Unfall   *accident*
die Marktanalyse *market research/analysis*
ein|stellen   *to discontinue* (production)

Match the clauses in the first section with those in the second:

1. Die Preise sind niedriger, denn
2. Früher gab es viele kleine Firmen, aber
3. Vor zehn Jahren war das Produkt noch gar nicht auf dem Markt, doch
4. Wir haben die Produktion ins Ausland verlagert, denn
5. Die Reklame muß junge Leute ansprechen, weil
6. Die Fernsehwerbung muß sich an Kinder wenden, denn
7. Der Direktor besichtigte die Werkshalle persönlich, nachdem
8. Wir sollten eine Marktanalyse durchführen, bevor

A. die Entwicklungskosten sind auch niedriger.
B. das Produkt nach jüngsten Marktforschungsergebnissen hauptsächlich von ihnen gekauft wird.
C. sie beeinflussen das Kaufverhalten der Eltern.
D. jetzt gibt es schon ein Dutzend Hersteller.
E. er über dem Unfall informiert worden war.
F. die Herstellungskosten waren hier zu hoch.
G. wir die Produktion dieses Artikels einstellen.
H. jetzt gibt es nur noch drei führende Unternehmen.

DICTIONARY PRACTICE 9
R & D (Forschung und Entwicklung)

Please study the following newspaper article (taken from Metro-Clubpost 12/1990) and (A) find the answers to these questions:

1) What did today's best-selling product look like yesterday?
2) How was it shaped into a 'bestseller'?
3) How does the Federal Republic see its future role?
4) What indicates in the text that economic development is likely to continue?
5) How big has the increase been in investment in research and development since 1970?
6) How much is invested in R & D in relation to economic output?
7) What is the level of investment in research in relation to GNP?
8) What is the common factor regarding Japan, Sweden and Germany?
9) Which sector pays two-thirds of the cost of R & D?
10) Where does the remaining third come from?

Jedes Jahr 70 Milliarden für deutsche Forschung

Was heute als Spitzenprodukt auf dem Weltmarkt gehandelt wird, war gestern oft nur eine Idee oder Skizze auf dem Reißbrett. Erst Forschung und Entwicklung haben daraus die „Bestseller" geformt. Die Forschung als Motor des Fortschrittes spielt daher für ein exportorientiertes, aber rohstoffarmes Land wie Deutschland eine herausragende Rolle, wenn es auch in Zukunft zu den führenden Industrienationen gehören will. Die Voraussetzungen dafür sind gut, denn Wirtschaft, Staat und verschiedenste Institutionen steigern von Jahr zu Jahr ihre Ausgaben für Forschung und Entwicklung. Waren es 1970 noch 15 Milliarden Mark, so hat sich die Summe bis heute nahezu vervierfacht. 70 Milliarden Mark werden die Forschungsausgaben 1990 voraussichtlich betragen, wie unser Schaubild zeigt. Damit stehen 2,9 Prozent der Wirtschaftsleistung für diese Investitionen in die Zukunft zur Verfügung. Neben Deutschland gehören Japan und Schweden zu den Ländern, die im Verhältnis zu ihrer Wirtschaftsleistung den größten Aufwand für Forschung und Entwicklung treiben. Ihre Ausgaben erreichen jeweils 2,9 Prozent des Bruttosozialproduktes. Rund zwei Drittel des Betrages bringt hierzulande die Wirtschaft auf. Den Rest steuert der Staat dazu.

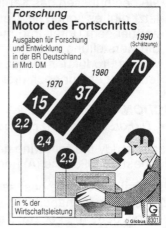

Forschung
Motor des Fortschritts

Ausgaben für Forschung und Entwicklung in der BR Deutschland in Mrd. DM

1990 (Schätzung)

1970 — 15
1980 — 37
70

2,2
2,4
2,9

in % der Wirtschaftsleistung

© Globus 8301

B) Please fill in the missing verbs (you'll find them all in the text!):

1) ein Produkt auf dem Weltmarkt _____
2) eine (herausragende) Rolle _____
3) zu den führenden Industrienationen _____
4) (seine) Ausgaben von Jahr zu Jahr _____
5) die Summe hat sich _____
6) die Forschungsaufgaben werden _____
7) für (diese) Investitionen zur Verfügung _____
8) Japan und Schweden _____ zu den Ländern, die ...
9) den größten Aufwand für Forschung und Entwicklung _____
10) den Rest _____

UNIT 12

Mixing business with pleasure

In this Unit the emphasis is on financial vocabulary and background information on the Federal Republic of Germany.

On the day after their visit to the trade fair, Mr Jackson has invited Frau Schneider to dinner, but business is never far from their minds. Mr Jackson takes the opportunity to ask a few questions about German business and banking practices. We join them at the end of their meal.

Frau S.: Das war ein ausgezeichnetes Essen. Jetzt fehlt mir nur noch ein starker Kaffee.

Mr J.: Da schließe ich mich gern an. Wenn es Ihnen recht ist, möchte ich Sie auch noch zu einem Drink einladen.

Frau S.: Das ist sehr nett von Ihnen, aber ich muß heute abend noch nach München fahren. Ich habe morgen früh einen Geschäftstermin bei einem unserer deutschen Lieferanten.

Mr J.: Dann will ich Sie auch nicht mehr lange aufhalten. Aber vielleicht können Sie mir noch einen Rat geben. Ich habe festgestellt, daß in Deutschland Kreditkarten nicht sehr populär sind. Ich spiele deshalb mit dem Gedanken, hier ein Bankkonto zu eröffnen. Wir könnten dann unsere laufenden Ausgaben per Scheck bezahlen. Was meinen Sie, wäre es sinnvoll, hier ein Bankkonto zu eröffnen?

Frau S.: Es stimmt schon, daß die Deutschen eine gewisse Reserviertheit in Bezug auf "Plastikgeld" an den Tag legen, denn bei uns sind die Gebühren dafür recht hoch. Aber die Unbeliebtheit der Kreditkarten als Zahlungsmittel ist meiner Meinung nach kein hinreichender Grund, hier ein Konto zu eröffnen. Die Kontoführungsgebühren für Geschäftskonten sind relativ hoch und die Habenzinsen sind extrem niedrig, die liegen zur Zeit bei 0,5 Prozent, und die Sollzinsen liegen weit über 10 Prozent!

Mr J.: Das war mir nicht bekannt. Ich wußte nur, daß ganz allgemein die Zinssätze in Deutschland niedriger liegen als in Großbritannien, aber Ihre Inflationsrate ist auch entsprechend niedrig.

Frau S.: Nun in finanzpolitischer Hinsicht wird es sicher in Europa in nächster Zeit eine gewisse Angleichung geben, aber bisher unterscheiden sich die einzelnen Länder jedoch in Bezug auf ihre Geschäftspraktiken noch ziemlich stark voneinander. In Deutschland bezahlen wir fast alle Rechnungen per Überweisung und nicht mit Schecks. Und für regelmäßige Zahlungen sind Einzugsaufträge die Norm. Obwohl Bildschirmtext (Btx) sehr praktisch ist, benutzt bisher nur eine verschwindend kleine Minderheit diesen Service der Bundespost, um ihre Bankgeschäfte per Bildschirm abzuwickeln.

Mr J.: Ich bin sicher, daß das kommt. In Zukunft werden die ISDN-Dienste der Post eine ebenso große Bedeutung haben, wie heute die Bargeldautomaten der Banken und Sparkassen. – Da wir gerade von Banken reden, ich bin übrigens überrascht darüber, daß die Banken sowohl in Deutschland als auch in Großbritannien eine immer breitere Palette von Dienstleistugen anbieten: vom normalen Bankgeschäft mit Kleinkrediten und Hypothekendarlehen über Geldanlagen in Renten- und Wertpapieren bis zu Versicherungsgeschäften.

Frau S.: Ja das stimmt wohl. Banken und Versicherungen arbeiten immer mehr Hand in Hand. Die waren auch die ersten als die Geschäfte im Osten anliefen. Es ist ja auch nur zu verständlich, daß eine Bank wie z.B. die Dresdner wieder im östlichen Landesteil vertreten sein will und das gilt natürlich auch für andere Unternehmen, die einmal ihren Stammsitz dort hatten.

Mr J.: Glauben Sie, daß Unternehmen in den fünf neuen Bundesländern Wettbewerbsvorteile vor anderen europäischen Firmen haben?

Frau S.: Sie denken da an die Panne mit den Übersetzungen der Gebrauchsanweisungen, nicht wahr? Da machen Sie sich mal keine Sorgen! Wenn Sie Ihre Liefertermine einhalten, gleichbleibend gute Qualität produzieren und den Kundendienst aufbauen, den Sie gesprächsweise erwähnt haben, dann haben Sie ganz bestimmt die besten Chancen, Ihr Verkaufsgebiet im Endeffekt auf ganz Europa auszuweiten.

Mr J.: Sie werden hoffentlich auch davon profitieren, wenn wir ganz groß herauskommen! Aber lassen Sie uns nicht weiter vom Geschäft reden. Das hat Zeit bis zu meinem nächsten Besuch! Ich will Sie nicht unnötig lange aufhalten, Sie haben noch eine lange Autofahrt vor sich. - Ich kümmere mich um die Rechnung. Schließlich habe ich Sie ja eingeladen! Sagen Sie mir nur bitte, ob Bedienung und Mehrwertsteuer im Endbetrag inbegriffen sind?

Frau S.: Ja, das schon, aber wenn man mit allem zufrieden ist, gibt man meist noch ein zusätzliches Trinkgeld. - Ich hole noch schnell meinen Mantel und dann können wir aufbrechen!
(Outside the restaurant.) Das war ein netter Abend. Nochmals vielen Dank für die freundliche Einladung.

Mr J.: Gern geschehen. Mir hat das Restaurant auch sehr gut gefallen. Sie haben wirklich eine gute Wahl getroffen. Darf ich Sie noch zu Ihrem Wagen begleiten?

Frau S.: Ja, gern. Wenn Sie möchten, kann ich Sie an Ihrem Hotel absetzen. Ich fahre sowieso in diese Richtung.

Mr J.: Das Angebot nehme ich doch gerne an. Ich wollte ja eigentlich zu Fuß gehen, aber an so einem regnerischen Abend ist es doch angenehmer, mit dem Auto zu fahren.

Frau S.: Mein Wagen steht dahinten auf dem Parkplatz. *(They walk to her car.)*
Herr Jackson, mit Ihrem perfekten Deutsch, führen Sie mir immer wieder vor Augen, daß ich meine Englischkenntnisse sträflich vernachlässigt habe. Vielleicht sollte ich mir so einen neuen Übersetzungscomputer anschaffen!

Mr J.: Für die Geschäftskorrespondenz reicht der wohl, aber bei alltäglichen Gesprächen ist so ein Gerät einfach zu umständlich. Wie könnte denn auch eine Maschine die Bedeutungsnuancen des Satzbaus, die Vielfalt der Ausdrücksmöglichkeiten und die Bedeutungsvariationen der Intonation imitieren! Auch heute geht's noch nicht ohne Anstrengung, trotz elektronischer Hilfsgeräte! Damit ich nicht aus der Übung komme, lese ich jede Woche eine deutsche Zeitung und treffe ab und zu einen deutschen Bekannten, mit dem ich mich immer nur auf Deutsch unterhalte. Und wie heißt's so schön: "Übung macht den Meister"!

TRANSLATION

Frau S.: That was an excellent meal. The only thing missing now is a strong coffee.

Mr J.: I'll gladly join you. I'd like to offer you a drink afterwards, if that's all right with you.

Frau S.: That's very kind of you, but I still have to drive to Munich tonight. I have a business appointment with one of our German suppliers first thing in the morning.

Mr J.: Then I won't keep you much longer, but perhaps you could give me some advice. I've noticed that credit cards aren't very popular in Germany. I'm therefore toying with the idea of opening a bank account here. Then we'll be able to pay our day-to-day expenses by cheque. What do you think, would it make sense to open a bank account here?

Frau S.: You're quite right that the Germans show a certain reluctance in relation to 'plastic money', as the fees are quite high. In my opinion, the unpopularity of credit cards as a method of payment is not a sufficient reason to open a bank account. The running costs for business accounts are relatively high. The interest rate on deposits is extremely low. At the moment it stands at 0.5%, and the interest rate on overdrafts stands at well over 10%.

Mr J.: I didn't know that. All I knew was that, generally speaking, interest rates were lower in Germany than in Great Britain, but then again, your rate of inflation is correspondingly lower.

Frau S.: Well, as far as financial policy is concerned, there will soon have to be a certain amount of homogenization in Europe, but, so far, individual countries still differ quite a lot from each other in respect of business practices. In Germany we pay nearly all bills by bank giro credit and not by cheque and for regular payments direct debit arrangements are the norm. Although Btx is very practical, up to now only a negligible number (of people) use this service of the Bundespost to carry out their banking transactions via the computer monitor.

Mr J.: I'm certain that will come! In future the ISDN [Integrated Services Digital Network] system of the post office will be as important as the automatic cash dispensers of banks and savings banks are today. As we're talking about banks, I'm surprised that the banks in Germany, as well as in Great Britain, offer an ever-increasing range of services from normal banking activities, i.e. small loans and mortgages, to investments in bonds and shares, and even insurance policies.

Frau S.: Well, yes, that's quite right. Banks and insurance firms work increasingly hand in hand. They were first off the mark, when trading with the East got underway. Then again, it's only natural that a bank like the 'Dresdner' wants to be represented in the eastern part of the country again and the same holds true for other businesses formerly established over there.

Mr J.: Do you think that firms in the five new regions are going to have a competitive edge over other European firms?

Frau S.: You're thinking of the mishap with the translations of the users' manuals, aren't you. Don't worry about that! If you keep to your delivery dates, produce consistently good quality (products) and set up the after-sales service you mentioned in the course of our conversation, then you're in with a winning chance to increase your sales area to cover the whole of Europe one day.

Mr J.: Hopefully, you'll benefit, too, when we make it in a big way! Let's stop talking shop. That can wait until my next visit! As you've still got quite a long drive in front of you, I don't want to detain you unnecessarily. I'll take care of the bill, as I invited you. Could you just tell me please, if service and VAT are included in the final figure?

Frau S.: Yes, they are, but if one is really satisfied (with everything), one would normally give an additional tip, I'll just go and fetch my coat and then we'll be able to leave.
(Outside the restaurant.) That was a very nice evening. I'd like to thank you again for the kind invitation.

Mr J.: My pleasure. I also liked the restaurant very much. You really made a very good choice. May I accompany you to your car?

Frau S.: That's very kind. If you like, I could drop you off at your hotel. I'll be driving in that direction anyway.

Mr J.: I'll gladly accept your offer. Originally I intended to walk, but on such a wet evening it is considerably more pleasant to go by car.

Frau S.: My car is over there, in the carpark. *(They walk to her car.)* Mr Jackson, with your perfect (command of) German, you always demonstrate to me that I have neglected my English terribly. Perhaps I ought to buy one of those translating machines.

Mr J.: That might well do for (your) business correspondence, but for everyday conversations such a machine is simply too inconvenient. How could a machine emulate all the nuances of syntax, the wide choice of vocabulary and the variations of meaning conveyed by intonation? Even in this day and age it can't be done without putting in some effort, despite all those electronic aids! So that I don't get out of practice, I read a German newspaper every week and sometimes meet a German friend with whom I always converse in German. What's the famous saying?... 'Practice makes perfect!'

Checklist 12

Masculine nouns:

der Lieferant, -en	*supplier*
der Rat (no pl.)	*advice*
der Grund, ˇ-e	*reason*
der Zinssatz, ˇ-e	*interest rate*
der Einzugsauftrag, ˇ-e	*direct debit*
der Bildschirm, -e	*screen, monitor*
Bildschirmtext (Btx)	electronic shopping and banking facility
der Service/Dienst, -e	*service*
der Automat, -en	*robot, electronic gadget, dispensing machine*
der Geldautomat, -en	*money dispenser*
der Kredit, -e	*loan*
der Kleinkredit, -e	*small loan*
der Osten	*east*
der Landesteil, -e	*region, part of the country*
der Stammsitz, -e	*base, place of origin*
der Wettbewerbsvorteil, -e	*competitive edge*
der Liefertermin, -e	*delivery date*
der Kundendienst	*customer services*
der Endbetrag, ˇ-e	*total amount*
der Mantel, ˇ-	*coat*
der Parkplatz, ˇ-e	*car park*
der Übersetzungscomputer	*translating machine*
der Satzbau	*syntax*
der Freund, -e	*close friend* (not a mere acquaintance!)
der Meister, -	*master craftsman* (in Germany normally holding a specialist diploma); *foreman* (in a factory)

Feminine nouns:

die Aufgabe, -n	*task*
die Beliebtheit	*popularity*
die Unbeliebtheit	*unpopularity*

die Gebühr, -en	charge; fee
die Kontoführungsgebühren	bank charges
die Inflationsrate	rate of inflation
die Angleichung	homogenization
die Überweisung, -en	bank giro credit
die Minderheit, -en	minority
die (Bundes-) Post	Federal postal services
die Bedeutung, -en	meaning; importance
die Sparkasse, -n	(local) savings bank
die Dienstleistung, -en	service
die Palette	range
die Versicherung, -en	insurance
die Panne, -n	mishap; breadown (car)
die Autofahrt, -en	car journey
die Bedienung	person serving; service (in a restaurant)
die Steuer, -n	tax
die Mehrwertsteuer (Mwst)	Value Added Tax (VAT)
die Richtung, -en	direction
die Kenntnis, -se	knowledge
die Englischkenntnisse	knowledge of English
die Bedeutung, -en	meaning
die Bedeutungsnuancen	nuances of meaning
die Bedeutungsvariationen	variations in meaning
die Vielfalt	great variety
die Ausdrucksmöglichkeit	way of expressing oneself
die Anstrengung, -en	effort
die Übung, -en	practice

Neuter nouns:

das (Bank-) Konto, -ten	(bank) account
das Plastikgeld	'plastic' money
das Zahlungsmittel, -	means of payment
das Darlehen, -	loan
das Hypothekendarlehen	mortgage
das Versicherungsgeschäft	insurance (business)
das Rentenpapier, -e	bond
das Wertpapier, -e	share
das Verkaufsgebiet	sales area
das Trinkgeld, -er	tip (given to waiters etc.)
das Hilfsgerät, -e	aid; gadget

Plural nouns:

die Habenzinsen	interest rate on deposits
die Sollzinsen	interest rate on overdrafts
die Geschäftspraktiken	business practices

Adjectives/adverbs:

laufend	current; running
gewiß (gewisser, -e, es)	certain

recht hoch	quite high
hinreichend	sufficient
weit	far
allgemein	general
entsprechend	correspondingly
politisch	political
finanzpolitisch	in relation to financial policy
stark	strong
regelmäßig	regular
verschwindend	negligible
überrascht (pp)	surprised
breit	wide; broad
verständlich	understandable
östlich	eastern
gleichbleibend	unchanged
unnötig	unnecessary
lange	a long time
zufrieden	pleased, satisfied
zusätzlich	additional
regnerisch	rainy
sträflich (coll.)	awfully, terribly
alltäglich	everyday
umständlich	complicated, awkward

Verbs:

auf|halten acc. *(st)*	to hold back, detain
sich untercheiden in dat. *(st)*	to differ in
benutzen acc.	to use; utilize
ab|wickeln acc.	to carry out (business transactions)
an|bieten (dat.) acc. *(st)*	to offer
an|laufen coll. (intr. *st*)	to get off the ground, get started
gelten für acc. (imp. *st*)	to be valid for
ein|halten acc. *(st)*	to keep, stick to
produzieren acc.	to manufacture
auf|bauen acc.	to build; set up
aus|weiten acc.	to widen, expand
profitieren von dat.	to take advantage of
(groß) heraus|kommen (coll.)	to make it in a big way
reden von acc.	to talk, chat about
auf|halten acc. (von dat.)	to detain, keep
sich kümmern um acc.	to take care of
ein|laden acc. (zu dat.) *(st)*	to invite someone
auf|brechen (intr. *st*)	to set off, leave
mir hat ... gefallen	I liked
begleiten acc.	to accompany
ab|setzen acc.	to drop someone off
an|nehmen acc. *(st)*	to accept
vor Augen führen	to show, demonstrate
vernachlässigen acc.	to neglect

an|schaffen (coll.) acc.	to get, buy
reichen (coll.) für acc.	to be adaquate for
es geht!	it works! it's possible!
treffen acc. *(st)*	to meet
sich unterhalten mit dat.	to hold a conversation with

Other expressions:

wenn es Ihnen recht ist!	*If it's all right with you*
mit dem Gedanken spielen	*to toy with an idea*
ein (Bank-)Konto eröffnen	*to open a (bank) account*
per/mit Scheck bezahlen	*to pay by cheque*
was meinen Sie?	*what do you think?*
es stimmt schon ... ... aber	*Admittedly ... ... , but*
in Bezug auf	*with regard to, concerning*
an den Tag legen acc.	*to display (openly)*
das war mir nicht bekannt!	*I didn't know that!*
in finanzpolitischer Hinsicht	*as far as financial policy is concerned*
sich voneinander unterscheiden	*to be different from one another*
ich bin überrascht darüber, daß ...	*I'm surprised that ...*
sowohl ... als auch ...	*... as well as ...*
eine breite Palette von dat Dienstleistungen an|bieten	*a wide range of to offer services*
von ... über ... bis zu	*starting at ... via .. up to*
Geschäfte ab|wickeln	*to conduct business*
per Scheck/Post/Bote	*by cheque/post/messenger*
das gilt für acc.	*that's valid for; holds true*
vom Geschäft reden	*to talk shop*
lassen Sie uns nicht weiter ...	*let's stop (doing something)*
das hat Zeit (bis...)!	*that can wait (until ...)!*
zufrieden sein mit dat	*to be satisfied with*
im Endbetrag inbegriffen	*included in the final sum/amount*
nochmals	*once more*
eine gute Wahl treffen	*to make a good choice*
sowieso	*anyway*
zu Fuß gehen	*to go on foot*
mit dem Auto/Zug/... fahren	*to go by car/train/...*
es ist doch angenehmer	*it's really (a lot) more convenient*
dahinten	*over there*
noch nicht	*not ... yet*
aus der Übung sein/kommen	*to be/get out of practice*
ab und zu	*now and then*
Wie heißt das auf Deutsch?	*How do you say that in German?*

CHECKNOTES

140 Polite comments and requests - Past subjunctive

When dealing with foreigners or doing business in a foreign country we normally use very polite language. So, when talking on the telephone, you might be a little surprised to hear the standard phrase: "Kann ich Herrn/Frau X sprechen?". You may have been expecting the German equivalent of 'May I?' rather than 'Can I?', but the Germans generally express themselves in a more direct manner and, of course, the intonation makes all the difference. Particles, too, may be used to make a request or statement more acceptable.

Let's now look at the way we make polite comments and requests in German (and listen to the cassette, if possible):

Könnten Sie mir sagen, ob/wann ...?	*Could you tell me if/when ...?*
Ich könnte morgen wiederkommen.	*I could come back tomorrow.*
Könnten wir den Termin nicht verlegen?	*Couldn't we change the date?*
Dieser Preis dürfte stimmen!	*This price should be right.*
Sie dürften gleich kommen!	*They ought to come any time now.*
Ich möchte dieses Modell bestellen.	*I'd like to order this model.*
Möchten Sie das Gerät umtauschen?	*Would you like a replacement?*
Wäre Ihnen Donnerstag recht?	*Would Thursday be all right?*
Ich wäre für die zweite Lösung.	*I'd be in favour of the second solution.*
Ich hätte da noch eine Frage.	*(Sorry, but) I still have a question.*
Hätten Sie auch preiswertere Modelle?	*Would you have any cheaper models?*
Gäbe es sonst noch 'was zu besprechen?	*Would there be anything else to discuss?*
Würde Ihnen Mittwoch passen?	*Would Wednesday suit you?*
Würden Sie mir das bitte schriftlich bestätigen?	*Could you please confirm that in writing?*
Wollten Sie den Preis wissen?	*Did you want to know the price?*
Sollten wir ihn nicht erst fragen?	*Shouldn't we ask him first?*

All the above are examples of the past subjunctive. This is normally formed by putting an umlaut on the simple past tense form, as you'll see from the following list of very frequently used subjunctive forms:

INFIN.	PRESENT INDICATIVE	SIMPLE PAST INDICATIVE	PAST SUBJUNCTIVE
können:	ich kann	ich konnte	**ich könnte**

	sie können	sie konnten	**sie könnten**
	wir können	wir konnten	**wir könnten**
dürfen:	er/sie/es darf	/sie/ durfte	**/sie/ dürfte**
	sie dürfen	sie durften	**sie dürften**
mögen:	ich mag	ich mochte	**ich möchte**
	Sie mögen	Sie mochten	**Sie möchten**
werden:	es wird	es wurde	**es würde**
	Sie werden	Sie wurden	**Sie würden**
geben:	es gibt	es gab	**es gäbe**
	sie geben	sie gaben	**sie gäben**
sein:	ich bin	ich war	**ich wäre**
	es ist	es war	**es wäre**
	sie sind	sie waren	**sie wären**
haben:	er hat	er hatte	**er hätte**
	Sie haben	Sie hatten	**Sie hätten**

Two verbs are missing from our list:

wollen:	Sie wollen	sie wollten	**Sie wollten**
sollen:	wir sollen	wir sollten	**wir sollten**

Please remember that the subjunctive forms of **sollen** and **wollen** do not have an umlaut, which means that the simple past and the past subjunctive forms are identical. As there are a great many verbs where the simple past and subjunctive forms are identical, e.g.: **kauften, zeigten, besichtigten, bezahlten**, Germans tend to use **würde/n** + the infinitive in order to simplify things. Examples:

Ich würde Ihnen gern die neuen Modelle zeigen.
I would like to show you the new models.

Sie würden sicher gerne unsere neuen Ausstellungsräume besichtigen.
I suppose you would like to visit our new showrooms.

Note that the past subjunctive is mainly used when making suggestions or assumptions. It is also used for reported speech which uses the past tense (**er sagte, .../sie fragte, ...**).

141 Talking about non-factual, imagined stituations

Please study the following examples:

Gäben Sie einen höheren Rabatt?
or: Würden Sie einen höheren Rabatt geben?
Would you give a bigger discount?

Führen Sie 1.Klasse nach Paris?
or: Würden Sie 1.Klasse nach Paris fahren?
Would you travel to Paris 1st class?

Entließen Sie eine so gute Sekretärin?
or: Würden Sie eine so gute Sekretärin entlassen?
Would you dismiss such a good secretary?

In the above sentences it is a matter of personal choice whether you use the traditional past subjunctive form or the alternative construction with **würden** + infinitive. For most verbs native speakers of Geman find the past subjunctive too stilted and, in the majority of cases, prefer to use **würde/n**.

142 Conditional sentences: fact vs. non-fact

Can you see an important difference in the meaning of the following pairs of sentences?

1a Wenn ich nach Hause komme, esse ich schnell zu Abend.
1b Wenn er jetzt käme, könnte er mit mir zusammen essen.

2a Wenn der Kunde mit der Qualität zufrieden ist, bleibt er uns treu.
2b Wenn der Kunde mit der Qualität nicht zufrieden wäre, bliebe er uns nicht treu!

3a Wenn ich Millionär bin, kaufe ich mir eine Hochseejacht.
3b Wenn ich ein Millionär wäre, würde ich mir eine Hochseejacht kaufen.

In all six sentences a condition is stated which starts off with **wenn**. In the a-sentences, however, an habitual, possible or probable situation is put before us, while the b-sentences are hypothetical and therefore the subjunctive must be used.

In case you wish to check your own translations:

1a *When I get home I have a quick evening meal.*
1b *If he came now, he could have a meal (together) with me.*
2a *The customer who is satisfied with the quality (of our goods), will remain loyal to us.*
2b *If the customer were not satisfied with the quality (of our goods), he wouldn't remain loyal to us!*
3a *When I'm a millionaire, I'll buy myself an ocean-going yacht.*
3b *If I were a millionaire, I'd buy myself an ocean-going yacht!*

Let's look at some more hypothetical sentences, expressed in two different ways:

1a Wenn ich höhere Betriebskosten hätte, könnte ich meine Ware nicht so preisgünstig anbieten.
If I had higher overheads, I wouldn't be able to offer my goods at such a competitive price.
1b Hätte ich höhere Betriebskosten, könnte ich meine Ware nicht so preisgünstig anbieten.
Had I not such high overheads, I'd be able ...

2a Wenn es keine Kunststoffe gäbe, müßte man sie erfinden!
If there were no man-made (lit. 'artificial') *fibres, one would have to invent them!*

2b Gäbe es keine Kunststoffe, so müßte man sie erfinden!
Were there no man-made fibres, one would have to invent them!

By putting the subjunctive at the beginning of the sentence, a clear indication of a contrary-to-fact conditional sentence is signalled and the opening **wenn** becomes superfluous. However, this is felt to be a more formal style and would not be used in normal everyday conversation.

143 Functional verbs and nouns (used in spoken German)

We'll need to give you the basic meaning of two words before you study the following examples: **der Abschied** = *farewell, leave;* **die Frage** = *question, query.* Now study these two sentences:

Nach dreißig Dienstjahren   *After thirty years he retired.*
nahm er seinen Abschied.
Drei Kandidaten kommen für   *Three candidates are suitable for this*
diese Position in Frage.   *position.*

In the first example the noun + verb combination is not far removed from the basic meaning and you wouldn't be far off the mark, if you were to translate the expression literally as 'he took his leave'. The second sentence, however, demonstrates that this cannot always be done! Here the meaning of the verb is quite different from its literal meaning.

The meaning of the two sentences given above is mainly conveyed through the noun, the verb mainly fulfils the grammatical function of indicating the person and the tense. You've already learnt quite a few combinations of nouns and verbs, where you could replace the noun by a pronoun, if you need to (cf. Checknote 137). In the above examples, however, this cannot be done, as the meaning would be obscured.

These so-called functional verbs are frequently found in written German, especially in administrative documents, the press and scientific papers. The following examples, however, are widely used in normal, everyday conversations:

Abschied nehmen   *to take one's leave*
Platz nehmen   *to take a seat*
Maß nehmen   *to take a measurement*

in Frage kommen   *to be suitable*
in Gang kommen   *to get going*

in Gang bringen	*to get started*
in Ordnung bringen	*to put in order; correct*
in Verlegenheit bringen	*to embarrass*
zur Debatte stehen	*to be under discussion/at issue*
zur Verfügung stehen	*to be at someone's disposal*
außer Frage stehen	*to be out of the question*
zur Debatte stellen	*to throw open for debate*
zur Verfügung stellen	*to place at someone's disposal*
in Frage stellen	*to call into question*

Here are some of these combinations used in complete sentences:

Wir müssen von altvertrauten Vorstellungen Abschied nehmen.
We have to let go of old familiar beliefs.

Sie müssen den Fehler wieder in Ordnung bringen.
You'll have to correct the mistake you made.

Eine Modelländerung steht noch nicht zur Debatte.
There is no question of a model change yet.

Können Sie uns einen Verhandlungsraum zur Verfügung stellen?
Could you make a room available for our meeting?

Ich möchte seine Motive nicht in Frage stellen, aber ich teile sie nicht!
I don't want to cast doubt on his motives, but I don't share them!

144 Functional verbs and nouns (written)

This Checknote deals with certain noun + verb combinations which are predominantly used in written German. You may be one of those people who occasionally have to work on official German documents, in which case you will find the following lists very useful – for reference only.

stellen (basic meaning: *to put in an upright position)*; takes an accusative:

in Aussicht stellen	*to hold out the prospect of*
in Rechnung stellen	*to charge, put on the bill*
zur Diskussion stellen	*to throw open for discussion*

stehen (basic meaning: *to stand*); takes only a nominative:

zur Entscheidung stehen	*to be waiting for a decision*
zur Verfügung stehen	*to be at someone's disposal*
zur Wahl stehen	*to have a choice*

kommen + in (basic meaning: *to come*): only needs a nominative:

in Bewegung kommen	*to start moving*
in Ordnung kommen	*to sort itself out*
in Schwierigkeiten kommen	*to get into trouble, difficulties*

kommen + zu/zum/zur:

zum Abschluß kommen	*to come to an end*
zu dem Ergebnis kommen, daß	*to arrive at the conclusion that ...*
zu der Erkenntnis kommen, daß	*to come to the realization that ...*
zur Kenntnis kommen	*to become general knowledge*
zur Sprache kommen	*to come up in a talk/debate*

bringen + in (basic meaning: *to bring*); takes an accusative:

in Bewegung bringen	*to set in motion*
in Erfahrung bringen	*to find out*
in Erinnerung bringen	*to remind someone of something*
in Gefahr bringen	*to endanger someone/something*
in Übereinstimmung bringen	*to make something agree*
in Verbindung bringen	*to associate, link*

bringen + zu/zum/zur:

zum Ausdruck bringen	*to express, voice*
zu Fall bringen	*to cause to collapse*
zum Halten bringen	*to bring to a stop*
zur Kenntnis bringen	*to inform, notify*
zur Sprache bringen	*to bring up, mention*

finden (basic meaning: *to find*); takes a nominative:

Absatz finden	*to find a market*
Anklang finden	*to be well received*
Unterstützung finden	*to get support*
Verwendung finden	*to have a use*
Zustimmung finden	*to meet with approval*

nehmen (basic meaning: *to take*):

Abstand nehmen (von + dat.)	*to refrain from*
Einfluß nehmen (auf + acc.)	*to influence something*
Einsicht nehmen (in + acc.)	*to examine, inspect*
Rücksicht nehmen (auf + acc.)	*to show consideration for*
Stellung nehmen (zu + dat.)	*to comment on*

145 so

The German word **so** can be translated into English in three ways:

1) *so* (as in 'so good', 'so quickly', etc.); 2) *in this way, in such a way*
3) *I see!*

Here are some examples:

Die Gewinnausschüttung ist so hoch, weil wir eine
Umsatzsteigerung von 20% hatten.
The dividend is so high, because we've increased our turnover by 20%.

Ich mache das immer so.
I always do it like this.

So, das hast du also den ganzen Tag gemacht!
I see! That's what you've been doing all day!

146 False friends

The expression 'false friends' refers to those German words which have a similar spelling to that of English words but which, in fact, mean something totally different. The German words **Fabrik** and **Warenhaus**, for example, do NOT mean 'fabric' and 'warehouse'; they mean 'factory' and 'department store'. Here's a short list of some other 'false friends':

aktuell	*topical, relevant, current*
also	*therefore, so*
Art	*way, manner, kind*
bei	*with, at, in, in case of*
bekommen	*to get, receive*
bilden	*to form*
dann	*then*
denn	*for, because, since*
eben	*just, exactly, precisely*
eventuell	*perhaps; possible*
Fall	*fall, BUT ALSO: case, instance*
fast	*nearly, almost*
Grad	*degree, extent, stage*
groß	*great, big, large*
halten (für)	*to hold, keep; take (for)*
handeln	*to act; trade*
konsequent	*logical, consistent*
Kritik	*criticism, critique*
lösen	*to solve; dissolve; loosen*
man	*one, you*
Maß	*measure, dimension*
Mittel	*means, medium; average (*first part in compounds: *middle,*
Objekt	*object, thing, BUT ALSO: subject matter* central)
passen	*to fit, suit*
prinzipiell	*in principle* (never: 'principally')
schauen	*to view, look* (never: 'to show')
vor	*before, in front of; ago* (never: 'for')
weil	*because*
wenn	*when, BUT ALSO: if*
wer?	*who?*
wo?	*where?*

Most of these words have appeared in the Checknotes or Fluency Practice exercises.

Comprehension Practice 12

Richtig oder falsch?

New words:

unbedingt	*definitely*
kaum	*hardly*
ab|weichen	*to differ*
der Einzahlschein	*paying-in slip*
gegeneinander	*against each other*
nur bedingt	*only under certain conditions*
die Rechnung	*bill*
auf|frischen	*to brush up*
selten	*rarely*
üben	*to practise*
Gelegenheit haben etwas zu tun	*to have the opportunity to do something*

1 Herr Jackson möchte Frau Schneider noch zu einem Drink einladen.
2 Frau Schneider hat einen späten Termin bei einem deutschen Lieferanten.
3 Kreditkarten sind in Deutschland sehr populär.
4 Herr Jackson möchte unbedingt ein Bankkonto eröffnen.
5 Die Habenzinsen sind sehr hoch.
6 Die Geschäftspraktiken der einzelnen europäischen Länder weichen kaum voneinander ab.
7 In Deutschland werden immer alle Rechnungen mit Scheck bezahlt.
8 Für regelmäßige Einzahlungen benutzt man Einzahlscheine.
9 Viele Deutsche benutzen Btx.
10 Banken und Versicherungen arbeiten immer gegeneinander.
11 Viele deutsche Unternehmen hatten einmal ihren Stammsitz im Osten.
12 Die fünf neuen Bundesländer haben nur bedingt Wettbewerbsvorteile.
13 Excel-Equip soll die Liefertermine einhalten.
14 Futura Büromaschinen wird auch davon profitieren, wenn Excel-Equip groß herauskommt.
15 Frau Schneider fährt am frühen Morgen nach München.
16 Die Mehrwertsteuer ist nicht in der Rechnung eingeschlossen.
17 Herr Jackson begleitet Frau Schneider zum Taxi.
18 Es ist ein angenehmer Abend und Herr Jackson geht gern zu Fuß.
19 Frau Schneider hat ihre Englischkenntnisse aufgefrischt.
20 Herr Jackson hat selten Gelegenheit, sein Deutsch zu üben.

DICTIONARY PRACTICE 10

Read the following topical conversation between Frau Schneider and Mr Jackson as often as necessary to follow their line of argument, then answer the comprehension questions in German. An English translation and the answers will be found in the Key.

Frau S.: Wie schätzen denn Ihre Landsleute die Wirtschaftsentwicklung der Bundesrepublik ein?

Mr J.: Im großen und ganzen positiv. Die vorhandenen Probleme werden zwar nicht bagatellisiert, aber auch nicht überbewertet. Ich habe übrigens einen interessanten Artikel über die "Treuhand" gelesen. Das ist ja wirklich eine schwierige Aufgabe, die die "Treuhandanstalt" zu bewältigen hat.

Frau S.: Da haben Sie recht. Bei uns gibt es allerdings einige Wirtschaftsexperten, die die Zukunft der Bundesrepublik mit den fünf neuen Bundesländern nur in den leuchtendsten Farben schildern und vom "Wirtschaftswunder ohne Grenzen" sprechen. Als ob das alles programmierbar wäre!

Mr J.: Ja, solche Prognosen standen auch bei uns in den Zeitungen!

Frau S.: Machen wir uns doch nichts vor: Sie wissen ebenso gut wie ich, daß es keine Patentrezepte für die Wirtschaft gibt. Ich glaube einfach nicht, daß das Zusammenwachsen von zwei Staaten eine einfache Sache ist. Keine Ehe ist einfach, schon gar nicht eine zwischen zwei so ungleichen Partnern.

Mr J.: Von dieser Seite habe ich das Problem noch gar nicht betrachtet! Für mich hat Deutschland einfach einen Standortvorteil für Geschäftsverbindungen mit dem Osten, der nicht zu überbieten ist.

Frau S.: Aber bisher läuft das Geschäft mit Osteuropa nur sehr schleppend. Auf Ihrem Gebiet haben Sie sicher auf absehbare Zeit keine Konkurrenz zu befürchten.

Mr J.: Wir sprechen uns in ein paar Jahren wieder. Dann wissen wir, ob Sie recht hatten!

Here are the questions:

1 Was möchte Frau Schneider wissen?
2 Wie werden die vorhandenen Probleme beurteilt?
3 Über welche Institution wurde in der Zeitung berichtet?
4 Wie schildern einige Wirtschaftsexperten die Zukunft?
5 Woven sprechen Sie?
6 Glaubt Frau Schneider an Patentrezepte?
7 Wie beurteilt sie das Zusammenwachsen der beiden deutschen Staaten?

8 Was für einen Vorteil hat Deutschland nach Herr Jacksons Meinung?
9 Wie beurteilt Frau Schneider die Konkurrenz aus Osteuropa?
10 Wann weiß Herr Jackson, ob Frau Schneider recht hatte?

FLUENCY PRACTICE 46
Polite comments and requests

New words:

schließen	*to close*
zurück|rufen	*to ring back*
in dieser Angelegenheit	*in this matter*
durchaus	*quite*
bereit sein	*to be prepared*
die Vertretung	*agency*
eine Aufgabe übernehmen	*to accept a task/job*
um|buchen	*to change a booking*
in Frage kommen	*to be suitable/acceptable*

Please find a more polite way of expressing the following:

1 Nehmen Sie bitte hier Platz!
2 Können Sie bitte das Fenster schließen?
3 Kann ich Sie morgen früh zurückrufen?
4 Können Sie uns das bitte schriftlich bestätigen?
5 Kann ich Sie nächste Woche in dieser Angelegenheit sprechen?
6 Ich habe da noch ein paar Fragen.
7 Herr Meier, fahren Sie nach Berlin!
8 Wir sind durchaus bereit, die Vertretung zu übernehmen.
9 Seien Sie so nett und buchen den Flug für mich um!
10 Kommen auch andere Farben in Frage?

FLUENCY PRACTICE 47
Find the right verb!

New words:

das Wörterbuch	*dictionary*
die Auslieferung	*delivery*

1 Sie können an diesem Tisch hier Platz ____ .
2 Können Sie mir einen Moment Ihr Wörterbuch zur Verfügung ____ ?
3 Eine Preiserhöhung ____ zur Zeit nicht zur Debatte.
4 Der Streik ____ die Auslieferung der Geräte in Frage.
5 Das neue Produkt ____ in der Presse großen Anklang.
6 Eine Vertragsänderung ____ außer Frage!

DICTIONARY PRACTICE 11
'Spiegel' interview

Study the following interview given by the American banker, James P. Miscoll, to *Der Spiegel*, a weekly news magazine. After hearing and reading so much about current developments in Germany you will no doubt be interested in Mr Miscoll's answers to the following questions:

1 When will the Bank of America open an office in East Berlin?
2 Where are they represented in the western part of the country?
3 What did Mr Miscoll do during his recent visit to Treuhand?
4 What are the biggest problems facing American investors in East Germany?
5 Which aspect had been neglected in the American teaching of economics in Mr Miscoll's view?
6 What advice would he give to the 'Treuhandanstalt'?
7 To which other achievements does he compare the Treuhand's task?
8 Given an annual investment figure of 100 billion US dollars, when will the former GDR have caught up with the West in Mr Miscoll's view?

„Bis der Dümmste es versteht"

SPIEGEL-Interview mit dem US-Banker James P. Miscoll über Investitionen in Deutschland

Miscoll, 56, ist Vorstandsmitglied der Bank of America, er hat für sein Institut die Büros in Moskau und Peking eröffnet.

SPIEGEL: Wann macht Ihre Bank eine Zweigstelle in Ostdeutschland auf?

MISCOLL: Eines Tages werden wir sicher in Berlin vertreten sein. Aber zur Zeit kommt der größte Teil unserer Kunden aus dem Westteil Deutschlands, und die bedienen wir von unserem Büro in Frankfurt.

SPIEGEL: Sehen Sie im deutschen Osten keine Chance für ein lohnendes Investment?

MISCOLL: Vor dem Zweiten Weltkrieg hat der Ostteil Deutschlands mit den USA mehr Handel getrieben als der Westteil. Das muß sich jetzt erst wieder entwickeln. Wir haben Gespräche mit dem Leipziger Unternehmen Takraf begonnen, das die größten Hafenkräne der Welt baut. Ich selbst war bei der Treuhand in Berlin und habe das berühmte rote Buch mit den Namen von 8000 ostdeutschen Betrieben durchgeblättert.

SPIEGEL: Mit welchem Ergebnis?

MISCOLL: Banker und Frauenärzte sollten keine Geheimnisse preisgeben.

SPIEGEL: Lohnt es im deutschen Osten zu investieren, oder lohnt es nicht?

MISCOLL: Es lohnt, auf ausgewählten Gebieten. Geld allein wird allerdings nicht weiterhelfen. Wir müssen den Ostdeutschen nicht nur Fisch bringen, wir müssen ihnen auch zeigen, wie man Fisch fängt.

SPIEGEL: Bisher sind die amerikanischen Investoren zögerlich. Warum?

MISCOLL: Die Ostdeutschen sprechen kein Englisch. Das ist das erste Problem. Hinzu kommen Schwierigkeiten mit den Unternehmensbilanzen, dem System der gesamten Rechnungsführung, ohne das nichts funktioniert. Wenn man etwas kauft, muß man den Wert der Sache kennen. Man kann nicht die Katze im Sack kaufen, denn am Ende öffnen wir den Sack, und es ist keine Katze drin.

SPIEGEL: Sie haben kürzlich kritisiert, daß amerikanische Firmen in Osteuropa zu wenig riskieren.

MISCOLL: Ich kritisiere, daß sie sich zum Teil überhaupt nicht engagieren. Schuld daran ist die Ausbildung unserer Manager. An der Harvard University, an der ich übrigens auch studiert habe, hat man erst jetzt den Lehrplan umgestellt, so daß nun ein längerfristiges ökonomisches Denken gelehrt wird. Nur wer langfristig denkt, wird Erfolg haben. Wer nur das schnelle Geld machen will, riskiert, daß er schon in naher Zukunft nicht mehr existiert.

SPIEGEL: Die Berliner Treuhandanstalt hat ausländischen Unternehmern das Investieren nicht gerade erleichtert.

MISCOLL: Es geht in Berlin sehr bürokratisch zu. Sie wissen, man muß sich da wirklich durchkämpfen. Alle Vorgänge dort sollte man sehr stark vereinfachen. Mein Motto wäre: Macht es so einfach, daß auch der Dümmste es verstehen kann. Alles andere verschreckt die Menschen. Denn warum soll ich nach Deutschland kommen, wenn ich dasselbe Geschäft in Ohio problemlos abwickeln kann.

SPIEGEL: Es gab in Deutschland sogar die Forderung, die Treuhand sofort aufzulösen.

MISCOLL: Ich würde nur das Verfahren vereinfachen. Wir haben einen Mann auf den Mond gebracht, Hannibal hat Elefanten über die Alpen geschafft. Also warum können wir nicht ein paar Betriebe verkaufen?

SPIEGEL: In welchem Zeitraum wird die ehemalige DDR-Wirtschaft das Westniveau erreichen?

MISCOLL: Ich kalkuliere mit ungefähr fünf Jahren bei einer jährlichen Investitionssumme von 100 Milliarden Dollar. Aber die Deutschen sollten nicht der Eile zum Opfer fallen. Es hat in Westdeutschland 40 Jahre gebraucht, um den heutigen Standard zu erreichen. Bringen Sie nun auch im Osten ein bißchen Geduld auf.

KEY TO EXERCISES

UNIT 1

Comprehension Practice (CP) 1: 1 f; 2 r; 3 r; 4 f; 5 r; 6 r.

Fluency Practice (FP) 2: [Your part in this conversation] Guten Tag. Mein Name ist – . Ich habe einen Termin bei Frau Schneider. ... Vielen Dank.

FP 4: doch, Wagen, Augenblick, bitte, Bescheid, Termin, bei, sofort, sagen, die, Karte, Empfangsdame, Platz, nehmen, ein.

FP 5: Guten Tag! Mein Name ist Müller. Ich habe einen Termin bei Frau Walter. ... Guten Tag, Herr Müller! Einen Auge·,blick, bitte. Ich sage Frau Walter Bescheid. ... Vielen Dank!

UNIT 2

CP 2: 1 f; 2 r; 3 f; 4 f; 5 f; 6 r.

FP 6: 1 Geschäftsführer.   2 Personalleiterin.   3 Produktionsleiter.
4 Finanzleiterin.   5 *[If your job description isn't listed, change jobs!]*

FP 7: 1 Haben Sie Faxgeräte im Programm?   2 Hat Herr Jackson eine Sekretärin?   3 Haben Sie einen Fotokopierer?   4 Kommen Sie aus England?   5 Verkaufen Sie Textcomputer?

FP 8: Es ist drei Uhr. Es ist zehn vor zwölf. Es ist halb fünf. Es ist Viertel nach acht.

FP 9: 1 der Deutsche, die Deutsche.   2 der Brite, die Britin (*or:* der Engländer, die Engländerin).   3 der Franzose, die Französin.   4 der Ire, die Irin.

FP 10: [your part in the dialogue] Guten Tag. Ich heiße/ich bin Richard Smith. Ich habe um drei Uhr einen Termin bei Herrn* Schwarz. ... Ja, sicher. Hier ist meine Karte. ... Ich bin der Verkaufsdirektor von Brown Engineering Ltd. ... Vielen Dank. *[*see note to CP 3]*

UNIT 3

CP 3: 1 r; 2 r; 3 f; 4 f; 5 r; 6 r.

FP 11: 1 organisieren;   2 bestellen;   3 importieren;   4 verkauft;
5 telefoniert;   6 unterschreibe;   7 warten.

FP 12: 1 haben ... organisiert;   2 haben ... bestellt;   3 haben ... importiert;
4 hat ... verkauft;   5 hat ... telefoniert;   6 habe ... unterschrieben;
7 haben ... gewartet.

FP 13: 1 Bringen Sie bitte zwei Tassen Kaffee!   2 Rufen Sie bitte Herrn XYZ an!   3 Beantworten Sie bitte den Brief von Interop!   4 Vereinbaren Sie bitte eine Besprechung mit M.!   5 Bestellen Sie bitte einen neuen Katalog.

FP 14: 1 Ich trinke gerne Kaffee, aber ich trinke lieber Tee. 2 Ich bestelle gerne bei Bürotec, aber ich bestelle lieber bei Excel-Equip. 3 Ich exportiere gern nach Frankreich, aber ich exportiere lieber nach Deutschland. 4 Ich importiere gern aus Japan, aber ich importiere lieber aus Deutschland. 5 Ich arbeite gerne am Empfang, aber ich arbeite lieber im Büro. 6 Ich organisiere gerne eine Messe, aber ich organisiere lieber eine Konferenz.

UNIT 4

CP 4: 1 f; 2 f; 3 r; 4 f; 5 r; 6 f.

FP 15: 1 mir; 2 ihr; 3 ihm; 4 ihnen.

FP 16: Müller: siebenundfünfzig, dreiundachtzig, achtunddreißig. Schuster: sechs, dreiundzwanzig, sechsundzwanzig, vierunddreißig. Maier: achtzig, zwanzig, sechzig. Kaufmann: zwei(zwo), neunzehn, einundachtzig. Bürger: fünf, achtzehn, siebenundneunzig, neununddreißig. Freund: dreiunddreißig, vierundvierzig, neunundneunzig.

FP 17: eintausend Berlin; zweitausend Hamburg; dreitausend Hannover; viertausend Düsseldorf; fünftausend Köln; sechstausend Frankfurt; siebentausend Stuttgart; achttausend München; fünftausenddreihundert Bonn; zweitausendachthundert Bremen; sechstausendfünfhundert Mainz; fünftausendvierhundert Koblenz; siebentausendvierhundert Tübingen; zweitausenddreihundert Kiel; sechstausendfünfhundertvierzig Simmern; siebentausendsiebenhundertfünfzig Konstanz; viertausendfünfzig Mönchen-Gladbach; zweitausendzweihundertzweiundvierzig Büsum; sechstausendsechshundertfünfunddreißig Schwalmbach.

FP 18: 1 die; 2 das; 3 der; 4 den; 5 die; 6 was.

Dictionary Practice (DP) 1: 1 all engagements; 2 a newspaper; 3 spend an evening in front of the big screen; 4 eleven; 5 in February.

UNIT 5

CP 5: 1 (Er versichert,) daß Excel-Equip in Frankreich einen guten Ruf hat. 2 Ja. 3 Frau Schneider fragt, wo sich die französische Niederlassung befindet. 4 (Sie liegt) an der Peripherie von Paris. 5 aus verkehrstechnischen Gründen. 6 Ja. 7 Eines Tages in die Außenbezirke ziehen. 8 Ja, extrem hoch!

FP 19: 1 bei der; 2 bei der; 3 beim; 4 beim; 5 beim; 6 Beim.

FP 20: 1 dem neuen; 2 dem pensionierten; 3 der netten .. einen neuen; 4 neuen; 5 den neuen ... unsere neuen.

FP 21: Wir wollen expandieren. Wir haben schon eine Niederlassung in

Frankreich. ... An der Peripherie von Paris. ... Sie wissen sicher, daß die Mieten in Paris extrem hoch sind. [*Or, used in spoken German only:* ..., die Mieten in Paris sind extrem hoch.]

FP 22: A 1; B 3; C 1; D 1; E 2; F 3.

DP 2: 1 c; 2 c; 3 a; 4 b; 5 a; 6 b; 7 c; 8 b; 9 c; 10 c; 11 a; 12 c.

UNIT 6

CP 6: 1 Die Produkte sind zuverlässig.   2 Die Preise sind konkurrenzfähig. 3 Ein (renomiertes) Marktforschungsinstitut.   4 Auf den Europäischen Binnenmarkt.   5 Die höchsten Zuwachsraten in Europa.   6 Das Wirtschaftswachstum.   7 Der Umsatz auf dem Inlandsmarkt. 8 Schlecht.   9 Sie wird immer internationaler.   10 In nationalen Kategorien.

FP 23: 1 Unsere Konkurrenz ist nicht fest etabliert!   2 Er hat nicht recht! 3 Sie haben unseren Brief nicht beantwortet!   4 Der Preis ist nicht zu hoch!   5 Wir sind nicht auf Bürotechnik spezialisiert!   6 Der Kunde hat die Lieferbedingungen nicht akzeptiert!

FP 24: 1 Er fragt, wo die Schere ist.   2 Er fragt, wann wir einen Kaffee bekommen.   3 Er fragt, wie die Kaffeemaschine funktioniert.   4 Er fragt, wer zuletzt die Heftmaschine gebraucht hat.   5 Er fragt, wem Sie den Bericht gegeben haben.   6 er fragt, ob Sie den Locher gesehen haben.

FP 25: 1 Wir haben einige Niederlassungen in Frankreich.   2 Wir haben mehrere Textverarbeitungsgeräte gekauft.   3 Wir haben einige Faxgeräte im Sortiment.   4 Wir wollen mehrere Mikrocomputer in unser Sortiment aufnehmen.   5 Die meisten Kunden wünschen gute Qualität.

FP 26: 1 Darf ich einmal Ihr Telefon benutzen?   2 Darf ich die neue Software ausprobieren?   3 Darf ich heute früher nach Hause gehen?   4 Darf ich vor dem Eingang parken?   5 Darf ich meinen Kollegen vorstellen?

FP 27: 1 Ich erlaube Ihnen, das Telefon zu benutzen!   2 Ich erlaube Ihnen, die neue Software auszuprobieren!   3 Ich erlaube Ihnen, heute früher nach Hause zu gehen!   4 Ich erlaube Ihnen, vor dem Eingang zu parken!   5 Ich erlaube Ihnen, Ihren Kollegen vorzustellen.

FP 28: 1 Aber natürlich dürfen Sie das Telefon benutzen!   2 Aber natürlich dürfen Sie die neue Software ausprobieren!   3 Aber natürlich dürfen Sie heute früher nach Hause gehen!   4 Aber natürlich dürfen Sie vor dem Eingang parken!   5 Aber natürlich dürfen Sie Ihren Kollegen vorstellen!

FP 29: 1 Sollen wir das Material in England einkaufen?   2 Sollen wir das Produkt unter dem Listenpreis verkaufen?   3 Sollen wir für den neuen Kunden Zugeständnisse machen?   4 Sollen wir das Gerät auf unsere Kosten reparieren?   5 Sollen wir den Bericht nach London faxen?

UNIT 7

CP 7: 1 Warum Frau Schneider nur deutsche Produkte verkauft. Ob Frau Schneider seine Meinung teilt. 2 Deutsche (Geräte). 3 In traditionellen, nationalen Kategorien. 4 An die Qualität der Geräte. 5 Daß nur deutsche Geräte ihren Ansprüchen genügen. 6 Diese Haltung. 7 Fax, Computer, Marketing, Management, Training und Business. 8 Diese Aufzählung / diese englischen Wörter. 9 Sehr hoch. 10 Weil im Bereich der Forschung und Entwicklung enorme Kosten anfallen. 11 Nach einer neuen Bezugsquelle. 12 Englische Geräte in die Produktpalette aufzunehmen. 13 Seine Prospekte. 14 Die Liefer- und Zahlungsbedingungen.

FP 31: The missing letters spell 'Produkt'.

FP 32: 1 um; 2 auf; 3 für; 4 über; 5 auf; 6 über; 7 an; 8 über.

FP 33: [Jackson's part] Darf ich Sie fragen, warum Sie nur deutsche Produkte verkaufen? ... Ich finde diese negative Haltung erstaunlich. Heutzutage kennen viele Deutsche eine Reihe von englischen Fachwörtern. Alle Welt spricht von 'Fax', 'Computer' und so weiter [usw.]. ... Das freut mich zu hören. Darf ich Ihnen unsere Prospekte zeigen. Dann/Danach können wir uns über (die) Zahlungs- und Lieferbedingungen unterhalten.

DP 3: 1 a; 2 c; 3 c.

UNIT 8

CP 8: 1 Im April. 2 Den dritten Mai neunzehnhundertzweiundneunzig. 3 Sechzehn. 4 Fünfzig. 5 Anfang/Mitte Juni. 6 Fünfzig Prozent. 7 Innerhalb/Binnen einundzwanzig Tagen. 8 Positiv auf die Produkte reagieren. 9 Über eine Tätigkeit als Agent. 10 Auf gute Geschäftsbeziehungen.

FP 34: 1 der; 2 des; 3 des; 4 des; 5 der; 6 der; 7 der; 8 der.

Practical Task 2 (sample answer):
Lieber Herr Wildemann,
Es tut uns sehr leid, daß die letzte Lieferung auf dem Transport beschädigt wurde. Natürlich nehmen wir die beschädigten Stücke zurück. Wir werden uns bemühen, in Zukunft solche Schäden zu vermeiden. Sie können sicher sein, daß die Ware ab sofort sorgfältiger verpackt wird.
Wir möchten uns nochmals für den Schaden entschuldigen und hoffen auf eine weitere erfolgreiche Zusammenarbeit mit Ihnen.
Mit freundlichen Grüßen, ...

FP 35: 1 einen ... guten; 2 eine kleine; 3 einen dicken; 4 dieses Buches; 5 der Verkäuferin einen neuen; 6 den unbequemen Kunden; 7 das genaue.

DP 4: 1 A; 2 B; 3 D; 4 E; 5 F; 6 C.

DP 5: 1 in 52 Schritten; 2 die Verwirklichung; 3 einer revolutionären Idee;

218

4 die Idee, eine Uhr zu schaffen;   5 nahezu diamanthart;
6 beispielsweise;   7 aufwendige Arbeitsschritte;   8 eines der
Geheimnisse;   9 beruht auf der gleichen Konsequenz;   10 höchste
Vollendung;   11 einzigartige Materialqualität;   12 aufwendige
Verarbeitung;   13 kompromislose Ästhetik;   14 bei;   15 unverbindliche
Preisempfehlung.

UNIT 9

CP 9: 1 Der Anrufbeantworter ist eingeschaltet.   2 Auf Band.   3 Daß
er (Herr J.) sich so schnell gemeldet hat.   4 Am Morgen.   5 Sie wollte
ihn so schnell wie möglich wissen lassen, was passiert war.   6 Es gab
Probleme mit der Verpackung.   7 Nein, nur eins.   8 Sie waren zu dünn.
9 Daß das nicht noch einmal passiert.   10 Der Versandabteilung eine
Hausmitteilung schicken.   11 Eine sachgemäßere Verpackung.   12 Er
ist defekt.   13 Sie soll ihn zurückschicken.   14 Sie lassen es überprüfen.
15 Nein, natürlich nicht.   16 Ein fabrikneues (Gerät).   17 Mit der
Gebrauchsanleitung.   18 Von einem Fachmann.   9 Er wird sie an Frau
Schneider faxen.   20 Die Kunden im In- und Ausland zufriedenzustellen.

FP 36 Dialogue translation:
Switch.: Futura Büromaschinen, good morning (*lit.* 'good day'). Who
would you like to speak to?
Mr J.: Good morning. Please put me through to Frau Schneider, in
the Purchasing Department.
Switch.: (What is) Your name, please?
Mr J.: Jackson, of (the firm) Excel-Equip, London.
Switch.: The line (*lit.* 'the connection') is very bad, unfortunately.
Could you please repeat your name?
Mr J.: Jackson. I('ll) spell (it for you): J - A - C - K - S - O - N.
Switch.: Just a moment, I'm putting you through.
Mr J.: Thank you (very much). ....
Switch.: (I'm afraid) Frau Schneider is talking on the other line. Would
you like to wait a moment?
Mr J.: Will it be long?
Switch.: (I assume) you are phoning from abroad, (aren't you)? I'll give
her a visual signal to let her know (lit. 'then she'll know') that
the next phone call is waiting for her.
Mr J.: That's very kind (of you). I'll hold the line (*lit.* 'I'll remain at the
receiver).
Frau S.: Hello, Mr Jackson! I hope you haven't been waiting long.

FP 36 answers: 1 the switchboard operator.   2 bad.   3 she's on
another line.   4 that Mr J. is phoning from abroad.   5 a visual signal
to Frau S.   6 hold on.   7 ... I hope you haven't been waiting long.

FP 37: 1 E; 2 B; 3 D; 4 A; 5 G; 6 H; 7 C; 8 F.

FP 38: 1 B; 2 A; 3 F; 4 C; 5 E; 6 G; 7 H; 8 D.

DP 6: 1 Kein Anschluß unter dieser Nummer! 2 Hier gibt es keinen Meier! 3 Bitte notieren Sie die neue Nummer! 4 Auskunft! 5 Falsch verbunden! 6 Der Name ist nicht aufgeführt! 7 Die Vorwahlnummer hat sich geändert! 8 Die Rufnummer hat sich geändert!

DP 7: 1 B; 2 E; 3 F; 4 D; 5 C; 6 H; 7 A; 8 G.

FP 39: 1 Der Chef wird gerufen. 2 Der Wein wird bestellt. 3 Das Auto wird repariert. 4 Die Anweisungen werden übersetzt. 5 Die Konferenz wird gedolmetscht. 6 Die neuen Modelle werden gezeigt.

FP 40: 1 Lassen Sie die Zahlen berichtigen! 2 Lassen Sie die Heizung in Ordnung bringen! 3 Lassen Sie den Scheck vom Direktor unterschreiben! 4 Lassen Sie den Flug nach Zürich stornieren! 6 Lassen Sie meine Filme entwickeln! 7 Lassen Sie den englischen Besucher vom Flughafen abholen! 8 Lassen Sie die Werbefotos noch einmal abziehen/vergrößern!

UNIT 10

CP 10: 1 Herr Mittermair. 2 In Herrn Mittermairs Büro. 3 Für eine Werbekampagne. 4 Den Umsatz steigern. 5 Einen tragbaren Textcomputer. 6 Um zu erfahren, welche Vorstellungen Frau Schneider hat. 7 Er fragt nach der Form der Werbung. 8 An etablierte oder potentielle Kunden. 9 Auf die Zielgruppe. 10 Kleinere Firmen. 11 Aus Kostengründen. 12 die Preise sind gefallen. 13 Ja, aber auch überregional. 14 In Zeitungen und Zeitschriften (und in der Fachpresse). 15 Daß sich Reklame aus einem Land nicht einfach in einem anderen europäischen Land einsetzen läßt. 16 Mehr sachliche Produktinformation. 17 Unter Zeitdruck zu arbeiten. 18 Die Auftragslage prüfen.

FP 41: 1 denn; 2 etwa; 3 eigentlich; 4 etwa; 5 denn; 6 denn; 7 eigentlich; 8 etwa; 9 denn; 10 etwa.

FP 42: A wann und wo; B wer; C wie; D wie lange; E warum; F welche; G was für einen; H seit wann.

FP 43: 1 tut; 2 machen; 3 hatten; 4 macht; 5 hat; 6 haben ... getan.

DP 8: 1 L; 2 B; 3 F; 4 E; 5 I; 6 D; 7 C; 8 G; 9 H; 10 A; 11 K; 12 J

UNIT 11

CP 11: 1 r; 2 f; 3 f; 4 r; 5 f; 6 f; 7 f; 8 r; 9 r; 10 r; 11 f; 12 r; 13 f; 14 f; 15 f; 16 f; 17 f; 18 f; 19 f; 20 f.

FP 44: habe; habe; bleibe; entwickle; seien; getan habe.

FP 45: 1 A; 2 H; 3 D; 4 F; 5 B; 6 C; 7 E; 8 G.

DP 9 section A: 1 It was just an idea or a sketch on a drawing board. 2 Through R&D. 3 Germany wants to belong to the leading industrial nations. 4 Industry, state and various other institutions keep increasing their spending on R&D. 5 Fourfold. 6 2.9%. 7 Equally high. 8 They are countries which spend the highest amount of money on R&D in relation to economic output. 9 Industry. 10 The public sector (state). *Section B:* 1 handeln; 2 spielen; 3 gehören; 4 steigern; 5 vervierfacht; 6 betragen; 7 stehen; 8 gehören; 9 treiben; 10 dazusteuern.

UNIT 12

CP 12: 1 r; 2 f; 3 f; 4 f; 5 f; 6 f; 7 f; 8 f; 9 f; 10 f; 11 r; 12 r; 13 r; 14 r; 15 r; 16 f; 17 f; 18 f; 19 f; 20 f.

DP 10: 1 Sie möchte wissen, wie Herr Jacksons Landsleute die Wirtschaftsentwicklung der Bundesrepublik einschätzen. 2 Die Probleme werden nicht bagatellisiert, aber auch nicht überbewertet. 3 Die Treuhandanstalt. 4 Sehr positiv (= in den leuchtendsten Farben). 5 Vom Wirtschaftswunder ohne Grenzen. 6 Nein (es gibt keine Patentrezepte). 7 Sie findet es problematisch (= keine einfache Sache). 8 Einen Standortvorteil. 9 Herr Jackson hat auf absehbare Zeit keine Konkurrenz zu befürchten. 10 In ein paar Jahren.

DP 10 Translation of dialogue:
Fr S.: How do your compatriots evaluate the economic development of the Federal Republic?
Mr J.: Overall, positively. The existing problems are neither played down, nor overemphasized. Actually, I read an interesting article about the 'Treuhand'. It's really a difficult task, which the 'Treuhandanstalt' *[Federal agency to dispose of former East German state property]* has to handle.
Fr S.: You're quite right, but there are some economic experts who paint the future of the Federal Republic with its five new states in the brightest colours and talk of a 'boundless' economic miracle. (Just) as if all that could be programmed!
Mr J.: Quite, such prognoses were also printed in our newspapers.
Fr S.: Let's not kid each other: you know as well as I do that there is no magic formula (*lit.* 'patented recipes') for the economy. I don't believe that a union (*lit.* 'growing together') of two states is easy. No marriage is easy, especially one between two such unequal partners.
Mr J.: I've never looked at the problem from this perspective. As far as I'm concerned (*lit.* 'for me') Germany definitely has a positional advantage for commercial links with Eastern Europe, with which we cannot compete.
Fr S.: Up to now business with Eastern Europe has been very slow. In your field you won't have to fear any competition in the near future.
Mr J.: We'll speak again (about this topic) in a couple of years. Then we'll know if you were right!

FP 46: 1 Würden Sie bitte hier Platz nehmen! 2 Könnten Sie ...

3 Könnte ich ... 4 Könnten Sie ... 5 Könnte ich ... 6 Ich hätte ...
7 Herr Meier, würden / könnten Sie (für uns) nach Berlin fahren? 8 Wir
wären ... 9 Würden Sie ... sein und ... umbuchen; 10 Kämen ...

FP 47: 1 nehmen; 2 stellen; 3 steht; 4 stellt; 5 findet; 6 steht.
DP 11: 1 One day for sure. 2 In Frankfurt. 3 Mr M. looked at the 'red
book' giving the names of 8000 East German firms. 4 East Germans
don't speak English and didn't keep proper accounts. 5 Long-term and
longer-term economic planning. 6 To simplify all their procedures,
according to the motto: 'Do it in such a simple way that even the most
stupid person can understand it.' 7 Landing on the moon and
Hannibal's crossing of the Alps with elephants. 8 In approximately
five years.

IMITATED PRONUNCIATION

UNIT 1

Mr J.: 'Goo-ten Tahk. Myn 'Nah-me ist Jackson. Ih 'hah-be 'y-nen
Tairr- 'meen by Frow 'Shny-der.

Recep.: 'Goo-ten Tahk, Hairr Jackson. 'Y-nen 'Ow-gen-blik, 'bit-e. Ih
'zah-ge Frow 'Shny-ders Zay-kray-'tair-rin Be-'shyt. 'Nay-men
Zee dokh 'bit-e Plutsl ... Hairr Jackson, Frow 'Shny-ders
Zay-kray-'tair-rin komt zoh-'forrt. Eer Bü-'roh ist im 'air-sten
Ge-'shoss.

Mr J.: 'Fee-len Dungk.

UNIT 2

Sec.: 'Goo-ten Tahk. Kunn ih 'Ee-nen 'hel-fen?

Mr J.: 'Goo-ten Tahk. Myn 'Nah-me ist Jackson.

Sec.: Ent-'shool-di-goong, vee 'hy-sen Zee?

Mr J.: Jackson. Ih 'kom-e owss 'Eng-lunt. Ih bin Fair-'kowfs-ly-ter by
Excel-Equip. Heer ist 'my-ne 'Karr-te. Ih bin füer elf 'Ooer
be-'shtell.

Sec.: Ukh yah [y as in 'yes'], Hairr Jackson. Frow 'Shny-der
air-'varr-tet Zee. 'Kom-en Zee 'bit-e mit!

UNIT 3

Fr S.: Hair-'ryn!

Sec.: Hairr Jackson fon Excel-Equip ist heer.

Fr S.: 'Goo-ten Tahk, Hairr Jackson. 'Kom-en Zee dokh 'bit-e
hair-'ryn! Veer 'hah-ben air-st 'gess-tern tay-lay-foh-'neerrt. Ess
froyt mih, Zee 'ken-en-tsoo-lairr-nen.

Mr J.: Gunts 'my-ner-zyts, Frow 'Shny-der.

Fr S.: 'Nay-men Zee 'bit-e heer umm Tish Pluts!

Mr J.: 'Fee-len Dungk.

Fr S.: 'Möh-ten Zee 'y-nen 'Kuff-ay, 'oh-der 'lee-ber 'y-nen Tay?

Mr J.: Ih 'tring-ke 'gairr-ne 'y-nen 'Kuff-ay. 'Bit-e shvarrts, 'y-nen 'Lö-fel
'Tsoo-ker. ...

Sec.: Yn 'Kuff-ay. Komt zoh-'forrt.

Fr S.: Hairr Jackson, Zee 'hah-ben meer 'gess-tern umm Tay-lay-'fohn ge-'zahkt, duss Zee Bü-'roh-ge-ray-te nahkh 'Doytsh-lunt eks-porr-'tee-ren 'vol-en.

Mr J.: Yah, duss shtimt. Veer zint fest owf daym 'bri-tish-en Marrkt ay-tuh-'bleerrt. Yetst 'vol-en veer dee 'Forr-ty-le dess Oy-roh-'pay-ish-en 'Bin-en-marrktes 'ows-nǫǫ-tsen. ...

Sec.: Heer ist Eer 'Kuff-ay. Shvarrts, mit 'Tsǫǫ-ker.

Mr J.: 'Fee-len Dungk. Duss ist zair net fon 'Ee-nen.

Sec.: 'Bit-e zair. Gairrn ge-'shay-en!

UNIT 4

Fr S.: Hairr Jackson, 'Ee-re 'Firr-ma *[i as in 'sit']* vill 'ull-zoh nahkh 'Doytsh-lunt eks-porr-'tee-ren. I*h* mǫǫs ge-'shtay-en, duss meer dair 'Nah-me Excel-Equip 'ly-der ni*h*t fair-'trowt ist. 'Kö-nen Zee meer mair 'ü-ber 'Ee-re 'Firr-ma air-'tsay-len?

Mr J.: Yah 'zi*h*-er! 'Qon-ze-re 'Firr-ma be-'shtayt zyt 'noyn-tsayn-hǫǫn-dert-'zeep-tsi*h*. Veer 'hah-ben ǫǫns owf Bü-'roh-'ows-shtatt-ǫǫng shpayts-yah-lee-'zeert; ǫǫm ess ge-'now tsoo 'zah-gen: owf ay-lek-'troh-nish-e Bü-'roh-ge-'ray-te. Veer'shtell-en 'Tish-re*h*-ner, ay-lek-'troh-nish-e 'Shryp-muh-'shee-nen, Mee-kroh-kom-'pyoo-ter, 'Fairrn-koh-pee-rer, 'Text-kom-pyoo-ter, ǫǫnt zoh 'vy-ter hair. Mit 'unn-de-ren 'Vorr-ten: veer proh-doo-'tsee-ren 'ull-ess, vuss munn füer yn moh-'dairr-nes Bü-'roh browkht.

Fr S.: Zee 'hah-ben zi*h* 'ull-zoh owf 'Shpit-sen-te*h*-noh-loh-'gee shpayts-yah-lee-'zeert!

Mr J.: Yah. Duss shtimt. Yetst 'zoo-khen veer 'y-nen Uh-'gent-en in 'Doytsh-lunt.

UNIT 5

Fr S.: Hairr Jackson, Darrf i*h* Zee nokh mahl 'frah-gen, vuh-'rǫǫm Zee nahk 'Doytsh-lunt eks-porr-'tee-ren 'vol-en?

Mr J.: Veer 'vol-en eks-pun-'dee-ren. Veer 'hah-ben shohn 'y-ne 'Nee-der-luss-ǫǫng in 'Frung-kry*h* ǫǫnt i*h* kunn 'Ee-nen fair-'zi*h*-em, duss veer dorrt 'y-nen zair 'goo-ten Roof 'hah-ben.

Fr S.: Voh be-'fin-det zi*h* denn 'Ee-re Frun-'tsö-zish-e 'Nee-der-luss-ǫǫng?

Mr J.: Unn dair Pay-ri-fay-'ree fon Puh-'reess. Duss ist fair-'kairss-te*h*-nish 'gün-stig-er ullss im 'Tsen-trǫǫm.

Fr S.: 'Qon-ze-re Bü-'rohs 'lee-gen im 'toy-ren 'Vest-ent fon 'Frungk-fǫǫrrt. Venn dee 'Mee-ten 'vy-ter zoh shtarrk 'shty-gen vee in dayn 'let-sten 'Yah-ren, dunn 'vairr-den owkh veer 'y-nes 'Tah-ges in dee 'Ow-sen-be-tsirr-ke *[i as in 'sit']* 'tsee-en 'mü-sen.

Mr J.: Zee 'viss-en 'zi*h*-er, vee eks-'traym hohkh dee 'Mee-ten in Puh-'reess zint.

Fr S.: 'Ull-er-dings! 'Ah-ber vuss zoll munn dah toon? Ess blypt 'y-nem ni*h*ts 'unn-de-res 'ü-bri*h* ullss tsoo 'tsah-len!

INDEX

The figures refer to Checknotes, *not* pages.